A FALLEN RECORD: THE CHRISTIAN TRANSGRESSION

LINWOOD JACKSON, JR.

PUBLISHED BY FIDELI PUBLISHING, INC.

© Copyright 2018, Linwood Jackson, Jr.

All Rights Reserved.

No part of this book may be reproduced, stored in a retrieval system, or transmitted by any means, electronic, mechanical, photocopying, recording, or otherwise, without written permission from the author.

ISBN: 978-1-948638-81-4

Cover created by artist Darko Hristov
@hristov_darko

For information, email the author at
LinwoodJackson@hotmail.com

Published by
Fideli Publishing, Inc.
www.FideliPublishing.com

Contents

1. Works Left Undone 1
2. Revelation's Benevolence 22
3. The Error Within The Mind Of The Church 36
4. The Holy Spirit Rejected 59
5. The Foundation Of Another Gospel 75
6. Engaging An Unlawful Exchange 90
7. From Whence They Had Fallen 103
8. Faith's Right End 126
9. Like Mother, Like Daughter 152
10. The Theology Of The Compromised Church 169
11. Reconciliation's Administration 188
12. Justification's Acknowledged Character 207
13. Transgression's Fever 232

Introduction

1. There is a reason why John counseled Christian elders, "If that which ye have heard from the beginning shall remain in you, ye also shall continue in the Son, and in the Father."[1] Christian elders were failing to do creation's course, which course the LORD's Christ blessed and ratified by His passing, regenerating, and high priestly appointment within the heavenly Sanctuary. Because they strayed from heaven's new will for man, they began doing what is "foolish, disobedient, deceived, serving divers lusts and pleasures, living in malice and envy, hateful, and hating one another."[2] To "hate" is to do contrary to the counsel, "Love one another,"[3] which "love," in reality, means, "Edify one another."[4] John sought to put priests and ministers in remembrance of creation due to the fact that creation did "good" to creation, which "good" is defined by the saying, "Let every one of us please his neighbour for his good to edification,"[5] and, "Let no corrupt communication proceed out of your mouth, but that which is good to the use of edifying."[6] For this cause, we should not take the words "hate" and "love," as they are here used in Scripture, to mean any secular or

---

1   1 John 2:2
2   Titus 3:3
3   1 Thessalonians 4:9
4   1 Thessalonians 5:11
5   Romans 15:2
6   Ephesians 4:29

sensual thing. To "love" is to edify, and edification is mental, and this mental refreshing occurring when "comparing spiritual things with spiritual"[7] to fortify the understanding. To "hate," then, also falls in line with mental activity, except it is contrary to edification, and means to retard, reduce, decline, limit, or decrease the conversation's conscience on heavenly things.

2. The "hate" that John saw from Christian elders was reminding him of the beginning of his LORD's operation, and not simply that record of Adam in Eden, but of before Eden's controversy, for "the earth was without form, and void; and darkness was upon the face of the deep. And the Spirit of God moved upon the face of the waters."[8]

3. This is a very disturbing image, especially since the record of creation states, "In the beginning God created the heaven and the earth."[9] What is evident, in the beginning, is that the earth is lame, but this is not what is only wrong. What is wrong is that the earth is lame because both "darkness" and the LORD's Word rest on the same waters. "The deep" are "the waters"; the two are one and the same illustration, even as it says, "The waters made him great, the deep set him up on high,"[10] and, "The waters are hid as with a stone, and the face of the deep is frozen."[11] When we hear of "waters" in vision, we shouldn't take them to mean literal seas, which is why it says, "The waters which thou sawest...are peoples, and multitudes, and nations, and tongues."[12] In reality, "darkness" and the Word are both joined together in one religious denomination without any distinction, and what suffers for this religious

---

7   1 John 2:13
8   Genesis 1:2
9   Genesis 1:1
10   Ezekiel 31:4
11   Job 38:30
12   Revelation 17:15

negligence is the earth. In the beginning, the LORD did create His world, but the earth that He created found itself in a spiritually degenerate condition, for it lacked His form, and if it lacked His form, then we may know that it adhered to another form, which form *blessed* His earth with "death."

4. The form of the LORD is the image of God, and because "God is a Spirit,"[13] to discern His "nature," it is well to comprehend the shape of His Spirit. We understand the Spirit's fashion according to the saying, "And God said, Let there be light: and there was light."[14] The fact that the Word pronounces a division between light and darkness reveals to us His image, which image is of One regenerating to provoke reform from what separates the spirit of the mind from His voice, for "that which is born of the Spirit is spirit."[15] Our mind, and the conscience of our conversation, is the Spirit's primary concern for our faith's wellbeing, which is why we are counseled, "Be renewed in the spirit of your mind,"[16] and, "Be ye transformed by the renewing of your mind, that ye may prove what is that good, and acceptable, and perfect, will of God."[17] The Spirit's concern can be for no thing but the mind because "a spirit hath not flesh and bones."[18] If flesh and bones, we may take the Spirit's Faith to be for what is flesh and bones, but since wholly Spirit, "that which is born of the Spirit is spirit."[19] Now, what is of flesh and bones is contrary to the Spirit's Faith because it forwards what lacks faith, and "whatsoever is not of

---

13 John 4:24
14 Genesis 1:3
15 John 3:6
16 Ephesians 4:23
17 Romans 12:2
18 Luke 24:39
19 John 3:6

faith is sin"[20] to heaven's new covenant will, "and the law is not of faith."[21]

5. This "law" that Paul mentions is in reference to the legal religious ordinance crafted by the hands of priests and elders. When it says, of what God's Man abolished by His flesh, "Blotting out the handwriting of ordinances,"[22] what is handwritten of priests and elders is for ever taken away from His LORD and Father's Faith, for "the sting of death is sin; and the strength of sin is the law."[23] "Having abolished in his flesh the enmity, even the law of commandments contained in ordinances,"[24] this Christ of Judah; of the seed of David, of them confessing, "I am an Hebrew; and I fear the LORD, the God of heaven";[25] took from out of His LORD's throne religion every legal religious commandment of every *Moses*; both in that age of the offering, and in every age thereafter. We understand this fact because "whatsoever God doeth, it shall be for ever: nothing can be put to it, nor any thing taken from it."[26] The illustration portrayed by this Christ on the tree is an illustration for ever condemning the inventing and employing of traditions and charges to His LORD's Faith by any one, and especially any priest or elder at any time after this act. And this the Spirit did, and this His Christ consented to do, because we are to be "written not with ink, but with the Spirit of the living God."[27] Thus, if it is that we find our religious conversation to be in service to teachings, and to *sabbaths*, and to charges, and to ceremonies not associated to Eden's LORD or Word, it is well to quit the craft of men to

---

20 Romans 14:23
21 Galatians 3:12
22 Colossians 2:14
23 1 Corinthians 15:56
24 Ephesians 2:15
25 Jonah 1:9
26 Ecclesiastes 3:14
27 2 Corinthians 3:3

personally learn of heaven's right will and doctrine, even as it says, "Acquaint now thyself with him."[28]

6. Herein is what the Spirit's Christ means when saying, "Repent ye, and believe the gospel."[29] We have to really understand the reality of what is here spoken. He is not speaking to any one but Jews of the LORD's assembly, for His mission did not remove away from the Jews, even as a companion of His states, "We are witnesses of all things which he did both in the land of the Jews, and in Jerusalem."[30] Our concern should be what it is that He is demanding repentance for and from, and what it is that we are to trust when penitent. Thus, remembering that "the strength of sin is the law,"[31] the Word's Minister taught a doctrine encouraging the people to quit legal religious laws for personally acquainting the conversation's conscience with the Spirit's will, for even He Himself did this, saying, "I know him, and keep his saying."[32] There is no liberty of mind within the legal religion, for the one without subjection to "the tradition of men, after the rudiments of the world,"[33] says, "Why is my liberty judged of another man's conscience?"[34] The understanding of the conscience's liberty from the rule of priests and elders to experience "the kindness and love of God our Saviour toward man"[35] is preached by this Christ, for He knew the position He should take up after His earthy mission, and, today, "we have a great high priest, that is passed into the heavens."[36] His heavenly intercession is for the

---

28 Job 22:21
29 Mark 1:15
30 Acts 10:39
31 1 Corinthians 15:56
32 John 8:55
33 Colossians 2:8
34 1 Corinthians 10:29
35 Titus 3:4
36 Hebrews 4:14

purpose of finishing His Father's will within our inward parts, but if "the strength of sin is the law,"[37] and we are continuing in what His sacrifice has accursed, must we think to faithfully execute His name without any carnal or sensual support?

7. "Whatsoever is not of faith is sin,"[38] and because "the law is not of faith,"[39] it must be blotted out from the Spirit's will and learning, for "without faith it is impossible to please him."[40] This is why it is well to understand what the Spirit means when saying, "He that is hanged is accursed of God,"[41] for "Christ hath redeemed us from the curse of the law, being made a curse for us: for it is written, Cursed is every one that hangeth on a tree."[42] As this Man lifelessly hangs on the tree, the illustration of His flesh represents the passing away of every handwritten ordinance of whatever *Moses* should come along, whether he exist in that age or in any other age thereafter. The principles of heaven's religion are therefore sealed with blood, which principles are ten laws of heaven's throne, which laws are blessed by the Faith that blood forwards, which Faith is illuminated by creation's seal, which seal reads, "God blessed the seventh day, and sanctified it."[43] John would have us remember that "in the beginning was the Word, and the Word was with God, and the Word was God,"[44] that we might not find ourselves honoring a *Christ* outside of the Hebrew tree, which tree begins in Eden, which Eden began with the LORD and His Word after creation, which creation, and Sabbath of creation, is blessed by this same Word for ever. This LORD's

---

37   1 Corinthians 15:56
38   Romans 14:23
39   Galatians 3:12
40   Hebrews 11:6
41   Deuteronomy 21:23
42   Galatians 3:13
43   Genesis 2:3
44   John 1:1

Christ preached this same Word and Spirit to alleviate the LORD's spiritual world, along with man's inwards, from that work and effect of "death," and He defines for us the "world" that He came in to by saying, "I spake openly to the world; I ever taught in the synagogue, and in the temple, whither the Jews always resort."[45]

8. This Christ of the Bible is that Christ for "the LORD God of the Hebrews,"[46] and Paul, understanding that Christian elders adhered to another *Christ*, counseled them, "Remember that Jesus Christ of the seed of David was raised from the dead."[47] Paul must say, "Remember," because Christian elders were doing contrary to the doctrine of that One the apostles referenced. This Christ preached putting away; from the personal religion; "the handwriting of ordinances"[48] of priests and ministers to receive a baptism that those ordinances can never provide, which baptism is "with the washing of water by the word."[49] Because it is by words, this baptism is greater than that occurring by any law of flesh for *consecration* or *conversion*, for conversion occurs only within the heart of the mind, which is why we are to be "perfect, as pertaining to the conscience."[50] Because the legal bill fails of rightly reaching the conscience, it is "sin" to the Spirit's learning, which learning states, "Through the Spirit wait for the hope of righteousness by faith."[51] The mind must personally spend time with the Spirit's voice if the conscience should know what to keep and dress the conversation with, and by this Christ on the tree, and then brought up by the Spirit into His LORD's heavenly Temple, what we have

---

45   John 18:20
46   Exodus 3:18
47   2 Timothy 2:8
48   Colossians 2:14
49   Ephesians 5:26
50   Hebrews 9:9
51   Galatians 5:5

depicted to us is the complete removal of handwritten charges from the Spirit's Faith, leaving only what the LORD of that Christ has decreed from out of His own mouth for observance, which is Ten Commandments highlighted by "the knowledge of his will in all wisdom and spiritual understanding."[52]

9. He or she passing through creation's course will understand why every one of the LORD's ten laws belong to their conversation, for by doing the will and saying of His Son's name, every law of liberty will be pronounced to their heart. And this will happen because we today have a King and a Priest over the LORD's name, even as it says of Aaron, "Aaron was separated...to burn incense before the LORD, to minister unto him, and to bless in his name for ever."[53] A "king" of God is a "priest" of the LORD's Faith, even as it says, "This Melchis'edec, king of Sa'lem, priest of the most high God,"[54] and, "And hast made us unto our God kings and priests."[55] How odd would it be for the LORD; who is that only King and God of heaven and earth; to have beside Him another King and God of heaven and earth? This is illogical. As a High Priest, the position of the LORD's Minister is not to be "God," but to bring His assembly to His LORD's wisdom and science, even as it says of this Christ today, "He shall stand and feed in the strength of the LORD, in the majesty of the name of the LORD his God."[56] This is important to understand because this Christ's sacrifice, and then this Christ's priestly ordination as His LORD's Chief Priest, establishes only one rule in heaven and earth, and that rule being the throne of the LORD His Father. Henceforward, every law or commandment put

---

52   Colossians 1:9
53   1 Chronicles 23:13
54   Hebrews 7:1
55   Revelation 5:10
56   Micah 5:4

forth by the pen and voice of priests and elders is accursed of the Word; "for he that is hanged is accursed of God";[57] seeing as how His High Priest's office eternally establishes the throne of His Father's Order.

10. Christian elders were not correctly giving enough attention to that Faith forwarded by this High Priest, and were therefore doing contrary to what His mediation taught, moving the apostles to say, "Ye yourselves are taught of God to love one another,"[58] and, "He was manifested to take away our sins; and in him is no sin."[59] Again, these things are written to Jews and pagan converts to Judaism, whose religion is determined by that "which stood only in meats and drinks, and divers washings, and carnal ordinances, imposed on them."[60] These carnal ordinances are legal religious laws, and the first apostles sought to help Christian elders understand that "the sting of death is sin; and the strength of sin is the law."[61] The "sin" that this Christ preached against was the very act that Christian elders were carrying out, which act was in inventing and regarding religious laws for *blessing*, which moved Paul to write, "After that ye have known God, or rather are known of God, how turn ye again to the weak and beggarly elements, whereunto ye desire again to be in bondage? Ye observe days, and months, and times, and years. I am afraid of you, lest I have bestowed upon you labour in vain."[62]

11. "Love" is in sweeping away the rubbish of what is not faith to encourage right learning by faith, but "hate" is in encouraging what is not faith as though it is of faith. "Hate"

---

57 Deuteronomy 21:23
58 1 Thessalonians 4:9
59 1 John 3:5
60 Hebrews 9:10
61 1 Corinthians 15:56
62 Galatians 4:9-11

is subjecting the conscience under legal rules and ordinances for *righteousness* to beautify the outward conversation, while "love" is in releasing the conscience from the legal charge by firstly spiritually discerning the LORD's voice, to then secondly act out that understand for, thirdly, knowledge to feed the heart to keep our faith soberly and intelligently on the hope of His Spirit. There is no faith in the legal religious bill, for, if all I must do is keep a tradition for *righteousness*, then I will only keep the tradition and have no mind to think any further. This is the religious philosophy of the serpent, and the end of this philosophy is witnessed, in the beginning, by the earth's condition. It is a fact that "where the Spirit of the Lord is, there is liberty,"[63] therefore when we find ourselves observing some desolate thing, we may know that the Spirit and confidence of liberty is not there. The earth adhered to the religion of darkness, even the religion "of the shadow of death, without any order, and where the light is as darkness."[64] Now, "the sting of death is sin; and the strength of sin is the law";[65] and when we are hearing about the earth's condition, we may know that the earth exists in a state of "hate," having its conscience under the rule of standards and judgments by a will without faith's learning.

12. Therefore to help Christian elders draw a clear reflection of their conversation, John wrote, "He that committeth sin is of the devil; for the devil sinneth from the beginning,"[66] and, "Know that he was manifested to take away our sins; and in him is no sin."[67] There is no "sin" in the knowledge of the living God's name, that is, there is no legal religious bill in

---

63 Job 10:22
64 1 Corinthians 15:56
65 2 Corinthians 3:17
66 1 John 3:8
67 1 John 3:5

heaven's new covenant Faith. The elder or minister preaching and subscribing to what is "sin"; that is, creating and employing legal religious laws and doctrines while professing service to *the LORD* and *Word* of *the Bible*; is a religiously erroneous and spiritually negligent *pastor*, for, "having abolished in his flesh the enmity, even the law of commandments contained in ordinances,"[68] such manners of worship and service are taken away from the Word's doctrine for ever. If it is that we accept the illustration of this LORD's Christ not simply on the tree, but also removed from the tree and brought in to the heavenly Sanctuary, it is that we accept what only remains by His mediation, which is every word that has ever come out of His LORD's mouth.

13. The serpent's philosophy is *righteousness* without faith in any thing but the charge of priests and elders. John hoped that Christian leadership could understand their false course, how that it mimicked the earth's original fall and Adam's transgression. Because the spirit of darkness ruled the earth, the earth found itself without a mind to properly dress its members with. But as soon as the earth heard how "God said, Let there be light,"[69] a loud cry came from the earth's heart, for, that Spirit pronouncing the sound of light said, "Are ye so foolish? having begun in the Spirit, are ye now made perfect by the flesh?"[70] The earth, only after receiving a fair reflection of its own self by the Word's impression, understood that the "good" it took for *righteousness* was only error that kept it asleep. "Darkness" only burdened the earth, and by that yoke, destroyed the earth, both inside and out. This was contrary to "love," for the earth only knew "hate," even an influence that refused to edify its core so that it could personally edify its

---

68 Ephesians 2:15
69 Genesis 1:3
70 Galatians 3:3

government. If "death" were right; and "the sting of death is sin; and the strength of sin is the law";[71] then the earth should experience no wrong thing against itself. Likewise, the apostles counseled them, "If righteousness come by the law, then Christ is dead in vain."[72] Thus, because "love" is understood to liberate the conversation from unnecessary chains, Paul counseled them, "Have no fellowship with the unfruitful works of darkness, but rather reprove them,"[73] and, "All things that are reproved are made manifest by the light: for whatsoever doth make manifest is light."[74]

14. The apostles told them, "Ye were sometimes darkness, but now are ye light,"[75] for like as the earth heard light's doctrine and never removed from it, the apostles expected the same from Christian elders, which is why they told them, "The darkness is past, and the true light now shineth."[76] The first regeneration of the earth spiritually resembled the LORD's plan for the creation of man's inward parts, and the apostles, discerning this, sought to help Christian elders understand the illustration put forth by creation's record. If they stayed faithful to "the light of the knowledge of the glory of God in the face of Jesus Christ,"[77] they would not do to the present creation what took place of old against the earth, and then against the earth again through Adam. If they took great care to beautify their faith's body by edifying their conscience, they would have understood that the legal religious law is "sin" because it "could not make him that did the service perfect, as pertaining

---

71   1 Corinthians 15:56
72   Galatians 2:21
73   Ephesians 5:11
74   Ephesians 5:13
75   Ephesians 5:8
76   1 John 2:8
77   2 Corinthians 4:6

to the conscience."[78] They would have understood why the name of the LORD's Christ is that Deliverer, and for what cause; they would have learned that "we might be justified by the faith of Christ, and not by the works of the law: for by the works of the law shall no flesh be justified."[79] But because they failed to investigate the Faith of this Christ, they began to do what is unjust before His LORD's Word, when if they had patiently and temperately sat with His words, they would have said, "That I may win Christ, and be found in him, not having mine own righteousness, which is of the law, but that which is through the faith of Christ."[80]

---

78   Hebrews 9:9
79   Galatians 2:16
80   Philippians 3:8,9

1

Works Left Undone

1. "I have no greater joy than to hear that my children walk in truth."[81] "This is the commandment, That, as ye have heard from the beginning, ye should walk in it."[82]

2. The apostle John longed to see the church remain in the name of the Father and His Son; this is that John who wrote, "He that saw it bare record, and his record is true; and he knoweth that he saith true, that ye might believe."[83] Because of the spirit that this man had within his heart, this man, who was ever "leaning on Jesus' bosom";[84] "whom Jesus loved";[85] "received a commandment from the Father"[86] for the Christian

---

81 3 John 1:4
82 2 John 1:6
83 John 19:35
84 John 13:23
85 John 13:23
86 2 John 1:4

church, saying, "Thou hast left thy first love. Remember therefore from whence thou art fallen."[87]

3. John was present when the LORD's Christ said, "I am the vine, ye are the branches,"[88] "and my Father is the husbandman."[89] John was there when He said, "I am the good shepherd."[90] "My sheep hear my voice, and I know them, and they follow me."[91] "I then, your Lord and Master,"[92] "have given you an example, that ye should do as I have done to you":[93] "ye also ought to wash one another's feet."[94] John heard and studied the Spirit's counsel from "looking upon Jesus as he walked,"[95] for this Christ said of His host, "They do follow My voice,"[96] therefore this same apostle wrote, "Follow not that which is evil, but that which is good,"[97] for "God anointed Jesus of Nazareth...who went about doing good, and healing all that were oppressed."[98]

4. It must have been heartbreaking for John to hear, concerning the Spirit's observation of ministers within the church, "I have somewhat against thee, because thou hast left thy first love."[99] It wasn't that long ago when "all that believed were together, and had all things common,"[100] yet the saying was fulfilling, "Of your own selves shall men arise, speaking

---

87	Revelation 2:4,5
88	John 15:5
89	John 15:1
90	John 10:14
91	John 10:27
92	John 13:14
93	John 13:15
94	John 13:14
95	John 1:36
96	John 10:27
97	3 John 1:11
98	Acts 10:38
99	Revelation 2:4
100	Acts 3:44

perverse things, to draw away disciples after them."[101] Herein we see why John wrote, when heading a letter, "Unto the elect lady and her children."[102] This elect church maintained "the faith of God's elect,"[103] for, at this time of which we speak, there "arose a question between some of John's disciples and the Jews,"[104] that is, between them that honored "the apostles' doctrine and fellowship"[105] and "the Jews which believed not,"[106] "the sect of the Pharisees which believed."[107] "To all the Jews and Greeks also dwelling at E'phesus";[108] the same ones professing the *Faith* of *the Father* and *His Son* that said, "Great is Diana of the Ephe'sians,"[109] and, "Keep the law of Moses";[110] came a word of caution from the Spirit's minister, saying, "Love not the world."[111] "He that saith he abideth in him ought himself also so to walk, even as he walked."[112] "This is love, that we walk after his commandments";[113] "that we should believe on the name of his Son...and love one another, as he gave us commandment."[114]

5. "That which was from the beginning"[115] of the Spirit's dispensation is the counsel of the "first love."[116] In the beginning, them dawning the spirit of Eph'esus were as a white horse

---

101 Acts 20:39
102 2 John 1:1
103 Titus 1:1
104 John 3:25
105 Acts 2:42
106 Acts 17:5
107 Acts 15:5
108 Acts 18:17
109 Acts 19:28
110 Acts 15:5
111 1 John 2:15
112 1 John 2:6
113 2 John 1:6
114 1 John 3:23
115 1 John 1:1
116 Revelation 2:4

that went forth conquering by the name of the living God, and to conquer for the name of the living God.[117] All "continued steadfastly in the apostles' doctrine and fellowship,"[118] "and the Lord added to the church daily such as should be saved."[119] "Believers were the more added to the Lord, multitudes both of men and women,"[120] yet it happened that "the unbelieving Jews stirred up the Gentiles, and made their minds evil affected against the brethren."[121] Thus, John wrote to them that had been damaged by "them which say they are apostles, and are not,"[122] saying, "These things have I written unto you concerning them that seduce you,"[123] for, the word had gone out some time ago, "In the latter times some shall depart from the faith, giving heed to seducing spirits, and doctrines of devils."[124] For this cause, it is well to inquire about where we are in the time of John's letters. The apostle himself tells us, saying, "It is the last time."[125] "The latter time" and "the last time" are one, and it was at this time in history that believers were to hear, concerning their conversation, that they should remain in "the power of God through faith unto salvation ready to be revealed in the last time."[126] At the end of this time or season of blessing, the faithful were to receive salvation; "The salvation of your souls,"[127] they were taught; but to reach that end, the people were to abide by the Faith and spiritual labor they first began with.

---

117 Revelation 6:2
118 Acts 2:42
119 Acts 2:47
120 Acts 5:14
121 Acts 14:2
122 Revelation 2:2
123 1 John 2:26
124 1 Timothy 4:1
125 1 John 2:18
126 1 Peter 1:5
127 1 Peter 1:9

6. This is why John says, "That we may have boldness in the day of judgment,"[128] for the apostles knew that, at the end of the times, a judgment would commence, for again he says, "When he shall appear, we may have confidence, and not be ashamed before him at his coming."[129] The apostles knew how that their High Priest had said, "I will come near to you to judgment,"[130] yet they, like the apostles after them, misunderstood the manner of His appearing, for it says, concerning this "coming," "The Lord, whom ye seek, shall suddenly come to his temple."[131] This appearing means that "he shall purify the sons of Levi...that they may offer unto the LORD an offering in righteousness,"[132] which is why the Spirit's Christ confessed of His witness, "John came unto you in the way of righteousness,"[133] for John taught "the righteousness which is of faith."[134]

7. The apostle John knew the ordinances given of the Spirit for the last time would keep the church as His faithful and honorable witness to the religious world, and if obeyed, would prepare every believer to accept the counsel of the position that the LORD's Christ should assume at the end of the last time, along with their new duty to that ministration. But from His observation of an unbelief that garnered discontent within Christian elders, the counsel of the Spirit to the church was, "Thou hast left thy first love. Remember from whence thou art fallen, and repent, and do the first works."[135]

8. That which was given to the early church was their "first love," and this "first love" was the doing of the "first works"

---

128   1 John 4:17
129   1 John 2:28
130   Malachi 3:5
131   Malachi 3:1
132   Malachi 3:3
133   Matthew 21:32
134   Romans 9:30
135   Revelation 2:4,5

of that "first love." What works are these? It was told them, "Be watchful, and strengthen the things which remain, that are ready to die."[136] Of old the LORD said, "Strengthen ye the weak hands, and confirm the feeble knees. Say to them that are of a fearful heart, Be strong, fear not...The eyes of the blind shall be opened, and the ears of the deaf shall be unstopped."[137] Because "wisdom strengtheneth,"[138] it was the responsibility of the early church to add the Spirit's wisdom to their spiritual understanding, for they had among them a heart that lacked sure "knowledge of his will in all wisdom and spiritual understanding."[139] If they took the time to comprehend heaven's new covenant will by discerning the old, the Spirit would have never acknowledged them as "them which say they are Jews, and are not, but are the synagogue of Satan."[140] It is because they failed to settle their heart on the LORD's Faith that John wrote of them, "They went out from us."[141]

9. Paul confirms, "The Gentiles should be fellowheirs, and of the same body, and partakers of his promise in Christ";[142] "for through him we both have access by one Spirit unto the Father."[143] "But when the Jews saw the multitudes, they were filled with envy, and spake against those things which were spoken by Paul, contradicting and blaspheming."[144] These Jews are them who Paul mentions when saying, "Forbidding us to speak to the Gentiles that they might be saved, to fill up their sins

---

136 Revelation 3:2
137 Isaiah 35:4,5
138 Ecclesiastes 7:19
139 Colossians 1:9
140 Revelation 2:9
141 1 John 2:19
142 Ephesians 3:6
143 Ephesians 2:18
144 Acts 13:45

always."[145] These priests found Paul's doctrine so grievous that, in the process of time, and after Paul had drawn injury to himself, "certain of the Jews banded together, and bound themselves under a curse, saying that they would neither eat nor drink till they had killed Paul...They were more than forty which had made this conspiracy."[146] The apostle John saw all of this happening against his band by a church who, when once honestly "believed were of one heart and one soul,"[147] and so knew within himself, when catching wind of their foreign state of mind, "Hereby know we the spirit of truth, and the spirit of error."[148]

10. It was around 65A.D. that Paul had been executed, and around 64A.D., the churches of Asia had been framed in their own government. The revelation given to John came during the years 90-100A.D., therefore even before he wrote his epistles and was given the Spirit's counsel "in the isle that is called Pat'mos,"[149] the word of the apostle Paul, concerning apostasy within the Christian church, was being fulfilled. This is why, during the time when a clear division was being drawn between the Spirit's apostles and them "of the sect of the Pharisees which believed,"[150] John expressed the prevailing character of church elders, saying, "Prating against us with malicious words: and not content therewith, neither doth he himself receive the brethren, and forbiddeth them that would, and casteth them out of the church."[151] Of this counterfeit assembly, the LORD's Christ says, "Ye have taken away the key of knowledge: ye entered not in yourselves, and them that

---

145   1 Thessalonians 2:16
146   Acts 22:12,13
147   Acts 4:32
148   1 John 4:6
149   Revelation 1:9
150   Acts 15:5
151   3 John 1:10

were entering in ye hindered."[152] Concerning such ministers, Paul writes, "Such are false apostles, deceitful workers, transforming themselves into the apostles of Christ,"[153] for to these elders he says, "By the deeds of the law there shall no flesh by justified in his sight,"[154] and, "The name of God is blasphemed among the Gentiles through you, as it is written."[155]

11. Godly love had perished due to "all deceivableness of unrighteousness in them that perish."[156] Our High Priest says, concerning the name of His intercession, "Whosoever believeth in him should not perish, but have everlasting life,"[157] which is why it says, "God hath given to us eternal life, and this life is in his Son."[158] What is "life"? Plainly the apostle says, "The Spirit is life."[159] Therefore in the name and knowledge of the LORD's High Priest; which name is "the law of Christ,"[160] "the word of righteousness";[161] is "the eternal Spirit"[162] to "purge your conscience from dead works to serve the living God."[163] It is for this reason that every believer is "complete in him";[164] that is, in the wisdom and operation of His Son's mediation; "for in him dwelleth all the fullness of the Godhead,"[165]

---

152 Luke 11:52
153 2 Corinthians 11:13
154 Romans 3:20
155 Romans 2:24
156 2 Thessalonians 2:10
157 John 3:16
158 1 John 5:11
159 Romans 8:10
160 Galatians 6:2
161 Hebrews 5:13
162 Hebrews 9:14
163 Hebrews 9:14
164 Colossians 2:10
165 Colossians 2:9

which is why it says, "Be filled with all the fullness of God,"[166] or rather, "Be filled with the Spirit."[167]

12. "By his Spirit in the inner man,"[168] "Christ may dwell in your hearts by faith"[169] to declare, "I delight in the law of God after the inward man."[170] Wherefore how is it that, in John's day, that white and perfect horse in vision could turn to become "another horse that was red"?[171] It is said, "He that keepeth the law, happy is he,"[172] therefore the Spirit's Minister says, "If ye know these things, happy are ye if you do them."[173] Thus, it was "men of corrupt minds, and destitute of the truth, supposing that gain is godliness,"[174] that compelled John to place the church in remembrance of what appeared when doing heaven's will, saying, "He that abideth in the doctrine of Christ, he hath both the Father and the Son,"[175] and, "He that acknowledgeth the Son hath the Father also."[176]

13. That which was to confess simple faith and obedience to the Spirit's doctrine was replaced with another doctrine of another spirit, and in salutation of another *God*. These "who changed the truth of God into lie,"[177] who "did not like to retain God in their knowledge,"[178] compelled the apostle to write, "Many deceivers are entered into the world, who confess not

---

166 Ephesians 3:19
167 Ephesians 5:18
168 Ephesians 3:16
169 Ephesians 3:17
170 Romans 7:22
171 Revelation 6:4
172 Proverbs 29:18
173 John 13:17
174 1 Timothy 6:5
175 2 John 1:9
176 1 John 2:23
177 Romans 1:25
178 Romans 1:28

that Jesus Christ is come in the flesh."[179] Because there was no honest searching after the LORD and Spirit of heaven's High Priest, because strange materials again began to consume the heart of priests professing His name, many began to "glory in appearance, and not in heart."[180] Joy in the knowledge of Christ's LORD and Father had again been removed from an assembly claiming devotion to Him, making the saying applicable for a second time, "I have written to him the great things of my law, but they were counted as a strange thing."[181] That which came by men "as they were moved by the Holy Ghost"[182] was "counted as beasts, and reputed vile,"[183] "less than nothing and vanity,"[184] and was exchanged for "Jewish fables, and commandments of men, that turn from the truth."[185] Because happiness in following the Spirit's law and decree concerning the benevolent Faith of heaven's LORD had vanished, for the vision of the Spirit's prayer had not been considered, leaving the saying, "Where there is no vision, the people perish,"[186] to be fulfilled.

14. The first apostles wrote, "concerning them that seduce"[187] "through philosophy and vain deceit, after the tradition of men, after the rudiments of the world, and not after Christ,"[188] "They speak great swelling words of vanity, they allure through the lusts of the flesh."[189] This is why John, when writing of his elect favorites in the Father and the Son,

---

179 2 John 1:7
180 2 Corinthians 5:12
181 Hosea 8:12
182 2 Peter 1:21
183 Job 18:3
184 Isaiah 40:17
185 Titus 1:14
186 Proverbs 29:18
187 1 John 2:26
188 Colossians 2:8
189 2 Peter 2:18

says, "I rejoiced greatly that I found of thy children walking in truth,"[190] for, before this time, John had said, "The Spirit is truth,"[191] therefore these had heard and obeyed the injunction, "Walk in the Spirit, and ye shall not fulfill the lusts of the flesh."[192] When once upholding the conversation by the Spirit's will and understanding, giving no power to the appetite within the members of the tongue of that conversation, what is the result? John writes, "Follow not that which is evil, but that which is good,"[193] that is, "Follow after righteousness, godliness, faith, love, patience, meekness,"[194] and, "Follow after the things...wherewith one may edify another."[195] Herein we have the general character "of the doctrine which is according to godliness,"[196] that is, "the doctrine of Christ."[197]

15. There is a reason why Paul says that the faith of the Spirit's host is "after the common faith,"[198] for, in one sense, when that of the Spirit is eaten without happiness, it becomes "common or unclean,"[199] for "the natural man receiveth not the things of the Spirit of God."[200] That which is to bring sinful and penitent man to the Spirit's will calls for a reform on diet. An evident attribute that one displays after accepting heaven's doctrine is the fruit of the knowledge of temperance concerning "the flesh with the affections and lusts,"[201] and without accepting the full work of righteousness, there will be

---

190   2 John 1:4
191   1 John 5:6
192   Galatians 5:16
193   3 John 1:11
194   1 Timothy 6:11
195   Romans 14:19
196   1 Timothy 6:3
197   2 John 1:9
198   Titus 1:4
199   Acts 10:14
200   1 Corinthians 2:14
201   Galatians 5:24

many "desirous of vain glory, provoking one another, envying one another."[202] This is why John writes, "I have no greater joy than to hear that my children walk in truth."[203] If there is a conversation in the Spirit's higher learning, then that conversation will bear witness of every right fruit of the LORD and Son of that Spirit, for "where the Spirit of the Lord is, there is liberty."[204] For this cause, every one keeping and dressing his or her mind with the wisdom of the Spirit's heavenly ministry says, "The law of the Spirit of life in Christ Jesus hath made me free from the law of sin and death."[205]

16. There is a spirit in the Faith of God's Man that is without "a shew of wisdom in will worship."[206] But Paul reports of spurious ministers, "They constrain you to be circumcised; only lest they should suffer persecution for the cross of Christ."[207] The banner that once read, "God forbid that I should glory, save in the cross of our Lord Jesus Christ, by whom the world is crucified unto me, and I unto the world,"[208] now needed to hear, "Thou therefore which teachest another, teachest thou not thyself?"[209] It was because of the vision given him revealing the new spirit that should arise in the church that John wrote, "Whosoever transgresseth, and abideth not in the doctrine of Christ, hath not God,"[210] for he knew that if there was to be any faithfulness among believers, any stance for reverencing the LORD's Government, it would have to be through "fellowship

---

202 Galatians 5:26
203 3 John 1:4
204 2 Corinthians 3:17
205 Romans 8:2
206 Colossians 2:23
207 Galatians 6:12
208 Galatians 6:14
209 Romans 2:21
210 2 John 1:9

of the Spirit,"[211] which fellowship manifested itself from personally doing "good." If the churches could hear these two points, "Believe on the name of his Son Jesus Christ, and love one another, as he gave us commandment,"[212] there would be no deception in the conversation of their ministers, but every trace of right confession. Therefore, "Hereby know ye the Spirit of God,"[213] said John to the churches, "every spirit that confesseth that Jesus Christ is come in the flesh is of God."[214]

17. Them that confess to the Spirit's will existing within the members of their heart and mind reveal their conversation with that Spirit's LORD and Father, and if the religion is of His Spirit, then the heart will confess, "God sent his only begotten Son"[215] "to be the propitiation for our sins"[216] "that we might live through him."[217] "Hereby perceive we the love of God, because he laid down his life for us: and we ought to lay down our lives for the brethren."[218] Yet why did the spirit of compassion and brotherly love vanish from within the early church? It was because many refused to sincerely and wholeheartedly confess, "We have known and believed the love that God hath to us."[219]

18. Nothing can be done for the mind in a state of unbelief. A refusal to allow the heart to accept, and by an active faith, the Spirit's counsel, is proof to His eye that the conscience of the conversation will not welcome reform by His voice. Yet when once the soul believes on and examines the instruction of the

---

211 Philippians 2:1
212 1 John 3:23
213 1 John 4:2
214 1 John 4:2
215 1 John 4:9
216 1 John 4:10
217 1 John 4:9
218 1 John 3:16
219 1 John 4:16

living God, the counsel is, "Let us love not in word, neither in tongue; but in deed and in truth."[220] That which testifies "of the truth that is in thee"[221] will "have born witness of thy charity before the church,"[222] and this is what it means to allow the Spirit's doctrine to birth indifferent beneficence within the soul, even as it says, "Doest faithfully whatsoever thou does to the brethren, and to strangers."[223] This is the doing of "good," the following after righteousness. Such a work for the one consecrated to the Spirit's voice is to bring the hopeful spirit forward on their journey after a godly conversation.[224] If the church does this, "Thou shalt do well,"[225] says John, or rather, "Doeth good."[226]

19. John heard the Spirit say, "Strengthen the things which remain, that are ready to perish,"[227] and, "Thou hast left thy first love";[228] "do the first works."[229] There was, at this time, a need to call the churches to remember the spirit from which they were born, which spirit teaches, "Except a corn of wheat fall into the ground and die, it abideth alone: but if it die, it bringeth forth much fruit."[230] Our High Priest says, "Follow me,"[231] and, "He that loveth his life shall lose it,"[232] but why say these things? This He teaches because this same Christ says, "I

---

220 1 John 3:18
221 3 John 1:3
222 3 John 1:6
223 3 John 1:5
224 3 John 1:6
225 3 John 1:6
226 3 John 1:11
227 Revelation 3:2
228 Revelation 2:4
229 Revelation 2:5
230 John 12:24
231 John 12:26
232 John 12:25

lay down my life";[233] "for even Christ pleased not himself";[234] which is why His beloved apostle writes, "He laid down his life for us: and we ought to lay down our lives for the brethren,"[235] that is, "Let every one of us please his neighbour for his good to edification."[236]

20. Because the church removed their attention from principles that witnessed to the effect of right unity by mental and spiritual recuperation, their faith and confidence in the hope promised by the Faith of the LORD's Son collapsed, causing a blow to the structure of the perfect harmony of the Spirit's new dispensation. Because the Spirit's will was not accepted among them, spiritual deception was entertained. When once deception entered into the fold, then came compromise, even "false prophets also among the people"[237] who encouraged "damnable heresies,"[238] "ungodly men, turning the grace of our God into lasciviousness."[239] Again, how could this have been accomplished? It was said, "Remember ye the words which were spoken before of the apostles of our Lord...how that they told you there should be mockers in the last time,"[240] "who separate themselves, sensual, having not the Spirit."[241] "These are murmurers, complainers, walking after their own lusts";[242] "mockers in the last time, who should walk after their own ungodly lusts."[243] John heard the Spirit say, "Thou hast tried them which say they are apostles, and are not, and hast

---

233 John 10:17
234 Romans 15:3
235 1 John 3:16
236 Romans 15:2
237 2 Peter 2:1
238 2 Peter 2:1
239 Jude 1:4
240 Jude 1:17,18
241 Jude 1:19
242 Jude 1:16
243 Jude 1:18

found them liars,"[244] and it was for this reason that he, trying to keep the thoughts of the elders heavenward, wrote, "Believe not every spirit, but try the spirits whether they are of God."[245] A spirit of error was striving with those of a spirit for truth and hopeful for birth by "the law of the Spirit of life,"[246] and the apostles felt the pangs of death beating against their heart due to the sight of growing apostasy within their camps.

21. What else could John say to them but, "This is the message that ye have heard from the beginning, that we should love one another."[247] As it was said, "Ye yourselves are taught of God to love one another,"[248] in reality, it was known, "Comfort yourselves together, and edify one another."[249] For, Paul wrote, to encourage them to experience heaven's learning, "We exhort you, brethren, warn them that are unruly, comfort the feebleminded, support the weak, be patient toward all men. See that none render evil for evil unto any man; but ever follow that which is good, both among yourselves, and to all men."[250] This charge forced them to quit the noise of the various *ministers* professing *the Spirit's Faith* to personally settle their own understanding, to the end they may know what good should appear by an experimental faith in the knowledge of God's Son to better value self, the Spirit's wisdom, and all others hopeful for the end of His ministry.

22. That which is "good" is a living expression of "your work of faith, and labour of love."[251] It was this labor; both to their own individual self and to one another; that they allowed

---

244 Revelation 2:2
245 1 John 4:1
246 Romans 8:2
247 1 John 3:11
248 1 Thessalonians 4:9
249 1 Thessalonians 5:11
250 1 Thessalonians 5:14,15
251 1 Thessalonians 1:3

to slip away from them. John knew that if the Spirit's voice was rejected, so too would pass away the betterment of free unity invoked by that Spirit, and if there should be no place found for heaven's labor and learning, it means that there has been a rejection of the Spirit's doctrine and that a breach has been made between them and the mediation of His High Priest. How, then, is it that a break from loyalty to heaven's pure Faith occurred? It is said, "He that hath no rule over his own spirit is like a city that is broken down, and without walls."[252] The elders of the early church had not received that promised conception of the Spirit within the spirit of their mind, for they had no right knowledge that "that which is born of the Spirit is spirit."[253]

23. "Eat so much as is sufficient for thee,"[254] counsels the Spirit, for "the righteous eateth to the satisfying of his soul."[255] Discontent and intemperance estranged the early church from the Godhead, for her elders became "mad upon their idols,"[256] so much so that they were counseled, "It is a shame to speak of those things which are done of them in secret."[257] It was because John saw this manner of worship and service at work that he wrote, "Little children, keep yourselves from idols."[258]

24. The heart of the apostles shattered when they saw how many ministers counted the Spirit's grace, and the understanding of Christ's priestly ministration, to mean nothing for their conversation's growth and development. The Word's man pleaded, "Behold";[259] Look and consider; "what manner

---

252 Proverbs 25:28
253 John 3:6
254 Proverbs 25:16
255 Proverbs 13:25
256 Jeremiah 50:38
257 Ephesians 5:12
258 1 John 5:21
259 1 John 3:1

of love the Father hath bestowed upon us";[260] what kindness the Father hath donated and imparted upon our faith's heart; "that we should be called the sons of God."[261] There was an ever-present zeal for heaven's instruction, but it was that "they being ignorant of God's righteousness, and going about to establish their own righteousness, have not submitted themselves unto the righteousness of God."[262] John desired to call the attention to the means for righteousness to properly execute love's service, which means was the express revelation of the Spirit's benevolence to our inward parts through His Son's name, which is why he wrote, "This is the promise that he hath promised us, even eternal life."[263] We should know that our High Priest "received of the Father the promise of the Holy Ghost"[264] for the development of our faith and mind in salvation's science.

25. "We might receive the promise of the Spirit through faith,"[265] said the apostle, therefore "we through the Spirit wait for the hope of righteousness by faith."[266] John saw the profession of the people preparing itself to rest "where Satan's seat is,"[267] and so sought to call the mind to the purpose of God's Man sacrificed on that tree, and to the only means for justification in the Spirit's sight, even as he says, "We have an advocate with the Father, Jesus Christ the righteous."[268] For this cause, John counseled, "Abide in him":[269] "the anointing which

---

260 1 John 3:1
261 1 John 3:1
262 Romans 10:3
263 1 John 2:25
264 Acts 2:33
265 Galatians 3:14
266 Galatians 5:5
267 Revelation 2:13
268 1 John 2:1
269 1 John 2:27

ye have received of him abideth in you, and ye need not that any man teach you";[270] "abide in him."[271] Years before, Paul had said of these same elders, "I marvel that ye are so soon removed from him that called you into the grace of Christ unto another gospel,"[272] for John now desired to bring an honest consideration to ministers regarding their religion and the proof of it, placing them in remembrance of how it was counseled, "By grace are ye saved through faith; and that not of yourselves: it is the gift of God."[273]

26. Thus, John wrote to the churches and said, "Behold the fashion and the form that the Spirit's love is given us for the purpose of adoption into the LORD our Father's heavenly Family. Contemplate and discern our Father's gift in order to provoke sincere acts of like tenderheartedness, for 'we believe that through the grace of the Lord Jesus Christ we shall be saved,'[274] that is, inwardly recovered." It is by "the Spirit of grace"[275] that "they which receive abundance of grace and of the gift of righteousness shall reign"[276] in heaven's conversation, and with the gift of righteousness there is only one work, and it says, "Every one that doeth righteousness is born of him."[277]

27. "Righteousness" is not a state of being, but is rather an assignment to accomplish. Such employment is by learning of and doing the Spirit's will, which is why we are counseled, "Acquaint now thyself with him,"[278] and, "Be ye transformed

---

270 1 John 2:27
271 1 John 2:27
272 Galatians 1:6
273 Ephesians 2:8
274 Acts 15:11
275 Hebrews 10:29
276 Romans 5:17
277 1 John 2:29
278 Job 22:21

by the renewing of your mind, that ye may prove what is that good, and acceptable, and perfect, will of God."[279] The end of the Spirit's will is the revelation of His righteousness within the constitution of our faith's body, and as we allow the Spirit of heaven's mediation to do His work within our mind, it is that the reformer is to also lead many, by their training under the wings of His Son, "forward on their journey after a godly sort"[280] as "fellowhelpers to the truth";[281] herein is the announcement that "Christ" has come in to the flesh. To the believer is given "the ministration of reconciliation,"[282] which is "the good pleasure of his goodness, and the work of faith with power,"[283] to accomplish within their heart by the knowledge of His Son through their own disciplined rule over self, to the end their consolation "not only supplieth the want of the saints, but is abundant also by many thanksgivings unto God."[284]

28. John desired the one who actively and diligently believes on the LORD's Faith to contemplate the manner of executing the promised redemption of the conversation. John desired church elders to understand that the root of their admiration for his LORD lay in the ground of self-sacrificing charity, which ground is watered by showers of grace, to the end the seed of faith, that the Spirit has placed within the person, may grow up by His own voice, and by their own efforts to soberly and intelligently learn of and do that voice. The end of this work is to ensure that the believer "walkest in the truth,"[285] that is, owns a conversation after His Son's doctrine and the knowledge of His name. For this to take place

---

279   Romans 12:2
280   3 John 1:6
281   3 John 1:8
282   2 Corinthians 5:18
283   2 Thessalonians 1:11
284   2 Corinthians 9:12
285   3 John 1:3

within the church, John instructed, "Be in health, even as thy soul prospereth,"[286] and, "Keep yourselves from idols,"[287] "for this is the will of God, even your sanctification, that ye should abstain from fornication."[288]

29. Faithfulness to only the LORD's Word would have resulted in blessings that would have encouraged pure movements of brotherly love and godly affection within the early church. One of the reasons that accounted for her fall from heaven's Faith was the fact that the members of the church lost sight of their own individual accountability before the wisdom of the LORD's Spirit and ministry. Spiritual senselessness "after the commandments and doctrines of men"[289] was advertised as the necessary prescribed practice for *salvation*, and a false religion was not known to have generated by that foolishness because there was a veiled atmosphere contrary to edification, for which cause John wrote, "He that hateth his brother is in darkness, and walketh in darkness, and knoweth not whither he goeth, because that darkness hath blinded his eyes."[290] Thus, through the example forwarded by the early Christian church, we may know that if individuals lack moral courage to rightly divide the LORD's speech, "I will spue thee out of my mouth,"[291] says His Spirit. This is why we today are counseled, "Remember therefore from whence thou art fallen, and repent, and do the first works."[292]

---

286   3 John 1:2
287   1 John 5:21
288   1 Thessalonians 4:3
289   Colossians 2:22
290   1 John 2:11
291   Revelation 3:16
292   Revelation 2:5

2

Revelation's Benevolence

1. "And there was in their synagogue a man with an unclean spirit; and he cried out, saying, Let us alone; what have we to do with thee, thou Jesus of Nazareth? art thou come to destroy us? I know thee who thou art, the Holy One of God. And Jesus rebuked him, saying, Hold thy peace, and come out of him. And when the unclean spirit had torn him, and cried with a loud voice, he came out of him. And they were all amazed, insomuch that they questioned among themselves, saying, What thing is this? what new doctrine is this? for with authority commandeth he even the unclean spirits, and they do obey him. And immediately his fame spread abroad throughout all the region round about Galilee."[293]

2. The words of this man may have been, "Let us alone; what have we to do with thee,"[294] but it is apparent that, "when

---

[293] Mark 1:23-27
[294] Mark 1:24

he saw Jesus afar off, he ran and worshipped him."[295] This man was sick, in that he carried a mind "which was diseased with an issue of blood,"[296] "and had suffered many things of many physicians"[297] "and was nothing bettered, but rather grew worse,"[298] declaring of such professed ministers, "Ye are forgers of lies, ye are all physicians of no value."[299] This man came to Christ, pleading in a language that only the LORD's Messenger could understand, which tone spoke of deliverance from a strange spirit within his heart. As Christ said to his troubled mind, "Hold thy peace,"[300] it was that His voice echoed the sentiment, "Know the truth, and the truth shall make you free."[301] But free from what? It is written, "He shall redeem their soul from deceit and violence,"[302] and, "Hath made me free from the law of sin and death."[303] This man was tired of purifying self, he was tired of having form of *righteousness* without the inward benefit, for he only knew the handwritten expression of *righteousness* by ordinances and commandments.

3. This man desired to be released from the bond of a gross spiritual labor without soul nourishment to possess self. The end of the living God's doctrine is a spirit benevolently regulating reason and religion, which is why the Spirit's course is for "the acknowledging of the truth which is after godliness."[304] Today, all that pray, "Create in me a clean heart, O God; and renew a right spirit within me,"[305] will have their prayer

---

295 Mark 5:6
296 Matthew 9:20
297 Mark 5:26
298 Mark 5:26
299 Job 13:4
300 Mark 1:25
301 John 8:32
302 Psalms 72:14
303 Romans 8:2
304 Titus 1:1
305 Psalm 51:10

heard and answered, but not before personally hearing and performing the counsel, "Guide thine heart in the way,"[306] and, "Let thine heart retain my words: keep my commandments, and live."[307] This Christ said, upon hearing this man's condition by the confession of his voice, "Know right possession and purchase liberty," therefore He sought to lead this man into a similar experience to that known of John, who confesses, "When I had heard and seen, I fell down to worship,"[308] for it is written, "Have ye not known? have ye not heard?"[309]

4. We may only hear our High Priest's voice when first taking knowledge of that voice. There is an experience awaiting the one who would be so bold as to move the living God to say, "Who is this that engaged his heart to approach unto me?"[310] The religion of His Christ is to be obtained by exercising faith on the merits and virtue of His name. As Christ opened up the mind of the people to the knowledge of His ministry, "they questioned among themselves, saying, What thing is this? what new doctrine is this?"[311] or rather "spake among themselves saying, What a word is this!"[312] It was no lie that "Jesus came into Galilee, preaching the gospel of the kingdom of God,"[313] for through this man, Christ "preached the word,"[314] insomuch that "his fame spread abroad,"[315] and it is said concerning "fame," "Have not heard my fame, neither

---

306 Proverbs 23:19
307 Proverbs 4:4
308 Revelation 22:8
309 Isaiah 49:21
310 Jeremiah 30:21
311 Mark 1:27
312 Luke 4:36
313 Mark 1:14
314 Mark 2:2
315 Mark 1:28

have seen my glory."[316] In this man, the LORD's Spirit "manifested forth his glory."[317]

5. What then is the knowledge of the Spirit's glory? What is the instruction of the Spirit's kingdom and dominion that His Christ preached? It is written, "To heal the brokenhearted, to preach deliverance to the captives, and recovery of sight to the blind, to set at liberty them that are bruised."[318] It is for this reason that it is said of Him, "A bruised reed shall he not break, and the smoking flax shall he not quench,"[319] for He says of them that make His faithful sick, "Ye pull off the robe with the garment"[320] and "pluck off their skin from off them, and their flesh from off their bones."[321] Our High Priest will not destroy any one who has even the smallest hint of a flame for His name. It is said of Him, "He shall gather the lambs with his arms, and carry them in his bosom,"[322] but of those consciously contrary to His understanding, He says, "Hypocrites! for ye compass sea and land to make one proselyte, and when he is made, ye make him twofold more the child of hell than yourselves."[323] Christ understood the plight of the soul in the hands of priests and ministers, and how "he that followeth vain persons is void of understanding"[324] and "shall have poverty enough."[325] This is why it is written, "The Son of God is come, and hath given us an understanding."[326]

---

316 Isaiah 66:19
317 John 2:11
318 Luke 4:18
319 Isaiah 42:3
320 Micah 3:2
321 Micah 3:2
322 Isaiah 40:11
323 Matthew 23:15
324 Proverbs 12:11
325 Proverbs 28:19
326 1 John 5:30

6. What was the understanding that this LORD's Christ established? It says, "He went out, and departed into a solitary place, and there prayed,"[327] for it is written, "God setteth the solitary in families: he bringeth out those which are bound with chains."[328] It is said of this Christ, "He went up into a mountain apart to pray: and when the evening was come, he was there."[329] He maintained personal communion with His LORD and Father, to the end He could confidently verify, "He that sent me is with me: the Father hath not left me alone,"[330] and, "I know him, and keep his saying."[331] This is why, as His Father's High priest, the LORD's Man can counsel His assembly, "Abide in me, and I in you,"[332] but in order to hear this commandment, the heart must confess to its own self, "I may know him."[333] For, concerning the one professing His name, our High Priest counsels, "Handle me and see"[334] "and be not faithless, but believing."[335]

7. By faith, the conscience of the conversation is to learn that "God imputeth righteousness without works,"[336] for an exercised "faith is counted for righteousness."[337] Christ could say of His Father, because He obtained personal knowledge of His intention, "I know that his commandment is life everlasting,"[338] and should He not care for us to confess to Him; because He is that mediator standing before the LORD

---

327 Mark 1:35
328 Psalms 68:6
329 Matthew 14:23
330 John 8:29
331 John 8:55
332 John 15:4
333 Philippians 3:10
334 Luke 24:39
335 John 20:27
336 Romans 4:5
337 John 12:50
338 John 12:50

His Father for the wellbeing of our mind; "When shall I come and appear before God?"[339] "Him that cometh to me I will in no wise cast out,"[340] He says. "Why are ye so fearful? how is it that ye have no faith?"[341]

8. The understanding preached to the people through this man shook them. The people said, "What new word and doctrine is among us," for they had known no other form of personal spiritual care or government than what had been prescribed for them by priests and elders. Here was a new doctrine that alleviated what the traditions and ordinances of ministers could not, for the digestion of His speech within the mind blessed the heart to rightly pick up the limbs of faith's body. This is why Paul taught them, "By him all that believe are justified from all things, from which ye could not be justified by the law of Moses."[342]

9. Of old it was said, "When a man shall have in the skin of his flesh a rising, a scab, or bright spot, and it be in the skin of his flesh,"[343] "and the plague in sight be deeper than the skin of his flesh, it is a plague of leprosy."[344] "It is an old leprosy in the skin of his flesh, and the priest shall pronounce him unclean";[345] for "when raw flesh appeareth in him, he shall be unclean";[346] "for the raw flesh is unclean."[347]

10. That which is raw is coarse, foul, filthy and indecent, and when the plague on the skin; that is, on the covering of the flesh; reaches deeper than the surface and into the flesh, an

---

339   Psalm 42:2
340   John 6:37
341   Mark 4:40
342   Acts 13:39
343   Leviticus 13:2
344   Leviticus 13:3
345   Leviticus 13:11
346   Leviticus 13:14
347   Leviticus 13:15

uncleanness is born within the man, turning that which is inside of him against himself and those around him. For "if it spread much abroad in the skin";[348] that is, "if the plague be spread in the garment,"[349] "in the garment, or in the skin";[350] "it is a fretting leprosy,"[351] "it is fret inward."[352] Because of this illness in him, "he shall dwell alone; without the camp shall his habitation be";[353] which is why it says of this man that approached the Spirit's Christ, "Who had his dwelling among the tombs,"[354] and, "Always, night and day, he was in the mountains, and in the tombs, crying, and cutting himself with stones."[355]

11. The condition of this man from Caper'naum was one of leprosy, and his individual error or frustration was sunken into the conversation of his spirit; the constitution of his personal religion; even as it says, "It reacheth unto thine heart."[356] "It is a fretting leprosy,"[357] "it is fret inward,"[358] says the Spirit, for there was nothing but a breach caused within the inward parts of this man, which is why the man knew, "By great force of my disease is my garment changed."[359] That of the skin is translated, in proper language, as "the garment which covereth,"[360] therefore that which changed in him was as it is said, "His countenance was changed in him."[361] The LORD's Christ told

---

348 Leviticus 13:27
349 Leviticus 13:51
350 Leviticus 13:49
351 Leviticus 13:51
352 Leviticus 13:55
353 Leviticus 13:46
354 Mark 5:3
355 Mark 5:5
356 Jeremiah 4:18
357 Leviticus 13:52
358 Leviticus 13:55
359 Job 30:18
360 Psalms 109:19
361 Daniel 5:9

him, "Thy thoughts trouble thee,"[362] and this is why the Word's Christ said, "Why reason ye these things in your hearts?"[363] That given of the Spirit is to be worked out by faith through His power and not in a self-sufficient spirit "after the commandments and doctrines of men."[364] For, "man's goings are of the LORD; how can a man then understand his own way?"[365]

12. "The Spirit of God searcheth all things, yea, the deep things of God,"[366] and the man or woman of this Spirit will be of the same mind. For this cause, the apostle counsels the believer, "Prove what is that good, and acceptable, and perfect will of God,"[367] but how? The Preacher counsels, "I proved by wisdom."[368] It is said, "He that getteth wisdom loveth his own soul,"[369] for, the spirit of the mind is to be nourished by the wisdom obtained by the Word's Spirit through an experimental faith on His voice, for we are to know that "wisdom giveth life,"[370] or rather, that "the spirit giveth life."[371] It is for this reason that we are counseled, "Be renewed in the spirit of your mind."[372]

13. This sick man was ready to know the Spirit's doctrine despite his inward perplexity. It is because there is no honest searching after the Spirit of heaven's throne, to compare every thought and perception with His understanding, that an inward fret develops wherein one distresses and torments self. The one professing Christ's name should know how it is

---

362   Daniel 5:10
363   Mark 2:8
364   Colossians 2:22
365   Proverbs 20:24
366   1 Corinthians 2:10
367   Romans 12:2
368   Ecclesiastes 7:23
369   Proverbs 19:8
370   Ecclesiastes 7:12
371   2 Corinthians 3:6
372   Ephesians 4:23

written, "Thou desirest truth in the inward parts,"[373] to the end they may "know wisdom."[374] It is the spirit of the mind that is to be "renewed in knowledge"[375] for the good of the personal conversation, for it is that, by the knowledge of His mediation, "the inward man is renewed day by day."[376] As the soul continues to exist without that nourishment ordained for it by the Creator through His Spirit, it will thin and cause an unbalance within the mind. Soon enough instability will reach into the heart, creating a wall to cease the reception of His Spirit's divine influence within the conscience.

14. "Without me ye can do nothing,"[377] says our High Priest of His mediation's course of learning, and why should He say so? This He says because He Himself confessed, and still confesses, "I can of mine own self do nothing."[378] For this cause He says, "Abide in me, and I in you,"[379] or rather, "Abide in me, and my words abide in you,"[380] for through an experimental faith on His Spirit's sayings, the mind is to find wisdom to overpower the conversation's natural or inherited mind of worship and service, which is why He says, "If a man keep my saying, he shall never see death."[381] This is why He says, "Abide in my love; even as I have kept my Father's name."[382]

15. One with an unclean spirit, or one with a heart troubled and in spiritual death for understanding, came to God's Christ, and through His doctrine, that coarse spirit "came out

---

373 Psalms 51:6
374 Psalm 51:6
375 Colossians 3:10
376 2 Corinthians 4:16
377 John 15:5
378 John 5:30
379 John 15:4
380 John 15:7
381 John 8:51
382 John 15:10

of him."[383] How could it have fled by His voice? It says, "Jesus rebuked him."[384] There is only One that may speak and have that which is spoken performed as it is said, and it reads, "He commanded, and it stood fast."[385] The people were amazed within themselves at the power of Christ's speech and said, "With authority commandeth he even the unclean spirits, and they do obey him,"[386] for among them stood that One speaking by that Word who, in the beginning, "commanded, and they were created."[387] It is for this reason that we are told of the LORD's Spirit, "All things were made by him."[388]

16. The one sick with leprosy was counseled, after they had fulfilled their ritual of purification, "The priest shall make an atonement for him, and he shall be clean,"[389] and even now it is told us, "We were reconciled to God by the death of his Son";[390] "by whom we have now received the atonement";[391] "for we have not an high priest which cannot be touched with the feeling of our infirmities."[392] Our offering for the sickness and confusion within and without us is not only finished, but the LORD of this offering accepts it; the only issue is whether we will accept the course that offering has ratified for our mental and moral wholeness. This is why we are counseled, "Look unto Abraham your father";[393] that is, learn of and do "the faith of Abraham";[394] because "faith was reckoned to Abraham for

---

383   Mark 1:26
384   Mark 1:25
385   Psalms 33:9
386   Mark 1:27
387   Psalm 148:5
388   John 1:3
389   Leviticus 14:20
390   Romans 5:10
391   Romans 5:11
392   Hebrews 4:15
393   Isaiah 51:2
394   Romans 4:16

righteousness."[395] Wherever faith is exercised, the true Spirit of the LORD and Father of Christ will be there also, "and where the Spirit of the Lord is, there is liberty."[396] This is the doctrine that Christ taught through this man, even the law of a liberated mind possessing reason by a simple and intelligent faith through His priestly mediation to honor His LORD and Father's name. The mind of this man was "saved," "redeemed," or "delivered" through faithfully accepting the means of his recovery, which recovery is according to the saying, "Through knowledge shall the just be delivered,"[397] for He took knowledge of the Spirit's voice. This is why we are counseled, "By grace are ye saved through faith; and that not of yourselves."[398] Your honest acceptance of, and diligent confidence in the illustration of the LORD's sacrifice, is to "purge your conscience from dead works to serve the living God."[399]

17. This man had grown tired of executing a theoretical profession for comfort. His cross-less and traditionally faithless religion left him without a reason as to why he labored for *blessing*; His flesh-based routine did not feed his spirit, nor did it touch his heart to relay right information on that LORD and Father he sincerely longed after. But what is written? It says, "Grace be with all them they love our Lord."[400] In this man, grace's creative power served as life's material through his own faith on what he had heard Christ say, and by the little knowledge and belief that he had, by bringing that charge of His voice into his heart, his mind was made whole and his being was reconstructed under a more sober spiritual constitu-

---

[395] Romans 4:9
[396] 2 Corinthians 3:17
[397] Proverbs 11:9
[398] Ephesians 2:8
[399] Hebrews 9:14
[400] Ephesians 6:24

tion. This is why it is said, "By grace you are recovered through faith,"[401] for by taking knowledge of the Spirit's voice; "for he whom God hath sent speaketh the words of God";[402] by knowledge he was regenerated.

18. "God hath not given us the spirit of fear; but of power, and of love, and of a sound mind."[403] God's Man expressed the knowledge of Himself to this faithful soul, for the man "heard him concerning the faith of Christ. And as he reasoned of righteousness, temperance, and judgment to come,"[404] the man declared, "By the law of faith,"[405] "the law of the Spirit of life in Christ Jesus hath made me free from the law of sin and death."[406] For, "By 'the law of Christ,'[407] he confessed, 'I delight in the law of God after the inward man.'"[408]

19. Our inward fret is over misapprehending the LORD's character, but when submitted to the instruction of His Son's mediation, when learning what it means to acknowledge the Faith of the Spirit's Christ as a personal Savior and Governor, the mind will be brought into closer relations with its Captain by its faithfulness to hear and do His counsel. This is the living God's doctrine, and "if any man will do his will, he shall know of the doctrine."[409] To know is to exceed fleshly and traditional principles of order and structure; it is to spiritually experience and cognitively determine; for the man or woman of knowledge

---

401   Ephesians 2:8
402   John 3:34
403   2 Timothy 1:7
404   Acts 24:24,25
405   Romans 3:27
406   Romans 8:2
407   Galatians 6:2
408   Romans 7:22
409   John 7:17

will confess, "I applied mine heart to know, and to search, and to seek out wisdom, and the reason of things."[410]

20. The unclean spirit heard the LORD's Faith and was removed out of the man only because he first obeyed the charge, "Come out of him."[411] Although the man came to God's Man frustrated and beside himself, yet "Jesus, moved with compassion, put forth his hand, and touched him."[412] In this is shown that in whatever state of mind we are in when appearing before the LORD's Priest to receive His manner of consolation, the measure of our faith, and the diligent activity of our mind, will determine how we should be accepted, and how far our refreshing will advance. Our Father ever "knoweth our frame; he remembereth that we are dust";[413] which is why "such an high priest became us,"[414] for "he also himself likewise took part of the same"[415] illness "in the likeness of sinful flesh, and for sin, condemned sin in the flesh."[416]

21. Today, our High Priest is our witness before the LORD our Father of what humanity can become when found subject to the Spirit of creation. The soul must know that it has "such an high priest"[417] "touched with the feeling of our infirmities,"[418] "who is set on the right hand of the throne of the Majesty"[419] "to make reconciliation for the sins of the people."[420] There are precepts of justification every believer must know in order to fall into harmony with the precepts of heaven's Majesty, for

---

410 Ecclesiastes 7:25
411 Mark 1:25
412 Mark 1:41
413 Psalms 103:14
414 Hebrews 7:26
415 Hebrews 2:14
416 Romans 8:3
417 Hebrews 8:1
418 Hebrews 4:15
419 Hebrews 8:1
420 Hebrews 2:17

our conversation's conscience is to be made whole by grace reigning within the inward parts that we may love the name of our High Priest's LORD and God, "and this is love, that we walk after his commandments."[421] "Wherefore gird up the loins of your mind, be sober, and hope to the end for the grace that is to be brought unto you at the revelation of Jesus Christ."[422]

---

[421] 2 John 1:6
[422] 1 Peter 1:13

3

The Error Within The Mind Of The Church

1. It was said, "In the last days perilous times shall come. For men shall be lovers of their own selves, covetous, boasters, proud, blasphemers, disobedient to parents, unthankful, unholy, without natural affection, trucebreakers, false accusers, incontinent, fierce, despisers of those that are good, traitors, heady, highminded, lovers of pleasures more than lovers of God; having a form of godliness, but denying the power thereof,"[423] therefore the apostle wrote, "Little children, let no man deceive you: he that doeth righteousness is righteous, even as he is righteous,"[424] and, "The darkness is past, and the true light now shineth."[425]

---

423 2 Timothy 3:1-5
424 1 John 3:7
425 1 John 2:8

2. The apostle John longed for the Christian church to remain in the confidence of their High Priest's name despite internal and external hardships. He told them, "We may have confidence, and not be ashamed,"[426] but what was the prevailing demeanor of the time? It is written, "Prophesy ye not, say them to them that prophesy: they shall not prophesy to them, that they shall not take shame."[427] That which exposes inward character defects, along with errors of thought and feeling concerning conversation and lifestyle, belongs to "the light of the glorious gospel."[428] As all things "are made manifest by the light,"[429] the Spirit's doctrine draws shame to the conscience by its reflected image of right worship and service by the mediation of His High Priest. The church, in the time of John, began to shy away from acceptable principles of reconciliation for the terror of fear and shame against spiritual recuperation. They had abandoned the counsel of their parents, even the "foundation of the apostles and prophets,"[430] and in turn had gathered "to themselves teachers, having itching ears."[431]

3. John wrote to the churches so that they might take confidence in the light of heaven's tidings, which is why he sought to put them in remembrance that "God is light,"[432] saying, "This then is the message which we have heard of him, and declare unto you."[433] John wanted the church to remember that the Spirit's voice is their light and confidence; that the Spirit's "law is light";[434] and if there should be a Christ-like spirit among

---

426   1 John 2:28
427   Micah 2:6
428   2 Corinthians 4:4
429   Ephesians 5:13
430   Ephesians 2:20
431   2 Timothy 4:3
432   1 John 1:5
433   1 John 1:5
434   Proverbs 6:23

them, that they need not cherish a spirit contrary to that of "the law of the Spirit of life,"[435] embracing self-indulgence at the expense of their own heart, and of one another. It is for this reason that he wrote, "If any man love the world (the religious world), the love of the Father is not in him,"[436] that is, said John, "The truth is not in him."[437]

4. John confesses, "The Spirit is truth,"[438] and another apostles writes, "The truth is in Jesus."[439] Again, this same John writes of the testimony given by God's Man, "The Spirit of truth, which proceedeth from the Father, he shall testify of me."[440] How is it that the Spirit should testify of Christ within the believer's conversation? He says, "Ye also shall bear witness,"[441] for the Spirit has said, concerning the good will of His name within the inward person, "Will ye not declare it?"[442]

5. It was because the church began to manifest qualities that displayed their removal from the Spirit's law of light; which removal spoke of their removal from His Christ as their High Priest; that compelled John to write, "Let us not love in word, neither in tongue; but in deed and in truth."[443] For, we know that "we dwell in him, and he in us, because he hath given us of his Spirit."[444] If we receive the Spirit of heaven's intercession then we receive the heart and mind of heaven's Chief Priest, even as it is written, "Let this mind be in you, which was also in

---

435 Romans 8:2
436 1 John 2:15
437 1 John 2:4
438 1 John 5:6
439 Ephesians 4:21
440 John 15:26
441 John 15:27
442 Isaiah 48:6
443 1 John 3:18
444 1 John 4:13

Christ."[445] "He humbled himself"[446] and "made himself of no reputation, and took upon him the form of a servant,"[447] "and became obedient unto death."[448] This is why John counseled them, "Our fellowship is with the Father, and with his Son,"[449] and, "Whosoever therefore will be a friend of the world is the enemy of God."[450] These things the apostles counseled Christian elders because the appetite of the religious world is not of the Father's enterprise or intention. If they possessed His Spirit, they would humble self under His voice to receive thorough correction in thought and feeling to better one another, but they handled a disagreeing spirit, and so began to display a character foreign to the LORD's Anointed Priest, making it needful to say to them, "Be ye all of one mind, having compassion one of another, love as brethren, be pitiful, be courteous."[451]

6. There was nothing for the church in the religious world, for which cause John wrote, "The world knoweth us not, because it knew him not."[452] John was present when Christ had said, "The Spirit of truth; whom the world cannot receive, because it seeth him not, neither knoweth him,"[453] for the religious world operates by a routine contrary to faith's exercise and learning. What stops the promise of the living God from reaching the world and her ministers? Our Priest says, "If a man love me, he will keep my words: and my Father will

---

445 Philippians 2:5
446 Philippians 2:8
447 Philippians 2:7
448 Philippians 2:8
449 1 John 1:3
450 James 4:4
451 1 Peter 3:8
452 1 John 3:1
453 John 14:17

love him, and we will come unto him."[454] Many elders within the early church did not keep the words and sayings of the LORD's Spirit, and of them He says, "Thou hast a name that thou livest, and art dead."[455] They maintained their practice by manners that the sacrificed flesh of His Christ abolished, rendering them a religious faction "having a form of godliness, but denying the power thereof."[456]

7. Man's natural eye cannot tell who does "preach Christ even of envy and strife";[457] "of contention, not sincerely";[458] "but all things are naked and opened unto the eyes of him with whom we have to do."[459] Only the eye of the one who will know the Spirit's voice may know religious falsehood, for He Himself says of His assembly, "They know the voice of strangers."[460] John wished to call attention to the proof of the reception and forwarding of salvation's science, and therefore wrote, "The Father sent the Son to be the Saviour of the world.[461]" If we believe on and learn of the illustration of this Man's act on that tree, then "we have passed from death unto life,"[462] seeing as how when "he saith, A new covenant, he hath made the first old."[463] With that first covenant predicated upon acts of the flesh for *righteousness*, understanding that such traditional laws can do no right thing for the person, "God sent forth his Son, made of a woman, made under the law, to redeem them that were under the law."[464] If the elders of the Christian church

---

454 John 14:23
455 Revelation 3:1
456 2 Timothy 3:5
457 Philippians 1:15
458 Philippians 1:16
459 Hebrews 4:13
460 John 10:5
461 1 John 4:13
462 1 John 3:14
463 Hebrews 8:13
464 Galatians 4:4

had knowledge of the Spirit's new will, they would not have subscribed to former manners of worship and service, for by accepting the offering of God's Man, it is that the mind is now inclined to quit a flesh-based conversation to hear and follow after the counsel, "Live according to God in the Spirit."[465]

8. By the offering of God's Man, the LORD has accursed every commandment and doctrine of flesh to "death" and "corruption," and because the religious world is centered upon such legal ordinances for *righteousness*, John advised the church to escape "the corruption that is in the world through lust"[466] by counseling, "We might live through him."[467] Thus, to help encourage them to maintain their conversation through the name of God's Man, and in hope of the promise of the Spirit's new will through His mediation, John wrote to Christian elders, "These things have I written unto you concerning them that seduce you,"[468] "that ye might believe that Jesus is the Christ, the Son of God; and that believing ye might have life through his name."[469]

9. What is "life"? We are counseled, "The Spirit is life."[470] Wherein is this "life" found? It is found in "the law of the Spirit of life"[471] that teaches, "By grace are ye saved"[472] "with the washing of water by the word."[473] This is why John writes, "He that hath the Son hath life,"[474] because he discerned the fulfillment of the saying within the Christian camp, "Woe to

---

465 1 Peter 4:6
466 2 Peter 1:4
467 1 John 4:9
468 1 John 2:26
469 John 20:31
470 Romans 8:10
471 Romans 8:2
472 Ephesians 2:5
473 Ephesians 5:26
474 1 John 5:12

them that devise iniquity, and work evil upon their beds! when the morning is light, they practise it, because it is in the power of their hand."[475] The "morning" is a term connoting "day" and the "light" is the Spirit's benevolence, for in the time or season when the Sun of the Spirit's doctrine was bright and full of revelation with regeneration, it was fulfilled within the early church, "Her sun is gone down while it was yet day."[476] This is why the apostles counseled Christian elders, "Ye are all children of the light, and the children of the day,"[477] for John saw, already nesting within the church, that seed which would eventually bring "out another horse that was red,"[478] until it should become "a black horse."[479]

10. John saw the Spirit's Revelation concerning the inevitable course of Asia's church and her daughters, therefore from what he presently observed taking place, and understanding that the Revelation given to him was already commencing, he said, "It is the last time: and as ye have heard that an'tichrist shall come, even now are there many an'tichrists; whereby we know that it is the last time."[480]

11. Them that do "evil" do not establish spiritual negligence during the night or at noon, but the Scripture says, "When morning is light."[481] This is why, when speaking to the first church of the Revelation, our Priest explains Himself to be one "that holdeth the seven stars in his right hand, who walketh in the midst of the seven golden candlesticks."[482] The church was to know that she was ever in the LORD's pres-

---

475 Micah 2:1
476 Jeremiah 15:9
477 1 Thessalonians 5:5
478 Revelation 6:4
479 Revelation 6:5
480 1 John 2:18
481 Micah 2:1
482 Revelation 2:1

ence, upheld by His Spirit and fed of His Son's hand, yet the saying was fulfilled in her, "What profit hath a man of all his labour which he taketh under the sun?"[483] As His Christ was head over the Spirit's assembly; His voice given all power of His Father's Word for the things that stood in heaven and on earth concerning His LORD's name; it was that even while under the dispensation of the Spirit and of His Faith, ministers took on "work that is wrought under the sun."[484] What was the result? Says one who experimented with this labor and documented the end of it, "I hated life."[485]

12. That apostasy which took place within the early church began with "profane and vain babblings,"[486] "foolish and unlearned questions."[487] "They will increase unto more ungodliness,"[488] warned Paul. "They do gender strifes,"[489] he continued, "and their word will eat as doth a canker."[490] The church was being devoured from the traditions, superstitions, and commandments brought into her by them that would not take full knowledge of heaven's will and wisdom, and the counsel was, "It 'shall eat your flesh as it were fire.'"[491]

13. Their manners of worship and service was not hidden to the LORD's vision, for His Spirit said, "Against this family do I devise an evil, from which ye shall not remove your necks; neither shall ye go haughtily: for this time is evil."[492] What was the "evil" given to the church at this time? The apostle writes,

---

483 Ecclesiastes 1:3
484 Ecclesiastes 2:17
485 Ecclesiastes 2:17
486 1 Timothy 6:20
487 2 Timothy 2:23
488 2 Timothy 2:16
489 2 Timothy 2:23
490 2 Timothy 2:17
491 James 5:3
492 Micah 2:3

"They that will be rich fall into temptation and a snare, and into many foolish and hurtful lusts, which drown men in destruction and perdition. For the love of money is the root of all evil: which while some coveted after, they have erred from the faith, and pierced themselves through with many sorrows."[493] Riches; both temporal and spiritual; that provoked unconverted and unsanctified ministers to confess, "Honour me now, I pray thee, before the elders,"[494] would form a yoke on the neck of the early church from which it would never recover, but from its error of perdition would birth "the son of perdition,"[495] for the apostles knew that "the mystery of iniquity doth already work."[496]

14. John heard and observed how that this church should transform itself from a white and pure church to a red and terrible institution, and upon this platform he heard the Spirit say to the believers of that time, "The devil shall cast some of you into prison."[497] Seeing as how the devil has never physically cast any one into prison, the actors fulfilling this vision are "the people of the prince."[498] Those "sons of the sorceress, the seed of the adulterer and the whore,"[499] acknowledged as "them which say they are Jews, and are not, but are the synagogue of Satan,"[500] would create, through this persecution against them, civil position to enact all that they would to hide themselves from the prophesied affliction. This people of the prince, they are chief men of the pagan Rome State, and the persecution of

---

493   1 Timothy 6:9,10
494   1 Samuel 15:30
495   2 Thessalonians 2:3
496   2 Thessalonians 2:7
497   Revelation 2:10
498   Daniel 9:26
499   Isaiah 57:3
500   Revelation 2:9

Diocletian against the church at this time opened up the door for the Christian camp to hold intercourse with her State.

15. The red horse of the second seal falls in line with the church of Smyrna, and in order for the devil to have cast any into prison, it must be that those Jews who were not Jews, but who were of the mind and craft of Satan's religion, should have gained some sort of favor with their State, for it says of this red horse, "Power was given to him."[501] It was not the devil that cast into prison, but rather men who practiced the devil's religious tradition acted out their glutinous impulses against the Christian church. Concerning this church that should suffer by the devil's band, Christ said of her elders, "Ye are of your father the devil, and the lusts of your father ye will do. He was a murdered from the beginning."[502] The Spirit therefore confirmed to the church at this time, "Ye shall have tribulation ten days: be thou faithful unto death."[503]

16. John saw an hierarchy developing among those who professed to be "apostles, and are not";[504] "them which say they are Jews, and are not, but do lie."[505] The spirit of Satan's religion is without truth's alleviating comfort, which is why it is prone to both physically and spiritually murder. It is because of this spirit existing within the early church that John wrote, "If we say that we have no sin, we deceive ourselves, and the truth is not in us."[506] What is that doctrine confessing the conversation to be without sin against the LORD's name? It says, "Thou hast said in thine heart, I will ascend into heaven, I will exalt my throne above the stars of God: I will sit also upon

---

501 Revelation 6:4
502 John 8:44
503 Revelation 2:10
504 Revelation 2:2
505 Revelation 3:9
506 1 John 1:8

the mount of the congregation, in the sides of the north."[507] This is the spirit and mind of Satan that began to exist in the church during her morning light. This spirit longs to exalt self's religious persuasion above the LORD's voice to sit as that chief confidence over the religious world, to the end its heart may say, "I am God, I sit in the seat of God, in the midst of the seas."[508]

17. This is the mystery of iniquity, even how ministers blatantly erroneous before the living God by their service to a lame and accursed conversation may claim their manners *righteous* and above His Spirit's good will. It was because of this developing spirit in the church that the Spirit said, "I know thy works, and where thou dwellest, even where Satan's seat is,"[509] for it is of the serpent's mind to do contrary to what the living God states. By failing to hear the counsel, "Christ hath redeemed us from the curse of the law, being made a curse for us: for it is written, Cursed is every one that hangeth on a tree,"[510] their adherence to what the sacrifice of Christ had accursed; which is all "handwriting of ordinances";[511] witnessed to the fact that they were transgressors of the LORD's will and commandment. For, by His Son's offering blotting out such legal religious ethics; not only in that age, but in every age after; it became needful to say to Christian elders, "If I build again the things which I destroyed, I make myself a transgressor."[512] Adhering to manners that the blood of God's Christ blotted out revealed the spirit within Christian understanding, for they preached devout loyalty to religious laws "after the tradition

---

507 Isaiah 14:13
508 Ezekiel 28:2
509 Revelation 2:13
510 Galatians 3:13
511 Colossians 2:14
512 Galatians 2:18

of men, after the rudiments of the world,"[513] moving Paul to confess, "If righteousness come by the law, then Christ is dead in vain."[514] Such manners remove the mind from heaven's new and right intention to frame a practice after the flesh's impulse to garner the *favor of God* for self-complacency, and the Christian church steadily advanced her apostasy in "fulfilling the desires of the flesh and of the mind."[515]

18. Satan's seat is the same seat as Judas, and of Judas Christ says, "None of them is lost, but the son of perdition."[516] It was written of Judas to fulfill the saying, "Give me my price,"[517] therefore as the church began to take a seat next to her State to accomplish her worldly ambitions, she began to say, "A measure of wheat for a penny, and three measure of barley for a penny."[518]

19. The church took on "the doctrine of Ba'laam"[519] and "the error of Ba'laam for reward";[520] "the way of Ba'laam the son of Bo'sor, who loved the wages of unrighteousness."[521] For, the church heard and accepted error's promise: "I will promote thee unto very great honour, and I will do whatsoever thou sayest unto me."[522] "All this power will I give thee, and the glory of them...if thou therefore wilt worship me."[523] The church accepted the bargain of heaven's enemy spirit, "and power was given...to take peace from the earth."[524] The

---

513 Colossians 2:8
514 Galatians 2:21
515 Ephesians 2:3
516 John 17:12
517 Zechariah 11:11
518 Revelation 6:6
519 Revelation 2:14
520 Jude 1:11
521 2 Peter 2:15
522 Numbers 22:17
523 Luke 4:6,7
524 Revelation 6:4

prophecy said, "When the morning is light, they practise,"[525] therefore it was fulfilled at this time, "A king of fierce countenance, and understanding dark sentences, shall stand up. And his power shall be mighty, but not by his own power: and he shall destroy wonderfully, and shall prosper, and practise."[526] "Through his policy also...he shall magnify himself in his heart, and by peace shall destroy many."[527]

20. Peace was taken from the earth by the legislative power invested within this church, which power did not come from the living God, but from her State. The synagogue of Satan was given a great sword, and with this sword came spiritual and civil death to all who would not acknowledge her claims. The spirit of greed and of self-righteousness left Christian elders with "their conscience seared with a hot iron,"[528] and all because they would not hear the counsel, "Thou hast left thy first love."[529]

21. Because the Spirit of Christ's mediation was quenched, pride and intemperance not only governed the throne of her elders' heart, but Satan's seat also manifests another distinct attribute, which character is called, "The accuser of our brethren."[530] Once "profane and vain babblings, and oppositions of science falsely so called"[531] began to cause many to "have erred concerning the faith,"[532] it was only natural that "there must also be heresies"[533] with "envying, and strife, and

---

525 Micah 2:1
526 Daniel 8:23,24
527 Daniel 8:25
528 1 Timothy 4:2
529 Revelation 2:5
530 Revelation 12:10
531 1 Timothy 6:20
532 1 Timothy 6:21
533 1 Corinthians 11:19

divisions."[534] For, "in the beginning of the gospel,"[535] this was done "that they which are approved may be made manifest,"[536] which is why John wrote, "If they had been of us, they would no doubt have continued with us: but they went out, that they might be made manifest that they were not all of us."[537]

22. The saying was being fulfilled, "Turning away he hath divided our fields."[538] For, amid her apostasy from His name, the LORD had said to this church, "I will go and return to my place, till they acknowledge their offense, and seek my face,"[539] but what was John told concerning this church? Says the Spirit, "I gave her space to repent of her fornication; and she repented not."[540] "Because thou hast rejected knowledge, I will also reject thee, that thou shalt be no priest to me,"[541] He continued. "Seeing thou hast forgotten the law of thy God, I will also forget thy children."[542] "I will cast her into a bed, and them that commit adultery with her into great tribulation, except they repent of their deeds."[543]

23. The elders of the church did not want the doctrine of the LORD's High Priest. "They shall not take shame,"[544] said the Spirit of these stubborn ministers, for they would "not hear the law of the LORD,"[545] and so they said, "Get you out of the way, turn aside out of the path."[546] It was at the sight of this

---

534   1 Corinthians 3:3
535   Philippians 4:15
536   1 Corinthians 11:19
537   1 John 2:19
538   Micah 2:4
539   Hosea 5:15
540   Revelation 2:21
541   Hosea 4:6
542   Hosea 4:6
543   Revelation 2:22
544   Micah 2:6
545   Isaiah 30:9
546   Isaiah 30:11

developing spirit that the apostle wrote, "Be not thou therefore ashamed of the testimony of our Lord,"[547] "for the which cause I also suffer,"[548] "nevertheless I am not ashamed."[549] He who saw the state of the church tried his best to prevent the seed of religious corruption from blossoming. Since all professed *righteousness* by *Christ's name* and yet failed to attain to the virtue that he knew of in that commandment, John wrote, "If ye know that he is righteous, ye know they every one that doeth righteousness is born of him."[550] Of old the LORD said, "Do not my words do good to him that walketh uprightly?"[551] "Ye pull off the robe with the garment,"[552] says the Spirit of dishonest priests, but the work of His Christ, who is today in the LORD's direct presence, is to leave the penitent soul "sitting at the feet of Jesus, clothed, and in his right mind."[553]

24. This was to be the spirit and rule among every church professing obedience to "the law of the Spirit of life,"[554] even that profession witnessed by following after the counsel, "In lowliness of mind let each esteem other better than themselves."[555] But because of a contrary burden growing within the Christian tribe, John was moved to write, "He that loveth his brother abideth in the light, and there is none occasion of stumbling in him."[556] "Let us not therefore judge one another any more,"[557] counseled Paul to her elders, "but judge this rather, that no man put a stumblingblock or an occasion

---

547 2 Timothy 1:8
548 2 Timothy 1:12
549 2 Timothy 1:12
550 1 John 2:29
551 Micah 2:7
552 Micah 2:8
553 Luke 8:35
554 Romans 8:2
555 Philippians 2:3
556 1 John 2:10
557 Romans 14:13

to fall in his brother's way."⁵⁵⁸ And again, "Follow after the things which make for peace, and things wherewith one man edify another."⁵⁵⁹ Remember, what is the record written of this church? We are told that she would eventually desire "to take peace from the earth."⁵⁶⁰ How can any one make peace without the material of peace? For, Christ said, "Peace I leave with you,"⁵⁶¹ in that He spoke of "abundance of peace"⁵⁶² in relation to "abundance of grace and of the gift of righteousness."⁵⁶³ If without the gift of righteousness; which righteousness is the Spirit's healing edification; what then do they that have no knowledge of this gift or righteousness preach? Herein the apostles were made to discern a very strange doctrine by "false brethren unawares brought in."⁵⁶⁴

25. With the material of grace comes the product of edification, yet when once the Spirit's grace is taken away, obtaining righteousness will be done through a spirit contrary to self-sacrificing love. John saw the prevailing spirit of *justification* by works and wrote, "Little children, keep yourselves from idols."⁵⁶⁵ And years before, Paul questioned the fortitude of them that had grown frustrated at doing heaven's new will, saying, "Are you so foolish? having begun in the Spirit, are ye now made perfect by the flesh?"⁵⁶⁶ "We might be justified by the faith of Christ, and not by the works of the law,"⁵⁶⁷ for the reforming Christian must confess, "The life which I now

---

558 Romans 14:13
559 Romans 14:19
560 Revelation 6:4
561 John 14:27
562 Psalms 72:7
563 Romans 5:17
564 Galatians 2:4
565 1 John 5:21
566 Galatians 3:3
567 Galatians 2:16

live in the flesh I live by the faith of the Son of God."[568] The believer must know how it is written, "Who gave himself for our sins, that he might deliver us"[569] "from every evil work, and will preserve me unto his heavenly kingdom."[570] Because the Spirit's doctrine failed among those who would not be fully converted by it, the balm of grace was replaced with images and forms, with customs, days, commandments and traditions, leaving it that Christ "was without in desert places."[571]

26. John tried to comfort the few remaining faithful ministers by saying, "If they had been of us, they would no doubt have continued with us."[572] What is it that these would not continue in? Says the Spirit, "They continued not in my covenant, and I regarded them not."[573] These would not accept the fact that Christ spoke of His name's spiritual reign for satiating the inward parts through spiritual blessings. Paul had written to them that it was the Father "who hath blessed us with all spiritual blessings in heavenly places in Christ,"[574] yet these would not accept the humility necessary to fall down at "the throne grace."[575] The corrupt spirit that worked among them within this church had so enflamed their heart that they began believing their church was the *kingdom of God*, therefore it was told them, "Who did hinder you that ye should not obey the truth? This persuasion cometh not of him that calleth you."[576]

27. Because they didn't care to diligently or intelligently examine creation's right science, they became ministers "that

---

568 Galatians 2:20
569 Galatians 1:4
570 2 Timothy 4:18
571 Mark 1:45
572 1 John 2:19
573 Hebrews 8:9
574 Ephesians 1:3
575 Hebrews 4:16
576 Galatians 5:7,8

obey not the gospel of our Lord,"[577] for, only by the new covenant promises may the believer "obtain salvation by our Lord,"[578] and that "salvation through sanctification of the Spirit and belief of the truth."[579] Thus, John saw a seed of rebellion growing into a most dreadful institution and wrote, "Whosoever denieth the Son, the same hath not the Father: [but] he that acknowledgeth the Son hath the Father also."[580]

28. The churches needed to first acknowledge the virtue and authority of the Spirit's doctrine before they could receive the blessing of the LORD and Father of His High Priest. To accept the knowledge of His Son is to accept the fact that "this is the true God, and eternal life."[581] It was to accept that His mediation was given of the LORD "a more excellent name,"[582] which is why He "gave him to be head over all things to the church."[583] It was to confess, "I bow my knees unto the Father of our Lord Jesus Christ, of whom the whole family in heaven and earth is named,"[584] and in so confessing, it would have to be said, "O come, let us worship and bow down: let us kneel before the LORD our maker."[585] But what is the word concerning the demeanor within this church? It says, "She repented not."[586] "Having a form of godliness, but denying the power thereof";[587] which wisdom and power came from learning of and doing the Spirit's new will and commandment; she began "to observe days, and month, and times, and

---

577 2 Thessalonians 1:8
578 1 Thessalonians 5:9
579 2 Thessalonians 2:13
580 1 John 2:23
581 1 John 5:20
582 Hebrews 1:4
583 Ephesians 1:22
584 Ephesians 3:14
585 Psalms 95:6
586 Revelation 2:21
587 2 Timothy 3:5

years."[588] "I am afraid of you,"[589] said Paul of such a people. Therefore through "teaching for doctrines the commandments of men,"[590] the church would eventually "cast a stumblingblock before the children of Israel, to eat things sacrificed unto idols, and to commit fornication."[591]

29. Observing the fact that the professed of *heaven's Faith* enjoyed "giving themselves over to fornication, and going after strange flesh,"[592] to help keep back the end of the spirit that Christian elders held intercourse with, John wrote, "If a man say, I love God, and hateth his brother, he is a liar."[593]

30. Temporal difficulties began to mingle with the mission and mind of the church, therefore the apostle said, "I endured: but out of them all the Lord delivered me."[594] The good fight of faith against the prevailing Roman customs of the day wore down her heart, therefore it was told her, "Be strong in the grace that is in Christ Jesus,"[595] and, "No man that warreth entangleth himself with the affairs of this life; that he may please him who hath chosen him."[596]

31. John saw that the souls of many men within the church were tired and beaten not only by the inward demands of heaven's higher learning, but also by the pagan State and age of Rome, so he encouraged them by saying, "These things have I written unto you that believe on the name of the Son of God; that ye may know that ye have eternal life."[597] Their

---

588   Galatians 4:9
589   Galatians 4:10
590   Mark 7:7
591   Revelation 2:14
592   Jude 1:7
593   1 John 4:20
594   2 Timothy 3:11
595   2 Timothy 2:1
596   2 Timothy 2:4
597   1 John 5:13

confidence needed to be established on the fact of their heart's perpetual recuperation, and this fact was held within the life of their High Priest's intercession, for "all the fullness of the Godhead"[598] is in His name. "The fullness of the blessing of the gospel of Christ"[599] teaches that, in regard to the knowledge of heaven's mediation, "In him should all fullness dwell,"[600] therefore the believer is to know that, within the spirit of their mind, an exercised faith on the knowledge of this Christ's mediation procures "the power of the Spirit of God"[601] into the inward parts, seeing as how we are "to be strengthened with might by his Spirit in the inner man."[602]

32. It is only by acknowledging this wisdom that believers on Christ's name might know the Spirit of His intercession to have better compassion on one another. For this cause John counseled, "If we love one another, God dwelleth in us, and his love is perfected in us."[603] The opportunity to edify not only blesses the one who hears, but also the one speaking. This is why Paul counseled church elders, "Strive not about words to no profit, but to the subverting of the hearers,"[604] and, "For meat destroy not the work of God."[605] Doctrines and precepts that gave no life to the conscience became a thing to stumble over within the church, until they were adopted and exchanged for the *sayings* of *God*. John saw that many elders among him were spiritually declining, and if the Spirit's doctrine could be taught and believed on in its right context, and the work of that law executed as ordained by the Spirit that gave the command-

---

598 Colossians 2:9
599 Romans 15:29
600 Colossians 1:19
601 Romans 15:19
602 Ephesians 3:16
603 1 John 4:12
604 2 Timothy 2:14
605 Romans 14:20

ment, then the spirit of the church would be in harmony with the LORD their Father's commandments, and before the religious age, she would witness to the power of His voice.

33. A true "servant of the church"[606] is one that "hath been a succourer of many,"[607] therefore John counseled, "Whoso keepeth his word, in him verily is the love of God perfected."[608] They of the Spirit's household are to know that "whosoever doeth not righteousness is not of God, neither he that loveth not his brother."[609] John pleaded with the members of the church, "This is the message that ye heard from the beginning, that we should love one another,"[610] for in so doing, it would cause many to hear the counsel, "Take away from the midst of thee the yoke, the putting forth of the finger, and speaking vanity...draw out thy soul to the hungry, and satisfy the afflicted soul,"[611] and, "Do the first works."[612] Amidst the prevailing religious errors, John longed to draw their attention to what he had heard in vision. "I heard a voice in the midst of the four beasts say...See thou hurt not the oil and the wine,"[613] he writes. All precepts and doctrines of men may be full of strange violence against the Spirit's will and Faith, yet the counsel of the Word's High Priest is the only instruction holding the oil of the Spirit's anointing grace that it may ever be fulfilled within the heart of every spirit, "They also that erred in spirit shall come to understanding."[614]

---

606 Romans 16:1
607 Romans 16:2
608 1 John 2:5
609 1 John 3:10
610 1 John 3:11
611 Isaiah 58:9
612 Revelation 2:5
613 Revelation 6:6
614 Isaiah 29:24

34. Reverence for heaven's will and wisdom is obtained by learning of and executing the precepts of the Spirit's righteousness, which precepts are those "ordinances of justice"[615] obtained through an experimental faith. Our labor of love is that route to relinquish inherited and self-cultivated religious error, and to also form a pure fondness for the character and sufferings of heaven's doctrine and High Priest, seeing as how the believer is instructed, "Be thou partaker of the afflictions of the gospel according to the power of God."[616] The one strengthened by the Spirit's saying may declare, "Christ which strengtheneth me,"[617] but how are they strengthened? It is written, "Wisdom strengtheneth."[618] Only by cultivating a culture for learning may the soul receive the education necessary for the flesh's constitution to command the members of the body to perform heaven-appointed worship and service; every other course has come under condemnation by the sacrificed flesh of the Spirit's High Priest.

35. The spirit of the mind is to rule the conversation's heart, and within the mind, the Spirit of heaven's mediation is to engrave the name and precepts of His LORD onto the heart, while also covering it in the garment of His praise for consistent advancement in heaven's course. Them of the early church did not care "to retain God in their knowledge,"[619] therefore "God gave them over to a reprobate mind"[620] "through the lusts of their own hearts, to dishonor their own bodies between themselves."[621] Because they willfully forgot "the law

---

615 Isaiah 58:2
616 2 Timothy 1:8
617 Philippians 4:13
618 Ecclesiastes 7:19
619 Romans 1:28
620 Romans 1:28
621 Romans 1:24

of Christ,"[622] they stubbornly endured "adultery, fornication, uncleanness...idolatry, witchcraft, hatred, variance...murders, drunkenness, revellings, and such like,"[623] and it is for us to know, from observing the history of this church, that shame found in the LORD's commandments, and in the Faith of His Son, forms a pit within the soul that the spirit of man is; in and of himself; unable to come up from.

---

[622] Galatians 6:2
[623] Galatians 5:19-21

4

The Holy Spirit Rejected

1. John heard how the Spirit said of the Christian church, "Thou hast left thy first love,"[624] therefore he wrote to the churches, "This commandment have we from him, That he who loveth God love his brother also."[625] Of old, concerning the definition of the word "commandment," the psalmist said, "Thy commandment,"[626] or, "The testimony of thy mouth,"[627] or, "The law of thy mouth,"[628] for the apostles were given a precept and law of the LORD's Spirit to give to Christian elders, and the keeping of this law of right charity; to the Word, to self, to their brethren, and to their assemblies; would have given witness to the great benevolence planned of the Godhead for them and their assemblies. If the church had left her first love, then it is that she had no right love, and we do know that "the love

---

624 Revelation 2:4
625 1 John 4:21
626 Psalm 119:96
627 Psalm 119:88
628 Psalm 119:72

of God is shed abroad in our hearts by the Holy Ghost."[629] If there was no proof of heaven-appointed kindness among them, it was because there was no true Spirit of the LORD within or among them. Beneficence emits from the soul connected to and educated by the Father's Spirit, and if there is a profession of His name, and through the name of His Son, the edifying works and influence of His Spirit should follow.

2. This is why John wrote, "Every one that loveth him that begat loveth him also that is begotten of him,"[630] or said in another way, "Every one that is fond of Him that begat holds dear to Him also that is begotten of Him." Who begat this Christ? It is written, "The Spirit of him that raised up Jesus from the dead,"[631] and, "Being put to death in the flesh, but quickened by the Spirit,"[632] and, "Jesus returned in the power of the Spirit,"[633] and, "The grace of God was upon him."[634] By His consistent reliance upon "the Spirit of grace,"[635] God's Man kept and dressed His conversation with the voice of His LORD's Spirit, and because "that which is born of the Spirit is spirit,"[636] by holding dear to the Spirit's commandment; as He says, "I know him, and keep his saying;"[637] He was able to become a living creature of His LORD and Father's will. This is why we are counseled, "Of his own will begat he us with the word of truth, that we should be a kind of firstfruits of his creatures."[638]

---

629 Romans 5:5
630 1 John 5:1
631 Romans 8:11
632 1 Peter 3:18
633 Luke 4:14
634 Luke 2:40
635 Hebrews 10:29
636 John 3:6
637 John 8:55
638 James 1:18

3. If there is one professing any confidence on the name of God's Man, then that same one born of His mediation should also be filled with that which begat Him. If there is to be any semblance of the LORD's Priest within our conversation's heart and mind, of any proof of an honest confidence under His wings, it must be that the believer accepts the fact that "God hath sent forth the Spirit of his Son into your hearts."[639] The Spirit's understanding come in to the spirit of the mind is the only means to own a pure conscience for the inward man to keep self by, to the end we might know what our LORD and Father "wrought in Christ, when he raised him from the dead."[640] After ascending on high, "being by the right hand of God exalted, and having received of the Father the promise of the Holy Ghost, he hath shed forth this"[641] privilege on us, to the end it might be known, "The love of God is shed abroad in our hearts by the Holy Ghost."[642]

4. Every one who admires, respects, and reverences Him that conceived this Christ, in like manner they too will be born of the living God. By exercising faith on the Spirit's law, "we shall be also in the likeness of his resurrection,"[643] for the apostle confirms, "Whosoever believeth that Jesus is the Christ is born of God."[644] If it is that we believe Jesus is that Christ, "whosoever shall confess that Jesus is the Son of God, God dwelleth in him, and he in God."[645] In what way does "God" dwell in us, and especially when "God is a Spirit"[646]? It is written, "By the

---

639 Galatians 4:6
640 Ephesians 1:20
641 Acts 2:33
642 Romans 5:5
643 Romans 6:5
644 1 John 5:1
645 1 John 4:15
646 John 4:24

Holy Ghost which dwelleth in us,"[647] and, "He that raised up Christ from the dead shall also quicken your mortal bodies by his Spirit that dwelleth in you."[648] If there is one who should say of the LORD and of His Son, "How amiable,"[649] it is that they must allow their spirit to inherit "love in the Spirit,"[650] which only occurs as the mind retains personal knowledge of the name of the Father and the Son. This is why we are counseled, "Be renewed in the spirit of your mind,"[651] and, "That which is born of the Spirit is spirit."[652]

5. John knew that "if any man have not the Spirit of Christ, he is none of his,"[653] therefore he hoped to move Christian elders to purify their understanding by writing, "I write no new commandment unto you, but an old commandment which ye had from the beginning. The old commandment is the word which ye heard from the beginning."[654] That which was "in the beginning of the gospel,"[655] "which we have heard of him and declare unto you,"[656] said the apostle, is "that God is light, and in him is no darkness at all."[657] This witness came from the beginning of creation, how Adam was removed from the LORD's Spirit because they entertained the serpent's tongue, which tongue is a practice challenging the Spirit's voice by employing a mediator contrary to faith for executing His commandment. John understood that the Spirit was failing from within the churches because they willingly gave themselves over to a form

---

647 2 Timothy 1:14
648 Romans 8:11
649 Psalms 84:1
650 Colossians 1:8
651 Ephesians 4:23
652 John 3:6
653 Romans 8:9
654 1 John 2:7
655 Philippians 4:15
656 1 John 1:5
657 1 John 1:5

of speech that did not reflect the new covenant's promise, but rather forwarded a spirit against the commandment they were to keep if rightly honoring the office of the Spirit's High Priest. For, because of their position against the Spirit's saying, it became necessary for the apostle to say, "Have no fellowship with the unfruitful works of darkness,"[658] that is, with "those things which are done of them in secret."[659] For, "all things that are reproved are made manifest by the light,"[660] therefore John wrote, "God is light,"[661] because he understood that, concerning the Spirit's will, His "law is light."[662]

6. If indeed the Spirit is light, and if they who profess "the law of the Spirit of life"[663] testify of the spirit and beauty of that light, it is that they should confess, "For the love of the Spirit,"[664] "strive together with me in your prayers to God."[665] Thus, "If there be therefore any consolation in Christ, if any comfort of love, if any fellowship of the Spirit, if any bowels and mercies,"[666] says the doer of heaven's commandment, "be ye kind one to another, tenderhearted, forgiving one another,"[667] "not rendering evil for evil, or railing for railing: but contrariwise blessing."[668] If there is found any alleviation in the doctrine of Christ, if any benevolent learning, there will be joined to heaven's comfort a perpetual fellowship with heaven's Spirit, and from communing with His voice, the soul will

---

658 Ephesians 5:11
659 Ephesians 5:12
660 Ephesians 5:13
661 1 John 1:5
662 Proverbs 6:23
663 Romans 8:2
664 Romans 15:30
665 Romans 15:30
666 Philippians 2:1
667 Ephesians 4:32
668 1 Peter 3:9

know, "Look not every man on his own things, but every man also on the things of others."[669]

7. John challenged the church to remember the Spirit's disposition, saying, "That 'he might shew the exceeding riches of his grace in his kindness towards us,'[670] 'he laid down his life for us: and we ought to lay down our lives for the brethren.'"[671] This is why John wrote, "He that saith he abideth in him ought himself also so to walk, even as he walked."[672] The elders failing to quit compromising their consciences, and the consciences of the people that heard them, witnessed to the fact that these ministers honored a commandment contrary to the Spirit of the LORD's Son. God's Man passed away and then resurrected symbolizes a former religious manner put to sleep for the regeneration of a new conversation by the spirit of the mind, which is why we are counseled, "Worship God in the spirit."[673] To see elders conducting a service contrary to the Godhead's science revealed that heaven's new will had not been embraced or experienced, which is why the conscience of that will had not moved them to rightly care for themselves, to the end they may properly care for one another.

8. Christ observed the commandments of His Father through the law of righteousness by an experimental faith on His Spirit's saying, and He kept the law of His Father's benevolence by the same faith wherewith He was encouraged by the Spirit of His God. John cared for the members of the churches to confess this one thing, "We are members one of another,"[674] for he had remembered how the apostle

---

669 Philippians 2:4
670 Ephesians 2:7
671 1 John 3:16
672 1 John 2:6
673 Philippians 3:3
674 Ephesians 4:25

exhorted the Corinthians at times before, saying, "Is Christ divided? was Paul crucified for you? Or were ye baptized in the name of Paul?"[675] Thus John, seeing the prevailing spirit among professed believers that the Spirit warned him of by that Revelation; for they began inventing manners of baptism against the Spirit's plain definition of baptism; and hoping to quell that mind, wrote, "Every one that loveth him that begat loveth him also that is begotten of him. By this we know that we love the children of God."[676]

9. If believers should honor the LORD's Spirit, them believing on the Spirit's mediation for comfort and consolation will care for the members of that same Spirit, for it is written, "The power of the Lord was present to heal them."[677] If indeed the Spirit's voice is cherished, the mind will care to learn a reform on mental and moral health; to be healed that it may heal another after the manner of its recuperation; and because of this fact, John wrote, "I wish above all things that thou mayest prosper and be in health, even as thy soul prospereth."[678] For failing to admit heaven's right will and commandment in to their inward parts, a departure from the Spirit meant a retreat from the intercession of the Spirit's High Priest, which opened Christian elders to the serpent's imprisonment, causing them to receive the rebuke, "I marvel that ye are so soon removed from him that called you into the grace of Christ unto another gospel."[679] The spirit of secrecy was developing in the church after the saying, "Hast thou seen what the ancients of the house of Israel do in the dark, every man in the chambers of his imagery? for they say, The LORD seeth

---

675   1 Corinthians 1:13
676   1 John 5:1,2
677   Luke 5:17
678   3 John 1:2
679   Galatians 1:6

us not."[680] But the apostle would have them know, "We being many are one bread, and one body: for we are all partakers of that one bread,"[681] and, "He that is joined unto the Lord is one spirit,"[682] and, "Stand fast in one spirit, with one mind striving together for the faith of the gospel."[683]

10. "The communion of the body of Christ"[684] translates the believer to "the love of God, and the communion of the Holy Ghost."[685] It is from the communion of the Spirit that the heart will confess, "I long after you all in the bowels of Jesus Christ"[686] "until Christ be formed in you."[687] The spirit of the one born of the Spirit is ever "endeavoring to keep the unity of the Spirit in the bond of peace,"[688] therefore when "false brethren unawares brought in"[689] "another gospel,"[690] and when the effect of such teachings were known by the loss of brotherly kindness; which kindness is a testament to the inward working of the LORD's Spirit; such tragedy caused John to write, "If a man say, I love God, and hateth his brother, he is a liar."[691] The work of division or disunion is not the Spirit's labor, for they that know Him confess, "How good and how pleasant it is for brethren to dwell together in unity!"[692]

11. Subtract the Spirit of charity from among professed believers and we have a spirit most "foolish, disobedient,

---

680 Ezekiel 8:12
681 1 Corinthians 10:17
682 1 Corinthians 6:17
683 Philippians 1:27
684 1 Corinthians 10:16
685 2 Corinthians 13:14
686 Philippians 1:8
687 Galatians 4:19
688 Ephesians 4:3
689 Galatians 2:4
690 Galatians 1:6
691 1 John 4:20
692 Psalms 133:1

deceived, serving divers lusts and pleasures, living in malice and envy, hateful, and hating one another."[693] It was this spirit that caused the Spirit to say of them in this church, "I have somewhat against thee,"[694] for they, professing to know and revere *His name*, were accomplishing the very spirit that His sacrifice took out of heaven's Faith. The "sin" abolished by His Christ's offered flesh is "the enmity, even the law of commandments contained in ordinances."[695] To observe Christian elders forwarding a form of worship that is ultimately abolished reveals a contrary force acting within them, for by them establishing legal religious traditions and commandments to *God*, they reveal the hate or disdain they actually have for the Spirit's voice, for self, and for one another, fulfilling the saying, "They crucify to themselves the Son of God afresh, and put him to an open shame."[696]

12. John knew that there could be no pure acceptance of Christ's doctrine, and no reverent carrying out of its principles of service for any individual; personally or for the church; unless there was an acceptance of the Spirit's will and saying. "If you love the living God, if you love His Spirit," said John, "do so also likewise with one another what that Spirit has done with and for you." But if we have not experienced that benevolence, must we think to have a mind to lawfully demonstrate it? Christ explained the Spirit's vocation, saying, "He will reprove the world of sin, and of righteousness, and of judgment."[697] If there is one who has communed with heaven's Faith by His Spirit, it is that they are entered into the knowledge of His refreshing love to know how it is written, "Rebuke

---

693 Titus 3:3
694 Revelation 2:4
695 Ephesians 2:15
696 Hebrews 6:6
697 John 16:8

thy neighbour, and not suffer sin upon him."[698] The reforming Christian is to have it recorded of them, in the log of their life's memories, "All the people that were with him, came weary, and refreshed themselves,"[699] for the sign of the Spirit existing within the heart is this confession of them that are around us: "He oft refreshed me, and was not ashamed of my chain."[700] For this cause, "Fulfill the law of Christ,"[701] counseled Paul to church elders. And again, "Use not liberty for an occasion to the flesh, but by love serve one another."[702]

13. The revelation of the law of Christ impressed upon the heart by the Spirit's finger will cause one to pray, "Renew a right spirit within me."[703] It is the law or doctrine of the LORD's Son that will cause the spirit to accept the fact that the Spirit's voice "is holy, and the commandment holy, and just, and good."[704] "By his Spirit in the inner man,"[705] "Christ may dwell in your hearts by faith"[706] "that the righteousness of the law might be fulfilled."[707] We are to bless one another according to the understanding of the Spirit's praise and righteousness, but if we have failed to capture this experience, must we believe we can sincerely "bear the infirmities of the weak, and not to please ourselves"?[708]

14. There is an obligation to live a conversation even as God's Man lived and still lives, therefore "let us also walk in

---

698 Leviticus 19:17
699 2 Samuel 16:14
700 2 Timothy 1:16
701 Galatians 6:2
702 Galatians 5:13
703 Psalms 51:10
704 Romans 7:12
705 Ephesians 3:16
706 Ephesians 3:17
707 Romans 8:4
708 Romans 15:1

the Spirit,"[709] for isn't it written, "In that he died, he died unto sin once; but in that he liveth, he lieveth unto God"?[710] That none would "be desirous of vain glory, provoking one another, envying one another,"[711] it was ordained "that like as Christ was raised up from the dead by the glory of the Father, even so we also should walk in newness of life,"[712] that is, "should serve in newness of spirit."[713] "That which is born of the Spirit is spirit";[714] the testimony of Christ is inward regeneration by the Spirit of His mediation within the spirit of the mind; and the reason such health is made available through His intercession is for us to properly bless one another after the manner of His comfort, which is why it says, "Let every one of us please his neighbour for his good to edification."[715] With this right spirit should come a demonstration of the Spirit's kindness, therefore John wrote, "We know that he abideth in us, by the Spirit which he hath given us."[716]

15. If there is no acceptance of God's Spirit, it will be known by "a division among the people because of him."[717] "God was in Christ,"[718] and this Christ confessed, "I came down from heaven, not to do mine own will, but the will of him that sent me."[719] There is no division in the Godhead. Having experienced the work of righteousness by faithfully obeying the Spirit's counsel, it is that the heart will care to be a laborer for the Spirit's will and cause, and not for "the imagination of the

---

709 Galatians 5:25
710 Romans 6:10
711 Galatians 5:26
712 Romans 6:4
713 Romans 7:6
714 John 3:6
715 Romans 15:2
716 1 John 3:24
717 John 7:43
718 2 Corinthians 5:19
719 John 6:38

thoughts of the heart."[720] Now that this mind of obedience and subjection to the Spirit's law has found a place in the heart, it should be said of us, "The bowels of the saints are refreshed by thee,"[721] to the end that "now at this time your abundance may be a supply for their want, that their abundance may be a supply for your want."[722]

16. The spirit of self-sacrificing love and impartial beneficence was removing from the Christian church. For this cause Peter counseled, "Seeing ye have purified your souls in obeying the truth through the Spirit unto unfeigned love of the brethren, see that ye love one another with a pure heart fervently."[723] Fervent love to the Spirit's will and ministry was quenched because the elders and the members of the church were no longer desirous to have their souls purified by heaven's instruction. The members of the church grew cold towards one another, and the only way this demeanor could have become prominent was if it should be fulfilled, "Iniquity shall abound, the love of many shall wax cold."[724]

17. Iniquity rested in the house, and so the words of the Preacher were fulfilled, "I saw under the sun the place of judgment, that wickedness was there; and the place of righteousness, that iniquity was there."[725] The professed of God's Son had rejected the Spirit of His priestly office, and in so doing had declared rebellion against His LORD's Faith and ten laws, wherefore John was moved to write, "If any man see his brother sin a sin which is not unto death, he shall ask, and he

---

720 1 Chronicles 29:18
721 Philemon 1:7
722 2 Corinthians 8:14
723 1 Peter 1:22
724 Matthew 24:12
725 Ecclesiastes 3:16

shall give him life for them that sin not unto death. There is a sin unto death: I do not say that he shall pray for it."[726]

18. Our Priest teaches, "He that shall blaspheme against the Holy Ghost hath never forgiveness."[727] "Whosoever shall speak a word against the Son of man, it shall be forgiven him: but unto him that blasphemeth against the Holy Ghost, it shall never be forgiven."[728] It is for this reason that Paul writes, "Let every one that nameth the name of Christ depart from iniquity,"[729] and because the church rejected the divine influence over her heart to personally know the living God's name, it was fulfilled, "God shall send them strong delusion, that they should believe a lie."[730] For, the Spirit says of the corrupt church in conflict with those who would be faithful to His name, "Against this family do I devise an evil,"[731] therefore to such ministers the Word has "made every thing beautiful in his time: also he hath set the world in their heart, so that no man can find out the work that God maketh from the beginning to the end."[732]

19. To warn the church, because of her spiritual negligence, of her inevitable fate, John sought to awaken her elders to the image they were assuming, saying, "The whole world lieth in wickedness."[733] These priests, who were "strangers from the covenants of promise,"[734] did not have heaven's wisdom within their inward person, and so honored what they served "in the vanity of their mind, having the understanding

---

726   1 John 5:16
727   Mark 3:29
728   Luke 12:10
729   2 Timothy 2:19
730   2 Thessalonians 2:11
731   Micah 2:3
732   Ecclesiastes 3:11
733   1 John 5:19
734   Ephesians 2:12

darkened, being alienated from the life of God."[735] This is why John wrote, "He that hath the Son hath life,"[736] and if indeed we have the life of God's Minister working within our conversation's conscience, then we "also are full of goodness, filled with all knowledge, able also to admonish one another"[737] on "the excellency of the knowledge of Christ"[738] "for the love of the Spirit."[739]

20. They who were without the Spirit and honored a lifeless religious conversation were to be persuaded of heaven's understanding by the powerful fellowship that its assembly had among themselves. The church was counseled, concerning the religious world, "Be not ye therefore partakers with them,"[740] but, "with all lowliness and meekness, with longsuffering, forbearing one another in love,"[741] "rather reprove them."[742] It was the task of the church to go "forth conquering, and to conquer"[743] by "the mystery of God, and of the Father, and of Christ,"[744] but the weight of consolation without the Word's refreshing Spirit devoured the spirit and passion of the church, causing her ministers to take hold of the carnal manners of the majority, mingling with the Spirit's doctrine a strange creed that called for works of the flesh for *righteousness*, which labor God's Man removed "out of the way, nailing it to his cross."[745]

21. If indeed the church was to fulfill her first work, she needed to engage herself towards her first love. This love

---

735 Ephesians 4:17,18
736 1 John 5:12
737 Romans 15:14
738 Philippians 3:8
739 Romans 15:30
740 Ephesians 5:7
741 Ephesians 4:2
742 Ephesians 5:11
743 Revelation 6:2
744 Colossians 2:2
745 Colossians 2:14

cannot be executed without full submission to the Spirit's will and commandment, and the proof of our surrendering is exhibited in the fact that we also benevolently care for those spirits around us, for it is from examining and doing the LORD's mind that the heart grows fond of His throne. From examining His voice, despite appearance or disposition, a love born of a faith desiring to know Him will swallow up the conversation, and it will be known to Him that we are willing to become servants of His name for one another. It is for this reason that Paul wrote of his mission, saying, "By manifestation of the truth commending ourselves to every man's conscience in the sight of God."[746]

22. The evidence of consecration and discipleship is expressed through a mind of unity with heaven's priesthood. Evident rejection of Christ's doctrine is division from that priesthood's manner of love and learning; this is why John wrote, "Whosoever believeth that Jesus is the Christ is born of God: and every one that loveth him that begat loveth him also that is begotten of him."[747] The doctrine of Christ is not without the healing, sealing, teaching, correcting, and converting Spirit of the LORD God. John does not say, "All who love the Begotten love also Him that begat." The soul temple is to welcome the Spirit's voice of counsel into its midst, and as the individual works with that Spirit to clean up and dispense with all the rubbish within it by His voice, it will be that "the love of God is shed abroad in our hearts by the Holy Ghost."[748] For this cause John warned Christian elders, "Many deceivers are entered into the world, who confess not that Jesus Christ is come in the flesh. This is a deceiver and

---

[746] 2 Corinthians 4:2
[747] 1 John 5:1
[748] Romans 5:5

an an'tichrist,"[749] and, "Whosoever transgresseth, and abideth not in the doctrine of Christ, hath not God. He that abideth in the doctrine of Christ, he hath both the Father and the Son. If there come any unto you, and bring not this doctrine, receive him not into your house."[750]

749　2 John 1:7
750　2 John 1:9,10

5

The Foundation Of Another Gospel

1. The apostle John heard the admonition of the Spirit, who said, "I know the blasphemy of them which say they are Jews, and are not, but are the synagogue of Satan."[751] It was because of this observation that John wrote, "Whosoever transgresseth, and abideth not in the doctrine of Christ, hath not God,"[752] and, "Whosoever committeth sin transgresseth also the law."[753] The Spirit surveyed the field of His believers, and finding a famine where there should be no drought, He came to them with a message, saying, "These things saith the first and the last, which was dead, and is alive."[754]

---

751 Revelation 2:9
752 2 John 1:9
753 1 John 3:4
754 Revelation 2:8

2. Because they had rejected the name of the LORD's High Priest, along with that Spirit to familiarize themselves with that name, "By swearing, and lying, and killing, and stealing, and committing adultery, they break out, and blood toucheth blood,"[755] said the Spirit of them. John saw the universal spirit that would lay the foundation for a complete removal from heaven's will and wisdom, and so he called their attention to consider that the one who violates the doctrine of Christ is a liar, and in being a liar, is caught up in religious error against the goodness of that will and understanding, and in sinning against the end of heaven's ministry, is become a breaker of the Spirit's ten immutable precepts. Without conserving reverence for these laws, the Spirit of the LORD of these commandments would not be heard, and the counsel explaining the relation of these laws to the violent would be disregarded, causing another *doctrine* to be accepted as a vehicle to achieve that which man cannot do for himself. For what is it that marks the error of "sin"? It is written, "Whatsoever is not of faith is sin."[756] To transgress heaven's doctrine would be to apply for righteousness by that which is not of faith's course, and from committing self to honor that which is not for rightly learning "his will in all wisdom and spiritual understanding,"[757] the Spirit's Faith is undermined, leaving another *gospel* to candidly enter into the fray.

3. John observed the strange behavior of ministers professing loyalty to *heaven's science*. The churches would not hear the counsel, "He that is perfect in knowledge is with thee,"[758] and so the church cultivated the saying, "Righteousness come by the law."[759] John saw among the professed of

---

755 Hosea 4:2
756 Romans 14:23
757 Colossians 1:9
758 Job 36:4
759 Galatians 2:21

heaven's will that law of "sinners of the Gentiles,"[760] in that these now did put off rightly discerning the Spirit's voice to be "now made perfect by the flesh."[761] This was evidence to John that there had been a removal from the Spirit's good tidings. "The truth of the gospel"[762] is "that a man is not justified by the works of the law, but by the faith of Jesus Christ."[763] To transgress the Spirit's commandment is to structure the conversation after the works of the flesh to receive *justification* before *His* voice. If indeed the religion is found within a legal religious bill serving to convince the conscience of its devotion, it is a fact that "they that are in the flesh cannot please God."[764] Why? "By the works of the law (the handwritten religious tradition) shall no fleshed be justified,"[765] but rather it is that "God would justify the heathen through faith."[766] Faith's work is to appropriate to the believer the goodness promised of the LORD to prolong their experience in His name, even "the promise of the Spirit through faith."[767]

4. That which took control of the early church was "another gospel"[768] "exceedingly zealous of the traditions"[769] "after the commandments and doctrines of men."[770] That which replaced justification by an experimental faith on the Spirit's saying became that instruction to "persuade men"[771]

---

760 Galatians 2:15
761 Galatians 3:3
762 Galatians 2:14
763 Galatians 2:16
764 Romans 8:8
765 Galatians 2:16
766 Galatians 3:8
767 Galatians 3:14
768 Galatians 1:6
769 Galatians 1:14
770 Colossians 2:22
771 Galatians 1:10

to "pervert the gospel of Christ"[772] by "the handwriting of ordinances."[773] Their understanding was "not another,"[774] but was rather a perversion of the LORD's Word that became "the Jews' religion"[775] to persecute "the church of God."[776] The doctrine of these ministers, of these "false brethren unawares brought in,"[777] would serve to fulfill the word that John heard and recorded: "Thou shalt suffer: behold, the devil shall cast some of you into prison...and ye shall have tribulation."[778] The current controversy was between two doctrines: one that confessed sanctification by the Faith of God's Man, who "abolished in his flesh the enmity, even the law of commandments contained in ordinances,"[779] and another "by the works of the law"[780] that taught, "You are justified by the law."[781] If the church continued to reject the counsel of redemption by faith on the Spirit's power and wisdom, "the law of sin"[782] would regenerate, causing many to take on that which is contrary to the LORD's new will, when all that need be done is take knowledge of His character's saying. This is one of the reasons why the LORD's Spirit came to them as one "which was dead, and is alive,"[783] for the churches were removing from the fact of righteousness without legal commandments and needed to remember what confidence the name of the Spirit's High Priest taught.

---

772 Galatians 1:7
773 Colossians 2:14
774 Galatians 1:7
775 Galatians 1:13
776 1 Corinthians 11:22
777 Galatians 2:4
778 Revelation 2:10
779 Ephesians 2:15
780 Galatians 2:16
781 Galatians 5:4
782 Romans 7:23
783 Revelation 2:8

5. If it is that we know that the LORD's Christ has died and is risen, it should also be understood that "our old man is crucified with him, that the body of sin might be destroyed, that henceforth we should not serve sin."[784] Again, what, according to Scripture, is "sin"? All that does not serve to cleanse the inward parts by an exercised faith in the Spirit's wisdom is "sin" against the living God's Faith. If the believer is crucified with God's Christ, they will never have to know that "if I build again the things which I destroyed, I make myself a transgressor."[785] It does not say, "The things which God destroyed," but it says, "The things I destroyed," for there is to be, within the conscience of the believer, a certain conversation destroyed by doing heaven's will and doctrine, which manners account for confirming our belief in redemption's science by our faith on the end of that will and learning. The only things that man may cultivate are works of the flesh that serve to persuade an excuse from right obligation, and if I am a transgressor to heaven's will, if I go against justification by faith's higher learning and adhere to a policy of *righteousness* by legal religious ethics, then my old devotional mind is not destroyed. I do not trust that I am buried with God's Man because my labor is proof that this Man neither lived in this flesh, saw death, nor resurrected to find Himself in the LORD's direct presence; I am therefore a transgressor of the Spirit's law and doctrine. Having built up again that which causes a separation from heaven's throne, the saying is indeed become a fact, "Your iniquities have separated between you and your God."[786]

6. The highest iniquity is taking the LORD's Spirit as being ignorant to personally lead, cleanse, seal, and perfect the

---

784 Romans 6:6
785 Galatians 2:18
786 Isaiah 59:1

conversation and conscience. The spirit attached to one who would seek *favor* of *God* from rites and customs, doctrines, traditions, charges, and commandments, is one that believes it has no sin against the LORD's name, and is before *God* in a position to be *blessed* of *Him*, seeing as how a physical brand of religion is done to appease *Him*, as though *God* were flesh. The LORD accepted the handwriting of Moses as that instrument to keep the people faithful to His ten laws, but the people perverted that covenant, taking the handwriting of Moses to be the end of the LORD's intention. Thus, concerning the oppression forwarded by priests who perverted the old manner, the LORD said, "I hate, I despise your feast days,"[787] to the end He would declare, "I will turn your feasts into mourning, and all your songs into lamentation."[788] Notice the LORD's counsel, how He says, "I desired mercy, and not sacrifice; and the knowledge of God more than burnt offerings. But they like men have transgressed the covenant: there have they dealt treacherously against me."[789] Because His people began to become as other priests; who were without right science; because they took on the mind of Gentiles to invent a scripted tradition, they could not hear, through the counsel within His voice, Him saying, "Let judgment run down as waters, and righteousness as a mighty stream."[790]

7. Instead of devoting their faculties to investigating His counsel, they rejected His Spirit and became as vain as the priests of the religious world in matters of worship and service, even as it is written, "There is among you envying, and strife, and divisions, are ye not carnal, and walk as men?"[791] God's

---

787 Amos 5:21
788 Amos 8:10
789 Hosea 6:6,7
790 Amos 5:24
791 1 Corinthians 3:3

Man spoiled every opportunity for obedience to ordinances crafted of elders by His passing away on that tree, for it is written, "He that is hanged is accursed of God,"[792] wherefore it is an eternal fact that this Christ "abolished in his flesh the enmity, even the law of commandments contained in ordinances."[793] Paul noticed how that men again cared to be governed by vain religious precepts, therefore he wrote, to help clarify what right service to the Father's Faith meant, "Henceforth know we no man after the flesh."[794] That which was to lead "to mourning, and to baldness, and to girding with sackcloth,"[795] strangely left men in "joy and gladness, slaying oxen, and killing sheep, eating flesh, and drinking wine."[796] The doctrine of Christ was becoming perverted, and John saw the saying fulfilling, "Confounded be all they that serve graven images, that boast themselves of idols,"[797] and, "Let their table become a snare before them: and that which should have been for their welfare, let it become a trap."[798] This is why he counseled them, "Keep yourselves from idols."[799]

8. A religion ordained to accept sensual works for *righteousness* removes the mind from observing the Spirit's righteousness, causing the heart to formulate its own craft, moving the person to forget learning how to confess, "In the flesh I live by the faith of the Son of God."[800] If the believer is passed away with His Christ, a mind fearing traditions and owning a spirit of shame and rebellion against the Spirit's voice is dead with Him

---

792 Deuteronomy 21:23
793 Ephesians 2:15
794 2 Corinthians 5:16
795 Isaiah 22:12
796 Isaiah 22:13
797 Psalms 97:7
798 Psalms 69:22
799 1 John 5:21
800 Galatians 5:24

also. If the inwards are crucified with the knowledge of God's Man, then that mind has "crucified the flesh with the affections and lusts,"[801] for it is from an unsanctified conscience that a spurious spirit and religion is born, wherefore Paul notes of some, before he had the opportunity to correct them, "I saw that they walked not up rightly according to the truth of the gospel."[802] Without observing that spirit of self-sacrifice as taught by the LORD's Priest, there would be no right compassion among those that professed His name. As John saw the result of mingling former religious practices with the Spirit's doctrine, he counseled, "If we walk in the light, as he is in the light, we have fellowship one with another, and the blood of Jesus Christ his Son cleanseth us from all sin."[803] If indeed we know that the law of Christ's intercession purifies our conversation's conscience, the unsanctified nature within the conversation's spirit is perished, but "if we say that we have no sin, we deceive ourselves, and the truth is not in us."[804]

9. John saw how ministers confessed that they did not know the living God. With the LORD's doctrine perverted, the Christian church began to repeat the history of the Jews, that is, "teaching for doctrines the commandments of men."[805] It is the law of the inward working of the blood of the Word's Christ that cleanses from all spiritual negligence. This is why, by exercising faith on the Spirit's doctrine to provide the heart with sin's remedy, heaven's Faith "might bring us to God."[806] If indeed these ministers were to be blessed, it was that they first needed to comprehend that they were all spiritually erro-

---

801 Galatians 5:24
802 Galatians 2:14
803 1 John 1:7
804 1 John 1:8
805 Mark 7:7
806 1 Peter 3:18

neous. "If there had been a law given which could have given life, verily righteousness should have been by the law (the legal religious laws of priests and elders),"[807] wherefore to pick up that which cannot give or forward life, and that which God's Man has abolished by His sacrificed flesh, witnesses to a conversation without right knowledge. Any law that takes the heart from observing a full intercourse with the Spirit's Word by faith is "sin" and religious error, and because "the law is not of faith,"[808] Paul counseled, "If any man preach any other gospel unto you than that"[809] "which we have preached unto you, let him be accursed."[810] For, Paul heard the lame doctrine of them that rebelled against heaven's new will, which is why he wrote, "They who seemed to be somewhat in conference added nothing to me,"[811] for such was the mind of those who "having swerved have turned aside unto vain jangling."[812]

10. If the Christian church could consider the law and judgment of Christ's heavenly ministry, John knew that health would immediately flourish within her, and that a right spirit of forgiven men would witness to the power of the LORD's voice. That which causes separation from the LORD's name is a spirit of self-righteousness, and as long as this mind should remain in man without a conscious effort to purge its reign from the inward parts of the heart, the person will not know its spiritual error. If indeed the members of the church were receiving His Spirit's strength; for we are "to be strengthened with might by his Spirit in the inner man";[813] it would be that they were coming to the conclusion of falsehood in their conversation

---

807 Galatians 3:21
808 Galatians 3:12
809 Galatians 1:9
810 Galatians 1:8
811 Galatians 2:6
812 1 Timothy 1:6
813 Ephesians 3:16

by stages of recovery through the law of Christ's mediation, to the end they should patiently wait on one another. To build again the foundation of dead religious works is to reject the fact that it is of the LORD's will to "purge your conscience from dead works to serve the living God."[814] The works of the flesh begin in none other place than an alienated heart, which is why the reforming Christian is counseled, "Be renewed in the spirit of your mind."[815] As you find that you are "alienated and enemies in your mind by wicked works,"[816] remember how it is written, "God commendeth his love toward us, in that, while we were yet sinners (yet servants to the pen of self and of ministers), Christ died for us (for the blessing of our conversation's conscience)."[817]

11. Herein is the religious error that John observed, for he saw many professing *sanctification* by *Christ's name*, but their actions only testified to the same old corrupt mind of worship and service under the first covenant. For this cause the Spirit says, "Every good tree bringeth forth good fruit; but a corrupt tree bringeth forth evil fruit."[818] This is why John says, "If we say that we have fellowship with him, and walk in darkness, we lie, and do not the truth."[819] John witnessed many unnecessarily working for blessing under the sun; that is, laboring for a free and an already purchased righteousness under the Spirit's kingdom and dispensation; and wondered to himself, when observing the resurrected character of the previous age, "There is no remembrance of former things,"[820] and, "What

---

814 Hebrews 9:14
815 Ephesians 4:23
816 Colossians 1:21
817 Romans 5:8
818 Matthew 7:17
819 1 John 1:6
820 Ecclesiastes 1:11

profit hath he that worketh in that wherein he laboureth?"[821] and, "What hath man of all his labour, and of the vexation of his heart, wherein he hath laboured under the sun?"[822] Thus, "Every one that loveth is born of God, and knoweth God. He that loveth not knoweth not God,"[823] he concluded. The burden of the apostle was that the reformer learn of and do heaven's will, for he was there when heaven's Christ said, "He that doeth truth cometh to the light,"[824] which is why John counsels, "He that doeth the will of God abideth for ever."[825]

12. If the church would only hear the counsel, "Only let your conversation be as it becometh the gospel of Christ,"[826] and, "Stand fast in one spirit, with one mind striving together for the faith of the gospel,"[827] they would not have received and preached "another Jesus"[828] "or another gospel."[829] The church moved away from the spirit that said, "Have I committed an offence in abasing myself that ye might be exalted,"[830] and took on the sentiment, by her re-establishing an abominable manner of worship and service, "All the congregation are holy, every one of them, and the LORD is among them."[831]

13. At what John saw, he said within himself, "The heads thereof judge for reward, and the priests thereof teach for hire, and the prophets thereof divine for money: yet will they lean upon the LORD, and say, Is not the LORD among us? none

---

821 Ecclesiastes 3:9
822 Ecclesiastes 2:22
823 1 John 4:7,8
824 John 3:21
825 1 John 2:17
826 Philippians 1:27
827 Philippians 1:27
828 2 Corinthians 11:4
829 2 Corinthians 11:4
830 2 Corinthians 11:7
831 Numbers 16:3

evil can come upon us."[832] The gentleness of the One which says, "They which are accounted to rule over the Gentiles exercise lordship over them,"[833] "but so shall it not be among you: but whosoever will be great among you, shall be your minister: and whosoever of you will be the chiefest, shall be servant of all,"[834] became a saying so filled with stubborn hatred that the apostle wrote, "Who hath bewitched you, that ye should not obey the truth, before whose eyes Jesus Christ hath been evidently set forth, crucified among you?"[835]

14. The body of the knowledge of the Spirit's Man was again crucified. The saying was being fulfilled, "In the latter times some shall depart from the faith, giving heed to seducing spirits, and doctrines of devils,"[836] wherefore John tried to encourage the church by saying, "Greater is he that is in you, than he that is in the world."[837] "We are of God, and the whole world lieth in wickedness,"[838] said John, and if in "wickedness" then in "sin," and "all unrighteousness is sin,"[839] for the accursed minister of the Word upholds "all ungodliness and unrighteousness of men, who hold the truth in unrighteousness."[840]

15. Herein John witnessed the formation of the mystery of lawlessness, in that he observed the Spirit's truth magnified by religious practices that conflicted with heaven's present understanding. Priests began to hold, or rather retain marks of observance to *the LORD's* will, by unlawful and unsatisfactory

---

832 Micah 3:11
833 Mark 10:42
834 Mark 10:43,44
835 Galatians 3:1
836 1 Timothy 4:1
837 1 John 4:4
838 1 John 5:19
839 1 John 5:17
840 Romans 1:18

means, proclaiming themselves *pure* by such ordinances and *justified* in His sight to keep them, and this routine forwarded while remaining evidently "dead in trespasses and sins."[841] As the Christian church moved away from the saying, "Whatsoever is not of faith is sin,"[842] justification; which is another term for sanctification; by every law of works took hold of the motivation and elevation of religion, and with this spurious administration in place, the faithful believer was reminded how it is counseled, "Be not among winebibbers; among riotous eaters of flesh."[843]

16. The church began to flirt with that spirit encouraging its adherent "to eat things sacrificed to idols."[844] John warned of the prevailing diet and wrote, "All that is in the world, the lust of the flesh, and the lust of the eyes, and the pride of life, is not of the Father, but is of the world."[845] The mind of the Father is not towards a routine of rehearsed *love*, but rather of free unity and benevolence made known to all who should come into contact with His name. The sign of the Spirit's accepted love would show forth in the tone of brotherhood, and because the instruction of that course for the soul returning to the image of its Creator had failed among Christian elders, John counseled, "He that loveth not his brother abideth in death."[846] That spirit teaching a gospel contrary to that stating, "Believe on him that raised up Jesus,"[847] is accursed of the LORD and His Spirit, and if accursed, the doer of it is become "alienated from the life of God through the ignorance that is in them, because of the blindness of their

---

841 Ephesians 2:1
842 Romans 14:23
843 Proverbs 23:20
844 Revelation 2:20
845 1 John 2:16
846 1 John 3:14
847 Romans 4:24

heart."[848] It was because of the willful slumber of their heart in regard to the true ordinances of justice that transgressors began to use "liberty for a cloak of maliciousness,"[849] fulfilling the word, "Through covetousness shall they with feigned words make merchandise of you; by reason of whom the way of truth shall be evil spoken of."[850]

17. Such a false religion prevailed because the church would not hear, "Thou hast left thy first love,"[851] and, "Do the first works."[852] Heaven's works are born of the Spirit's will for the believer to know Him and His High Priest, thereby developing the fruit of the Spirit within the conscience of the conversation. Not one soul within the Spirit's church is to be void of their primary vocation after passing through faith's higher learning, namely, "the perfecting of the saints,"[853] "the work of the ministry,"[854] "the edifying of the body of Christ."[855]

18. With the *body* of *Christ* universally rejecting the renewal of their mind to obtain the pleasure of salvation for their soul and spirit, and applying to flesh-based works of penance for *righteousness*, the church began "desiring to be teachers of the law; understanding neither what they say, nor whereof they affirm."[856] With sanctification by faith on the Spirit's saying trampled under the feet of Christian ministers, the apostle wrote, "Whosoever transgresseth, and abideth not in the doctrine of Christ, hath not God."[857] The Spirit's Priest

---

848 Ephesians 4:18
849 1 Peter 2:16
850 2 Peter 2:1-3
851 Revelation 2:14
852 Revelation 2:5
853 Ephesians 4:12
854 Ephesians 4:12
855 Ephesians 4:12
856 1 Timothy 1:7
857 2 John 1:9

teaches, "God is a Spirit,"[858] therefore if none are in fellowship with the Spirit's words and saying, it is that they are not receiving "salvation through sanctification of the Spirit and belief of the truth."[859] Thus, if indeed heaven's throne religion is upheld, it is that "ye turned to God from idols to serve the living and true God."[860] With that being said, one "that ministereth to you in the Spirit, and worketh miracles among you, doeth he it by the works of the law, or by the hearing of faith?"[861]

---

[858] John 4:24
[859] 2 Thessalonians 2:13
[860] 1 Thessalonians 1:9
[861] Galatians 3:5

6

Engaging An Unlawful Exchange

1. Hurt at their blatant display of irreverence towards the judgment of the Spirit's will, John wrote to Christian elders, "If we say that we have not sinned, we make him a liar, and his word is not in us,"[862] and, "If we confess our sins, he is faithful and just to forgive us our sins, and to cleanse us from all unrighteousness."[863]

2. John knew how that "if righteousness come by the law, then Christ is dead in vain,"[864] and how that "if Christ be not raised, your faith is vain; ye are yet in your sins."[865] The apostle wanted all professed believers to know that their LORD and Father is faithful and just in His operation, that is, "just, and

---

[862] 1 John 1:10
[863] 1 John 1:9
[864] Galatians 2:21
[865] 1 Corinthians 15:17

the justifier of him which believeth in Jesus,"[866] because all are "justified freely by his grace through the redemption that is in Christ Jesus."[867] If it is that He is just, and the justifier of the one who should surrender their will and spirit to His will and Spirit by faith on the knowledge of His Son's mediation, it is that blessing is imparted to the one who would be justified, or sanctified, by faith's exercise and learning, as it says, "We are saved by hope."[868] This hope in the Spirit's will is nothing but that which was displayed of old by Abraham, as it says, "Who against hope believed in hope."[869] "Abraham believed God, and it was imputed unto him for righteousness,"[870] and as John saw the church removing from sole devotion to the doctrine of Christ to "ten thousand instructors in Christ,"[871] he counseled the churches, "Your sins are forgiven you for his name's sake."[872]

3. Should the church remember to believe that the LORD gave His Son "to be a propitiation through faith in his blood,"[873] it would be that they would not violate the spiritual law that He established through His Son's name and blood for their redemption from a lame devotional spirit. It is God's Man "who gave himself for our sins,"[874] "who for the joy that was set before him endured the cross,"[875] "who his own self bare our sins in his own body on the tree, that we, being dead to sins, should live unto righteousness."[876] Of old, it was said, "It shall

---

866 Romans 3:26
867 Romans 3:24
868 Romans 8:24
869 Romans 4:18
870 James 2:23
871 1 Corinthians 4:15
872 1 John 2:12
873 Romans 3:25
874 Galatians 1:4
875 Hebrews 12:2
876 1 Peter 2:24

be our righteousness, if we observe to do all these commandments before the LORD our God, as he hath commanded us";[877] for the old covenant revolved around "meats and drinks, and divers washings, and carnal ordinances, imposed on them";[878] wherefore, to impress upon Christian ministers their present obligation to heaven's new covenant promise, John wrote, "Every one that doeth righteousness is born of him."[879]

4. The Psalmist declares, "All thy commandments are righteousness,"[880] and the Spirit says, "My righteousness shall not be abolished."[881] The Spirit's commandment regarding the conversation's redemption is in sanctifying the mind by faith's exercise, and such a course need not be disturbed, for the principles of "the ordinances of justice"[882] are as "written with a pen of iron, and with the point of a diamond."[883] Refusing to accept the work of acceptable righteousness, many ministers began to confess, "Righteousness come by the law (the legal religious bill),"[884] when in reality the counsel given by God's Priest is, "I will; be thou clean."[885]

5. The LORD's Minister suffered the inevitable woe that man would have been dealt if He had never interceded. For "he saw that there was no man, and wondered that there was no intercessor."[886] "And being found in fashion as a man, he humbled himself, and became obedient unto death"[887] "that he might be a merciful and faithful high priest in things pertaining to God, to

---

877 Deuteronomy 6:25
878 Hebrews 9:10
879 2 John 2:29
880 Psalms 119:172
881 Isaiah 51:6
882 Isaiah 58:2
883 Jeremiah 17:1
884 Galatians 2:21
885 Matthew 8:3
886 Isaiah 59:16
887 Philippians 2:8

make reconciliation for the sins of the people."[888] It is this Christ who has established reconciliation's course for every soul sorry for how they honor the living God. For, "with his stripes we are healed,"[889] "that the righteousness of the law might be fulfilled in us."[890] Therefore, "by the righteousness of one,"[891] "we have now received the atonement"[892] "unto justification of life,"[893] which is why John writes, "We might live through him."[894]

6. If indeed the believer would obtain heaven's ordained manner of righteousness, it should only be through an experimental confidence on the fact that the Father "sent his Son to be the propitiation for our sins."[895] The person must prove that "now the righteousness of God without the law is manifested,"[896] diligently examining and doing the knowledge of His Son's name to obtain a spirit wholly consecrated for honoring the LORD by the Word of His Son's mediation, even as it says, "I will meditate in thy precepts, and have respect unto thy ways."[897] For, "all our righteousnesses are as filthy rags,"[898] therefore "if our unrighteousness commend the righteousness of God, what shall we say?"[899]

7. John would have every minister know that, "by the law of faith,"[900] we have "victory through our Lord Jesus Christ,"[901]

---

888 Hebrews 2:17
889 Isaiah 53:5
890 Romans 8:4
891 Romans 5:18
892 Romans 5:11
893 Romans 5:18
894 1 John 4:9
895 1 John 4:10
896 Romans 3:21
897 Psalm 119:15
898 Isaiah 64:6
899 Romans 3:5
900 Romans 3:27
901 1 Corinthians 15:57

which is why he wrote to the churches, "This is the victory that overcometh the world, even our faith."[902] John saw how that the church was welcoming the seed of the religious world into its fellowship. "The lust of the flesh, and the lust of the eyes, and the pride of life"[903] is "all that is in the world,"[904] "but after that the kindness and love of God our Saviour toward man appeared,"[905] it is that "this commandment have we from him, That he who loveth God love his brother also."[906] A tried faith exercised by the law of the Spirit's righteousness will stop, within the conscience, all reliance on the law of *perfection* by the works of a legal traditional ethic. John saw that many ministers went about their conversation as though they had no sin against heaven's manners by the fact that they refused submission to the Spirit's simple instruction concerning worship and service, which counsel states, "Live according to God in the spirit,"[907] for "Christ hath redeemed us from the curse of the law (of the religious bill and ordinance of elders), being made a curse for us: for it is written, Cursed is every one that hangeth on a tree."[908]

8. If we would love one another as we claim to love the living God, it is that the soul must know its wrong against His throne's religion. The mind must be drawn to honest repentance from receiving conviction by the sentence against it, and it must know the power of the weight of the LORD's Spirit to provoke godly sorrow for true and purposeful confession of religious negligence, thereby coming into the knowledge that His High Priest's voice not only rescues the conversation from flesh into the Spirit's higher education, but that His name also

---

902 1 John 5:4
903 1 John 2:16
904 1 John 2:16
905 Titus 3:4
906 1 John 4:21
907 1 Peter 4:6
908 Galatians 3:13

delivers the heart from such a cold slumber that it may receive warmth to rightly feel. To say that we have no sin against heaven's course is to maintain a profession through a law of religious works or policies, and such a conversation relays the fact that it is believed that God's Man need not pass away, for what is perceived to be acceptable is so falsely maintained due to a deluded heart. John was seeing how Paul's counsel concerning "profane and vain babblings, and oppositions of science falsely so called,"[909] "which some professing have erred concerning the faith,"[910] was ever relevant. As more and more professed Christian elders began to draw back from the precious faith bestowed onto them, John took knowledge of their conversation and wrote, "Many deceivers are entered into the world, who confess not that Jesus Christ is come in the flesh."[911]

9. The lust of our faith's flesh and of the eyes of our understanding, and with the pride of such a conversation's understanding, had "hardened through the deceitfulness of sin"[912] the members of the church, exposing the fact that there was some open intercourse among them with the manners of that spirit nailed to the tree of the LORD's Christ, for which cause John wrote to the faithful few in fellowship with the apostles' doctrine, "The world knoweth us not."[913]

10. The material contained within the spirit of the religious age cannot recognize the fabric of right liberty and assurance; this is why John counseled, "They are of the world: therefore speak they of the world,"[914] and, "Hereby know we the spirit of truth, and the spirit of error,"[915] and, "The world knoweth us

---

909 1 Timothy 6:20
910 1 Timothy 6:21
911 2 John 1:7
912 Hebrews 3:13
913 1 John 3:1
914 1 John 4:5
915 1 John 4:6

not."[916] Of old, it was said, "Know how that the LORD doth put a difference between the Egyptians and Israel,"[917] and by taking knowledge of the fact of their peculiarity, it was of the LORD that they "put difference between holy and unholy, and between unclean and clean."[918] It was known, "There is no difference between the Jew and the Greek,"[919] yet the apostle would have every Jew professing the LORD's new will remember, "We who are Jews by nature,"[920] "even we have believed in Jesus Christ, that we might be justified by the faith of Christ, and not by the works of the law."[921] It was to emphasize this fact of a reform from their former Jewish mind in service to commandments and judgments of elders that John wrote, "Hereby know we the spirit of truth, and the spirit of error."[922]

11. The mind established on and advancing in truth subscribes to "the ministration of the spirit,"[923] which ministration knows justification "by the law of faith,"[924] for which cause this ministration is also known as "the ministration of righteousness."[925] "The ministration of death"[926] belongs to that spirit and conversation of religious error nailed to the tree, which is of "the law of sin and death"[927] after "a shew of wisdom in will worship."[928] The Spirit of heaven's will quiets the members of our faith's body that the mind may regain an

---

916 1 John 3:1
917 Exodus 11:7
918 Leviticus 10:10
919 Romans 10:12
920 Galatians 2:15
921 Galatians 2:16
922 1 John 4:6
923 2 Corinthians 3:8
924 Romans 3:27
925 2 Corinthians 3:9
926 2 Corinthians 3:7
927 Romans 8:2
928 Colossians 2:23

ever growing government within its body, to the end it may instruct the conversation's heart to hear the counsel, "Yield yourselves unto God, as those that are alive from the dead, and your members as instruments of righteousness."[929]

12. It is written, "The Spirit is life because of righteousness,"[930] and as righteousness appears from learning of and doing every word of the Father's Spirit by faith on the hope procured by His voice, it is that the LORD's Spirit will influence the spirit of man to regain his abused and decrepit faculties to soberly honor His name and precepts. The absence of this Spirit means an absence of His manner of righteousness within the conversation, and if there is an absence of the Spirit's righteousness, then man exists falsely within self. John sought to call attention to righteousness by the Spirit of heaven's ministry by teaching, "The Spirit is truth,"[931] for he tried to get the elders of the churches to understand that "he that saith, I know him, and keepeth not his commandments, is a liar, and the truth is not in him."[932]

13. The spirit of truth is after "the word of the truth of the gospel,"[933] and this word or counsel is "that we might be justified by the faith of Christ."[934] John saw how that many called the LORD and His Word a liar by the fact that they sought atonement to *Him* by their own ways and laws of order. For this cause John wrote to the churches, "We have an advocate with the Father, Jesus Christ the righteous,"[935] yet many elders

---

929 Romans 6:13
930 Romans 8:10
931 1 John 5:6
932 1 John 2:4
933 Colossians 1:5
934 Galatians 2:16
935 1 John 2:1

still declared, "Neither is there any daysman betwixt us, that might lay his hand upon usboth."[936]

14. "If any man sin against heaven's new will and covenant," said John, "there is One in the LORD our Father's direct presence, and 'he is able also to save them to the uttermost that come unto God by him,'[937] for 'this man, because he continueth ever, hath an unchangeable priesthood,'[938] 'seeing he ever liveth to make intercession.'"[939] But as it would happen, the observation of what took place of old would again find itself fulfilled, for He said, when observing Christian elders, "My people would not hearken to my voice; and Israel would none of me."[940] The LORD's blessing is in His commandment, for of old He said, "A law shall proceed from me,"[941] and, "The isles shall wait for his law."[942] Therefore His Christ confirmed, "I proceeded forth and came from God,"[943] and charged, "Hear the voice of the Son of God,"[944] which is how we know that "we have received a commandment from the Father."[945] What then is needed to receive the benefit of this commandment? It is written, "As soon as they hear of me, they shall obey me."[946]

15. If all that is necessary to receive the Spirit's righteousness is to simply hear and do the counsel of His voice, it is that upon mentally reverencing "the name of Jesus Christ for

---

936 Job 9:33
937 John 7:25
938 Hebrews 7:24
939 Hebrews 7:25
940 Psalms 81:11
941 Isaiah 51:4
942 Isaiah 42:4
943 John 8:42
944 John 5:25
945 1 John 2:4
946 Psalms 18:44

the remission of sins,"[947] "ye shall receive the gift of the Holy Ghost."[948] Now, the Holy Ghost is given to them that learn of and do the LORD's voice, and within the Spirit is a gift, a gift of His Spirit forwarding "the promise of the Spirit through faith,"[949] which gift is "abundance of grace and of the gift of righteousness."[950] Within the Spirit is the blessing of grace, and "by grace are ye saved through faith; and that not of yourselves: it is the gift of God."[951] The purpose of grace; the same power of the Spirit that in the beginning called all things into existence, yet now has for us been drawn up in showers of blessing to recover man's inward parts; is that we may have the remedy to conquer sin against heaven's educational course, as it says, "Where sin abounded, grace did much more abound."[952] This is why John said, "Whosoever is born of God sinneth not; but he that is begotten of God keepeth himself,"[953] for the one imbued with the Spirit's wisdom is impregnated "with all the fullness of God"[954] that they may confess, "Hereby know we that we dwell in him, and he in us, because he hath given us of his Spirit,"[955] and, "The Father sent the Son to be the Saviour of the world."[956]

16. One born of the LORD is one born of His Spirit's commandment, as His Christ says, "Every one that is born of the Spirit."[957] "That which is born of the Spirit is spirit,"[958] and

---

947   Acts 2:38
948   Acts 2:28
949   Galatians 3:14
950   Romans 5:17
951   Ephesians 2:8
952   Romans 5:20
953   1 John 5:18
954   Ephesians 3:19
955   1 John 4:13
956   1 John 4:14
957   John 3:8
958   John 3:6

"the spirit giveth life,"[959] therefore His Christ teaches, "It is the spirit that quickeneth."[960] He, having passed through the Spirit's course to be "perfect, as pertaining to the conscience,"[961] knows "that wisdom giveth life to them that have it";[962] this is why He says, "I know him, and keep his saying."[963]

17. As the spirit digests the fact of the Spirit's saying, the heart will confess, "Deliver me: quicken me according to thy word,"[964] for the person now accepts that "through knowledge shall the just be delivered."[965] Only diligent obedience to Spirit's judgment can bring deliverance to the understanding, which deliverance will quicken the inward faculties by the wisdom obtained from that counsel. This is why His Christ says, "I know him, and keep his saying,"[966] for He knows that the words of His LORD's Spirit are "life unto those that find them, and health to all their flesh,"[967] which is why He confessed, "I have not spoken of myself; but the Father which sent me, he gave me a commandment,"[968] and, "I know that his commandment is life everlasting: whatsoever I speak therefore, even as the Father said unto me, so I speak."[969]

18. Herein is the Spirit's voice, even an instruction concerning the complete "redemption that is in Christ."[970] It was because there was a falling away from the Father's commandment that there was a removal from His Spirit's

---

959 2 Corinthians 3:6
960 John 6:63
961 Hebrews 9:9
962 Ecclesiastes 7:12
963 John 8:55
964 Psalms 119:154
965 Proverbs 11:9
966 John 8:55
967 Proverbs 4:22
968 John 12:29
969 John 12:50
970 Romans 3:24

healing. As the Christian church left His name for *another*, they set *justification*, and the work of *righteousness*, by a code of unnecessary religious laws, and once the pure Spirit of righteousness was removed from their camp, so too went the gift of righteousness, even the Spirit's grace and strength for creation. Without surrendering the heart to receive heaven's medicine, when refusing to "have obeyed from the heart that form of doctrine which was delivered"[971] to it, then comes that spirit of error to convince the heart that the flesh must maintain right devotion in what is uncertain. Thus, it was because of a progressive effort to remove the LORD from His own doctrine, and to exist without His Son and Spirit's ministry, that John wrote, "If we confess our sins, he is faithful and just to forgive us our sins, and to cleanse us from all unrighteousness,"[972] and, "Our fellowship is with the Father, and with his Son Jesus Christ."[973]

19. At a time before these things were written, Paul, observing how the LORD and His Priest were finding themselves without Their own doctrine, warned Christian elders, saying, "Christ is become of no effect unto you, whosoever of you are justified by the law."[974] John was realizing what the Spirit had moved Paul to utter, for "another gospel"[975] had mingled a perverse spirit within "the truth of the gospel."[976] The faith of the Christian church now became *righteousness* and *justification* by "the tradition of men, after the rudiments of the world,"[977] therefore, "I justify myself,"[978] said her men.

---

971 Romans 6:17
972 1 John 1:9
973 1 John 1:3
974 Galatians 5:4
975 Galatians 1:6
976 Galatians 2:14
977 Colossians 2:8
978 Job 9:20

20. If man can sanctify the conscience of their conversation, the LORD's Christ need not die on that tree. If man could fully and knowledgeably account for his schism against the living God's name, the LORD need not have suffered the Word and Christ of His Spirit to execute a mission for humanity's plight. If there is in man a promise for acceptable *righteousness*, this Christ of the LORD God need not offer up His own name and course of righteousness as a gift, placing the Government of the Majesty in jeopardy, and receiving the full and complete wrath of His Spirit in place of man for the violation of His Father's throne religion. Thus, due to the revelation of the spirit working within the Christian church, as witnessed to him by the actions of her elders, John warned, "If we say that we have no sin, we deceive ourselves, and the truth is not in us."[979] "Ye are fallen from grace,"[980] said the apostle at the sight of spiritual apostasy, for it is that when grace is rejected, man believes self to be the creator and governor of his conversation, yet we know how it is counseled, "Through the Spirit wait for the hope of righteousness by faith."[981]

---

[979] 1 John 1:8
[980] Galatians 5:4
[981] Galatians 5:5

7

From Whence They Had Fallen

1. Said the apostles to church elders, "Am I therefore become your enemy, because I tell you the truth?"[982] "All that is in the world, the lust of the flesh, and the lust of the eyes, and the pride of life, is not of the Father, but is of the world."[983]

2. The apostles were exposed to ministers openly rejecting the Spirit's will and commandment while praises went towards *His name*, therefore they taught, "If we say that we have no sin, we deceive ourselves,"[984] and, "If a man think himself to be something, when he is nothing, he deceiveth himself."[985] As the church began to invent rites and customs that were to act as proof of devotion and loyalty to *the Faith*, the counsel was forgotten, "Let every man prove his own

---

982 Galatians 4:16
983 1 John 2:16
984 1 John 1:8
985 Galatians 6:3

work,"[986] and, "Examine yourselves, whether ye be in the faith."[987] Self-investigation is to lead the heart to confess, "In the cross of our Lord...the world is crucified unto me, and I unto the world,"[988] for it says, "They that are Christ's have crucified the flesh with the affections and lusts."[989] The spirit of the religious world is constructed after the error within "the lusts of our flesh, fulfilling the desires of the flesh and of the mind,"[990] and is "corrupt according to the deceitful lusts."[991] The apostles observed the movement of this spirit of error within unsanctified ministers and hoped to place them in remembrance of where they had fallen from, for they knew and had heard what the Spirit had said to them, counseling, "Remember from whence thou art fallen, and repent, and do the firstworks."[992]

3. The church was building up her self on Eve's violation. The lust of the flesh and of the eyes, and the pride of life's knowledge by that vain flesh, these were those attributes exemplified by Eve, in that "the woman saw that the tree was good for food, and that it was pleasant to the eyes, and a tree to be desired to make one wise."[993] Intemperance and inactivity governed the woman Eve, and it was because of this that she not only violated the LORD's commandment, but also placed an addition onto His voice due to her uneducated appetite. Because Eve existed in a wrong spirit, when she had enough proof to convince herself of the majesty of a certain accursed tree; for even the creation had sided with her inward motions;

---

986 Galatians 6:4
987 2 Corinthians 13:5
988 Galatians 6:14
989 Galatians 5:24
990 Ephesians 2:3
991 Ephesians 4:22
992 Revelation 2:5
993 Genesis 3:6

she saw that the tree was not only delightful to look on for food, but she added that it was also good to make one's conversation wise and outwardly beautiful. The Spirit has said, "What thing soever I command you, observe to do it: thou shalt not add thereto, nor diminish from it,"[994] for it is known, "The love of money is the root of all evil: which while some coveted after, they have erred from the faith."[995]

4. Eve didn't care to investigate the Spirit's instruction for her self's good. In her conviction is the revelation of her heart, which revelation was, "A tree to be desired."[996] Eve heard, "Ye shall be as gods, knowing good and evil,"[997] but if she had paused to collect herself, she would have noticed that knowledge of good and evil already existing within her. There was no thing greater in this tree of strange knowledge than in any other tree. God made every tree in the same fashion from out of the ground,[998] yet there was a tree of life that the pair could "eat, and live forever."[999] It was simply the fact that the LORD had said, "Do not," to one of the trees, that He knew a certain special reverence would be given to it by an untrained conscience, which reverence had a cursed attached to it by His commandment. Such a tree contained no greater knowledge than what was already in the woman, yet because of her innocence, because she knew no thing apart from Adam's verbal tradition; and would not stir up her self to know any better; in the moment her error had fully crossed her mind; when, after the fact, she became finally cognizant of her mistake; she knew no thing besides woe, guilt, bitterness, and shame.

---

994 Deuteronomy 12:32
995 1 Timothy 6:10
996 Genesis 3:6
997 Genesis 3:5
998 Genesis 2:9
999 Genesis 3:22

5. Because of her mental laziness, Eve did not want to prove the LORD's voice, nor her self by that doctrine, but rather wanted easy *knowledge* for a *blessed* appearance of *righteousness*. The tree became to her, as it was continually fixed in her thoughts, a *God* above the living God, so much so that she had fulfilled the saying, "The time will come when they will not endure sound doctrine; but after their own lusts shall they heap to themselves teachers, having itching ears."[1000] This woman began to hold the material of this tree in her heart as one "saying to a stock, Thou art my father; and to a stone, Thou hast brought me forth."[1001]

6. "The LORD God formed every beast"[1002] from out of the same ground as her and the tree, yet it was that the woman inevitably "worshipped and served the creature more than the Creator."[1003] Herein is witnessed an odd mystery, namely, how the creature of creation is believed to hold more understanding than creation's Creator. A creature, the serpent, a "beast of the field which the LORD God had made,"[1004] said, "Ye shall not surely die,"[1005] and the woman left off the plain counsel of her God, exchanging the truth for a lie. The woman would later report, "The serpent beguiled me,"[1006] for she lied to the LORD, seeing as how she desired knowledge of what she believed only belonged to gods. Scripture reports, "God standeth in the congregation of the mighty; he judgeth among the gods,"[1007] for the woman wanted to be one of might in the congregation and at the head of the mighty stewards of Eden,

---

1000 2 Timothy 4:3
1001 Jeremiah 2:27
1002 Genesis 2:18
1003 Romans 1:25
1004 Genesis 3:1
1005 Genesis 3:4
1006 Genesis 3:13
1007 Psalms 82:1

thus, concerning the vocation of such ministers, it is written, "Shew us what shall happen."[1008] "Shew the things that are to come hereafter, that we may know that ye are gods: yea, do good, or do evil, that we may be dismayed, and behold it together."[1009]

7. The knowledge contained in the tree, Eve believed, was a deep understanding, but she didn't know how to attain such knowledge so easily. It is written of the LORD's Spirit, "The Spirit searcheth all things, yea, the deep things of God,"[1010] therefore "he that is spiritual judgeth all things."[1011] But in Eve, the saying was fulfilled, "In the latter times some shall depart from the faith, giving heed to seducing spirits, and dcotrines of devils; speaking lies in hypocrisy."[1012] This is why John counsels the church, "He that doeth the will of God abideth forever,"[1013] for of old, the LORD's will was in consuming the tree of life, and to "eat, and live for ever."[1014] What can suffice the heart after the mind has tasted His thoughts and intention? Our counsel today is no different than that of old, for there still exists an accursed tree and a blessed tree of life to choose from. God's Man did nail to that tree an abominable religious course, "for he that is hanged is accursed of God."[1015] This is why John wrote to those who would have the testimony of Christ with falsehood, and this is why it is well to know heaven's right "record, that God hath given to us eternal life,

---

1008 Isaiah 41:22
1009 Isaiah 41:23
1010 1 Corinthians 2:10
1011 1 Corinthians 2:15
1012 1 Timothy 4:1
1013 1 John 2:17
1014 Genesis 3:22
1015 Deuteronomy 21:23

and this life is in his Son,"[1016] and that is not in "philosophy and vain deceit, after the tradition of men."[1017]

8. Today, a decision must be made: will we take that accursed tree and the old *knowledge* it represents to be for *salvation's right course*, or will we take knowledge of the ministry of the LORD's Son and Spirit to know salvation's science? Understanding that it is the serpent's intention to change the Spirit's science into a subtle lie; for his religion, being centered upon a tree, or a cross, will beguile the untrained spirit to believe that it, being accursed by the LORD God, will not curse our eyes; it is well for us to understand which tree we would and should be loyal to, lest the saying is fulfilled in us, "God shall send them strong delusion, that they should believe a lie: that they all might be damned who believed not the truth, but had pleasure in unrighteousness."[1018] For, it is said of old, "The tree of the field is man's life,"[1019] wherefore in the garden they were instructed to choose the minister of life or the minister of religious error, in whom is no life or right counsel for newness. John tried to get Christian elders to remember that "God was manifest in the flesh"[1020] within the spirit of His Son, whose doctrine came as "the express image of his person,"[1021] and "who through the eternal Spirit"[1022] "became the author of eternal salvation,"[1023] therefore he wrote to church elders, "The life was manifested, and we have seen it, and bear witness, and shew unto you that eternal life, which was with the Father."[1024]

1016 1 John 5:11
1017 Colossians 2:8
1018 2 Thessalonians 2:11,12
1019 Deuteronomy 20:19
1020 1 Timothy 3:16
1021 Hebrews 1:3
1022 Hebrews 9:14
1023 Hebrews 5:9
1024 1 John 1:2

9. The same issue with Eve was arising within the Christian church, therefore John wrote, to help church elders escape the mistake that she made, "That which was from the beginning, which we have heard, which we have seen with our eyes, which we have looked upon, and our hands have handled."[1025] Because Eve did not correctly hear the LORD's voice for her own self, she believed in a rehearsed tradition that said, "God hath said, Ye shall not eat of it, neither shall ye touch it, lest ye die,"[1026] which tradition, and every other after its kind, "could not make him that did the service perfect, as pertaining to the conscience."[1027] Eve passed away in her mind by the tradition imposed upon it, and Christian elders, by failing to personally examine heaven's will, were passing away within their understanding by the religious philosophies they imposed upon one another.

10. That Spirit saying, "Handle me, and see,"[1028] would have freely blessed Eve with understanding to clear the thoughts of her heart. He who says, "Reach hither thy finger, and behold my hands; and reach hither thy hand, and thrust it into my side,"[1029] would have loved for Eve to push and to challenge Him to explain whatever made no sense to her, for He Himself says, "Ask me of things to come concerning my sons, and concerning the work of my hands command ye me."[1030] This is why the LORD's man writes, "If any of you lack wisdom, let him ask of God, that giveth to all men liberally, and upbraideth not; and it shall be given him."[1031] The living God does not care about who we are or what we have done or what

---

1025 1 John 1:1
1026 Genesis 3:3
1027 Hebrews 9:9
1028 Luke 24:39
1029 John 20:27
1030 Isaiah 54:11
1031 James 1:5

we think we know. He doesn't care for what level of intellect we may carry in the knowledge of His name; should we *know* a lot, enough, a little, or no thing; for He ever says, "Come now, and let us reason together."[1032] All Eve and her husband had to do was simply ask for understanding, and after asking, fulfill the saying, "He gave good heed, and sought out, and set in order many proverbs."[1033]

11. Adam and Eve had free intercourse with the LORD's Spirit, and we may know this from how the Scripture tells of their communion with Him, saying, "They heard the voice of the LORD God walking in the garden in the cool of the day."[1034] The pair uninterruptedly communed with God face to face every morning and every evening, even as it is said, "In the morning sow thy seed, and in the evening withhold not thine hand."[1035] But creation's science is more than communion, seeing as how "the LORD is a God of knowledge, and by him actions are weighed."[1036] All of the communion in the world will mean nothing if the mind does not personally register the living God's voice, and this is why John approached Christian elders by saying, "We have heard,"[1037] and, "We have seen with our eyes,"[1038] and, "We have looked upon, and our hands have handled."[1039] Until "the eyes of your understanding"[1040] digest the wisdom of His High Priest's name, prostration before an accursed tree will consume the conversation to the injury of the conversation's mind and character.

1032 Isaiah 1:18
1033 Ecclesiastes 12:9
1034 Genesis 3:8
1035 Ecclesiastes 11:6
1036 1 Samuel 2:3
1037 1 John 1:1
1038 1 John 1:1
1039 1 John 1:1
1040 Ephesians 1:18

12. The LORD would have us commune with Him as we did in the beginning, and He has re-established such a course for us through the life, death, regeneration, and high priestly appointment of His consecrated High Priest. Because the Christian church had lost sight of the fact that pure religion is active in experimenting with faith on the Spirit's voice, and is not without inward labor to perfectly regulate the person away from the religious world in to His heavenly Sanctuary, John desired to remind them of the principle held by the true apostles, which principle states: "Of that wherewith the LORD thy God hath blessed thee thou shalt give,"[1041] and, "I will not dare speak of any of those things which Christ hath not wrought by me, to make the Gentiles obedient."[1042] The church was beginning to compromise her true doctrinal positions in order to gain supporters. Intercourse with the heart of the religious world above the living God ceased the flow of pure and blessed doctrines within her, for if she had remained patient and content in that given to her, applying to the Spirit for mental and moral health with all spiritual advancement, this church would have remained untainted in both the Father and His Son.

13. For this cause apostle counseled, "Let the peace of God rule in your hearts, to the which also ye are called in one body; and be ye thankful."[1043] "I have learned, in whatsoever state I am, therewith to be content,"[1044] he said, wherefore he advised, "Mark them which cause divisions and offences contrary to the doctrine which ye have learned; and avoid them. For they that are such serve not our Lord Jesus Christ, but their own belly."[1045]

1041 Deuteronomy 15:14
1042 Romans 15:18
1043 Colossians 3:15
1044 Philippians 4:11
1045 Romans 16:17,18

14. When Eve came to Adam, compelling his conscience to embrace a conflict against the commandment to be observed, she came to him as one "having the understanding darkened, being alienated from the life of God."[1046] Here was Eve, sitting in the LORD's presence and hearing His voice, and all that could be said to her was that said to certain sons of her own spirit: "The foxes have holes, and the birds of the air have nests; but the Son of man hath not where to lay his head,"[1047] and, "If thou doest well, shalt thou not be accepted? and if thou doest not well, sin lieth at the door. And unto thee shall be his desire, and thou shalt rule over him."[1048]

15. While Eve sat with the Word and Adam, her heart was not with them. As Judas beheld the works of this same Spirit's Christ, as He witnessed the Son of the Majesty actually lay out the seed of redemption and the beauty of His name's dominion, his heart was so untouched that Scripture says of him, "Set thou a wicked man over him: and let Satan stand at his right hand,"[1049] for which cause it is written, "Then entered Satan into Judas,"[1050] making him that one "lost,"[1051] even "the son of perdition."[1052] Because of a discontented and greedy spirit, Eve drifted from simple obedience to a complex disobedience. She sat quietly while God spoke of the earth's elements and her relation to it, of her diet and education, of who she and her husband were to be for the creation, and of the work that they were to accomplish on earth, but as the LORD saw their face, He knew their thoughts. Herein "the foundation of God standeth sure, having this seal, The Lord knoweth them that

---

1046 Ephesians 4:18
1047 Matthew 8:20
1048 Genesis 4:7
1049 Psalms 109:6
1050 Luke 22:3
1051 John 17:12
1052 John 17:12

are his."[1053] How is it that His own are known to Him? John confessed to the churches, "Every one that loveth is born of God, and knoweth God."[1054]

16. During the creation, of all that God saw in what He had made, He said that it was good, to where on the final day, "God saw every thing that he had made, and, behold, it was very good."[1055] Every thing, not everything, but rather every article, every element and creature of creation was good, in that every thing provoked "good to the use of edifying, that it may minister grace."[1056] Every thing in creation ministered to creation for vigor, for stability and for right function, and the message relayed by nature was to subdue the mind of man to remember, "As we have therefore opportunity, let us do good unto all men."[1057] For even before there was a man, "there went up a mist from the earth, and watered the whole face of the ground,"[1058] there being no division between the mist and the ground, the elements openly caring for one another. This is why John wrote, "Whoso keepeth his word, in him verily is the love of God perfected."[1059] By experiencing the wisdom of the LORD's Spirit to correct the thoughts and intentions of the heart, we enter into communion with His manner of love so that the imprint of His character would be engraved within the spirit of our mind, to the end we would care for one another according to the benevolence shown to us.

17. "If you love God's Spirit," said John to Christian elders, 'he that saith he abideth in him ought himself also so to walk,

---

1053 2 Timothy 2:19
1054 1 John 4:7
1055 Genesis 1:31
1056 Ephesians 4:29
1057 Galatians 6:10
1058 Genesis 2:6
1059 1 John 2:5

even as he walked.'"[1060] God's Man was not without obedience, godly love, or His LORD's wisdom, which is why Scripture instructs, "Say unto wisdom, Thou art my sister,"[1061] and, "Wisdom is the principal thing; therefore get wisdom,"[1062] and, "She shall preserve thee: love her, and she shall keep thee."[1063] This is why the apostle counsels, "Above all things put on charity, which is the bond of perfection,"[1064] and, "Let the word of Christ dwell in you richly in all wisdom."[1065]

18. If the church could pick up love and wisdom's right manner by exercising faith on the Spirit's will and revelation, John confirmed to them, "Whatsoever we ask, we receive of him, because we keep his commandments, and do those things that are pleasing in his sight."[1066] The church was to know her LORD's will and intention, and it was that many were to let their heart know His voice by living a personal religion, to the end the power of the Spirit may freely work in the congregated body by His individual impression upon the heart of their understanding. Thus, John counseled them, "We should believe on the name of his Son Jesus Christ, and love one another, as he gave commandment,"[1067] for the elders and their members were turning to their own religious inventions, erecting their own spiritual laws and judgments, fulfilling the saying, "When the bridegroom shall be taken from them...then shall they fast."[1068]

19. They that know and love the Spirit's bridegroom confess, "The friend of the bridegroom, which standeth and

---

1060 1 John 2:6
1061 Proverbs 7:4
1062 Proverbs 4:7
1063 Proverbs 4:6
1064 Colossians 3:14
1065 Colossians 3:16
1066 1 John 3:22
1067 1 John 3:23
1068 Mathew 9:15

heareth him, rejoiceth greatly because of the bridegroom's voice."[1069] They that love the voice of the Spirit's Priest will love His voice and none other, for, didn't the Father charge, "Hear ye him"?[1070] Doesn't His Son say, "If any man hear my voice, and open"?[1071] Because Eve failed to train her heart to recognize the counsel of the LORD's Spirit, by failing to acknowledge Him in what things He had created, she trusted a voice that *God* had made, but that He had not blessed with any power or understanding. Because of her desire, Eve forsook her LORD's will and wisdom to obtain that which was vain and imaginary, and her issues could have been resolved had she practiced right temperance, humility, and industry. Due to her lacking self-control, her mental health vanished in to a realm of self-righteousness and self-sufficiency, desiring to *know* more than what was necessary for peace and regeneration. John saw the seed of her error fast creeping into Christian folds, and so counseled, "If we walk in the light, as he is in the light, we have fellowship one with another, and the blood of Jesus Christ his Son cleanseth us from all sin."[1072]

20. What is in the "light" of God? Because "God is a Spirit,"[1073] it is that we should be mindful of the light within the Spirit of our Intercessor's mediation. For, if the Spirit is light, and if in His will and voice is no darkness, what then is the material of His "light" composed of? It is written, "The law is light,"[1074] and, "Light and understanding and excellent wisdom."[1075] If the believer should dwell in light, they should be receiving and practicing that knowledge of "the law of the

---

1069 John 3:29
1070 Matthew 17:5
1071 Revelation 3:20
1072 1 John 1:7
1073 John 4:24
1074 Proverbs 6:23
1075 Daniel 5:14

Spirit of life,"[1076] "understanding what the will of the Lord is."[1077] It is therefore a fact that it is this Christ of the LORD's Spirit "who gave himself for our sins, that he might deliver us... according to the will of God."[1078] The Spirit's will is "according to the promise of life which is in Christ Jesus,"[1079] which is why John writes, "This is the promise that he hath promised us, even eternal life."[1080] That promise of "life" obtained by doing the Spirit's will is "the grace that is in Christ,"[1081] and this grace is "the salvation which is in Christ."[1082] Therefore as God's Christ says, "Whosoever believeth in him should not perish, but have everlasting life,"[1083] in reality the believer should receive right "honour and power everlasting"[1084] "being sanctified by the Holy Ghost,"[1085] that is, sanctified "by the power of the Spirit of God."[1086] It is because of this fact that John taught the elders, "God hath given to us eternal life, and this life is in his Son. He that hath the Son hath life,"[1087] and, "If any man have not the Spirit of Christ, he is none of his."[1088]

21. The word was being fulfilled, "They profess that they know God; but in works they deny him."[1089] John knew that if all should care for Him that begat as they also devoted themselves

---

1076 Romans 8:2
1077 Ephesians 5:17
1078 Galatians 1:44
1079 2 Timothy 1:1
1080 1 John 2:25
1081 Galatians 1:44
1082 2 Timothy 2:10
1083 John 3:16
1084 1 Timothy 6:16
1085 Romans 15:16
1086 Romans 15:19
1087 1 John 5:11,12
1088 Romans 8:9
1089 Titus 1:16

to *Him* that was begotten of Him, that "by this we know that we love the children of God"[1090] and "have the mind of Christ."[1091] John saw how the church had grown to abandon the instruction, "Do good, that they be rich in good works, ready to distribute, wiling to communicate,"[1092] and, "To do good and communicate forget not: for with such sacrifices God is well pleased."[1093] For, the spirit that took over the church said, "Men shall be lovers of their own selves, covetous, boasters, proud, blasphemers, disobedient to parents, unthankful, unholy, without natural affection, trucebreakers, false accusers, incontinent, fierce, despisers of those that are good, traitors, heady, highminded, lovers of pleasures more than lovers of God; having a form of godliness, but denying the power thereof."[1094] Due to her disobedience, the Christian church left the ones that said, "I have espoused you to one husband,"[1095] and, "I travail in birth again until Christ be formed in you,"[1096] for her elders forgot their parents and their face, and began to detest them that were "good," that is, them that were "a good soldier of Jesus Christ."[1097]

22. Because the sign of forgetfulness through hate emphasized her decline from purity, John wrote, "This commandment have we from him, That he who loveth God love his brother also."[1098] If the church should "strive not about words to no profit, but to the subverting of the hearers,"[1099] it would be proof that her members were individually receiving the

---

1090 1 John 5:2
1091 1 Corinthians 2:16
1092 1 Timothy 6:18
1093 Hebrews 13:16
1094 2 Timothy 3:1-5
1095 2 Corinthians 11:2
1096 Galatians 4:19
1097 2 Timothy 2:3
1098 1 John 4:21
1099 2 Timothy 2:14

power and wisdom of the Father's grace from obeying the doctrine of His Son. If the members of the church received His Spirit, then His power to recover them "according to his own purpose and grace"[1100] would show forth. "Not according to our works,"[1101] "not by works of righteousness which we have done,"[1102] counseled the apostles, but rather, through "the righteousness of God which is by faith of Jesus"[1103] we are "justified freely by his grace through the redemption that is in Christ."[1104] If the members of the church could study after the maintenance of sanctification by faith on the Spirit's voice through grace's creative power, it would be understood that "to him that worketh is the reward not reckoned of grace, but of debt."[1105] The reward of faithfulness to the LORD's voice is righteousness, even His manner of kindness within the conversation's inward parts; for "God imputeth righteousness without works";[1106] which is why the apostle counseled the elders, "I testfy to every man that is circumcised, that he is a debtor to do the whole law."[1107]

23. Now, of old, the controversy between righteousness by faith on God's voice and righteousness by the labor of legal religious ordinances had so affected the church that, in a letter, the apostles wrote, "Certain which went out from us have troubled you with words, subverting your souls, saying, Ye must be circumcised, and keep the law: to whom we gave no such commandment."[1108] To the churches, John would have them

---

1100 2 Timothy 1:9
1101 2 Timothy 1:9
1102 Titus 3:5
1103 Romans 3:22
1104 Romans 3:24
1105 Romans 4:4
1106 Romans 4:6
1107 Galatians 5:3
1108 Acts 15:24

remember that apostate denomination, saying, "They went out from us, but they were not of us; for if they had been of us, they would no doubt have continued with us."[1109] They that went out from the light of the Spirit's knowledge sunk their teeth into their flesh, "lest they should suffer persecution for the cross of Christ."[1110] The act of circumcision was held by the Jews as that which was above or equal to every precept of the LORD, thereby causing an act in the flesh to portray *righteousness* equal to that concerning any precept of His voice. That which portrays a legal traditional ethic to adhere to for supposed *favor* of *God* is understood by the act of circumcision, for they believed that it was given of *God*, is forever of *God*, and is forever their *righteousness* to do, but man so served the creation that they missed the voice of the Creator saying, "Circumcision is nothing, and uncircumcision is nothing,"[1111] and, "In Christ Jesus neither circumcision availeth any thing thing, nor uncircumcision, but a new creature."[1112]

24. Herein religious error against the Spirit's new covenant will is understood, for many of profession were not created by the knowledge of the Spirit's Christ, but rather by the legal religious bill, and as a result were not in the LORD His Father's judgment and wisdom. Circumcision; which is a moniker used to denote every law of works to obtain the *righteousness* and *favor* of *God*; is now eternally dead and forgotten by the sacrificed flesh of God's Man, for when He said, "A new covenant, he hath made the first old,"[1113] wherefore this Christ "taketh away the first, that he may establish the second. By the which will we are sanctified through the offering of the body of Jesus

---

1109 1 John 2:19
1110 Galatians 6:12
1111 1 Corinthians 7:19
1112 Galatians 6:15
1113 Hebrews 8:13

Christ once for all."[1114] Thus, "having abolished in his flesh the enmity, even the law of commandments and ordinances,"[1115] do we express a right conversation by adhering to what is now acknowledged as accursed and abominable?

25. The reformer is sanctified by learning of and doing the divine promises of God's Spirit within His will for mental and moral deliverance from religious error, which promise is found only in that covenant ratified by the blood of His Christ. Man cannot save or recover their faith's conscience or conversation from the corruption of death; whether mental, moral, emotional, or spiritual; but it is that "according to his good pleasure which he hath purposed in himself,"[1116] "if any man be in Christ, he is a new creature: old things are passed away,"[1117] for a new spirit moves the heart of the believer to pick up a "faith which worketh by love."[1118] By the saying of this Christ of the living God existing within the inward parts, the works of the flesh will be quenched by inward creation that outward benevolence may result. In His name, "love, joy, peace, longsuffering, gentleness, goodness, faith, meekness, temperance,"[1119] all rule the throne of the heart, for "against such there is no law."[1120]

26. If such a right spirit could find a home in the conscience of the leaders of the Christian churches, there would be neither error nor division from the apostles' doctrine and communion. But the laws of works captivated the church, removing the spirit of self-sacrificing love from her, which spirit was a testimony to the fact that the Spirit was not welcomed among them. Like her

---

1114 Hebrews 10:9,10
1115 Ephesians 2:15
1116 Ephesians 1:9
1117 2 Corinthians 5:17
1118 Galatians 5:6
1119 Galatians 5:22,23
1120 Galatians 5:23

that saw the tree was "a tree to be desired to make one wise,"[1121] so the church was filled with "perverse disputings of men of corrupt minds, and destitute of the truth, supposing that gain is godliness,"[1122] when cajoled by that body "whom they slew and hanged on a tree."[1123] John beheld; and even among his dearest associates; those that did "resist the truth,"[1124] who had ceased to acknowledge the fact that "godliness with contentment is great gain,"[1125] and that stillness of the conversation is by "the doctrine which is according to godliness."[1126] Temperance is an attribute that the one in communion with the Spirit will adopt, and the loss of this spirit among ministers confirmed to John that none were hearing the counsel, "If any man will come after me, let him deny himself."[1127] The apostle counseled, "Every man that striveth for the mastery is temperate in all things,"[1128] and, "If a man strive for the masteries, yet is he not crowned, except he strive lawfully,"[1129] for to have "the Lord give thee understanding in all things,"[1130] one must labor to regain right digestion of the mental and moral faculties, and as John saw the churches grossly intemperate, he knew the fever among them flourished due to the diet of their eyes.

27. It was because of this that John wrote, "I wish above all things that thou mayest prosper and be in health, even as thy soul prospereth."[1131] Good health to our physical and mental bodies is needed when searching for knowledge of the

---

1121 Genesis 3:6
1122 1 Timothy 6:5
1123 Acts 10:39
1124 2 Timothy 3:8
1125 1 Timothy 6:6
1126 1 Timothy 6:3
1127 Luke 9:23
1128 1 Corinthians 9:25
1129 2 Timothy 2:5
1130 2 Timothy 2:7
1131 3 John 1:2

Godhead's science. There can be no one professing the Spirit's will and law while remaining intemperate without an effort to patiently embrace reform by the Spirit's wisdom and power, for it is that if one keeps "not his tongue,"[1132] he "deceiveth his own heart,"[1133] leaving it that their "religion is vain."[1134] But he or she that may, through the power of the Spirit's grace, educate their conversation to a higher existence by faith, "the same is a perfect man, and able also to bridle the whole body."[1135] And perfect how? It says, "Perfect, as pertaining to the conscience."[1136] True perfection is the full ordination of the spirit's organs to regulate the faculties and members of the personal religion's heart that service to the Word and man may be executed efficiently and in a right mind. Therefore due to a lack of care being devoted to the organs of their faith's body, Paul counseled them, "Ye cannot do the things that ye would. But if ye be led of the Spirit, ye are not under the law,"[1137] that is, by the Spirit's impression, you are not bound to believe that you are "made perfect by the flesh."[1138]

28. There is no thing given to man of the Spirit unless they sincerely and diligently ask for it, and in so asking would also cooperate with the conditions necessary to receive what is asked for. It is the power of grace that enhances the particular and individual gift within the Spirit's reformer. Upon reception of that gift from doing heaven's will and learning, diligence to obtain knowledge of His name will open the receiver to the gift of righteousness to obtain His name's righteousness, thereby providing entrance for His Spirit to pass into the domain of the

---

1132 James 1:26
1133 James 1:26
1134 James 1:26
1135 James 3:2
1136 Hebrews 9:9
1137 Galatians 5:17,18
1138 Galatians 3:3

soul for recovery and education in right service to the Spirit, self, and to other spirits. The Spirit will teach the spirit of the talent entrusted to it by the LORD their Father, and how to use that talent for its right purpose. Therefore, "Study to shew thyself approved unto God,"[1139] counsels the apostle, for "the soul of the diligent shall be made fat"[1140] and not the flesh; "the flesh profiteth nothing."[1141] The fact that the flesh should adhere to its own policies of *righteousness*, or even if the one professing the name of His Son should adhere to that which the Word has for ever left off, even adding to that dead manner of worship and service presumptuous error, is proof that the LORD's new will is not known or cared for, that none have subscribed to His grace and manner of righteousness, and that none desire to feel after His name's cause in the earth. This is why Paul said to the elders of the churches, "Be renewed in the spirit of your mind,"[1142] for he longed for them to understand why the apostles counseled, "Live according to God in the spirit."[1143]

29. It is because John saw and understood what maintained the present religious error that he wrote, "He that loveth his brother abideth in the light, and there is none occasion of stumbling in him."[1144] For this cause Paul wrote, "Ye are all complete in him,"[1145] advising their elders to learn how to "speak the mystery of Christ."[1146] The Spirit is given "that your love may abound yet more and more in knowledge and in all judgment; that ye may approve the things that are

---

1139 2 Timothy 2:15
1140 Proverbs 13:4
1141 John 6:63
1142 Ephesians 4:23
1143 1 Peter 4:6
1144 1 John 2:10
1145 Colossians 2:10
1146 Colossians 4:3

excellent,"[1147] for it is written, "His name alone is excellent."[1148] The LORD's understanding is not bound; the Agent and Educator of His benevolence is not bound; and He has done this to familiarize His believing reformer with those things most excellent concerning His name and person. When there is no advancement in the doctrine of the Spirit's will and righteousness, the heart will stand still in self-government and out of fear will govern self, even enduring the unnecessary pain of self-violation until it can no longer feel any good and warm thing of the Spirit.

30. A lacking of faith in the Spirit's voice within the church meant a lacking of self-sacrificing love, and a lacking of godly affection meant a lacking of knowledge and wisdom, therefore the apostle wrote, "There is no fear in love."[1149] Therefore if "we have known and believed the love that God hath to us,"[1150] "we ought also to love one another"[1151] according to the Spirit's commandment. Thus, hurt that no minister recognized the root of his behavior, John continued, "If we say that we have fellowship with him, and walk in darkness, we lie, and do not the truth."[1152] "He that saith, I know him, and keepeth not his commandments, is a liar, and the truth is not in him."[1153] "Let that therefore abide in you, which ye have heard from the beginning. If that which ye have heard from the beginning shall remain in you, ye also shall continue in the Son, and in the Father."[1154]

1147 Philippians 1:9,10
1148 Psalm 148:13
1149 1 John 4:18
1150 1 John 4:16
1151 1 John 4:11
1152 1 John 1:6
1153 1 John 2:4
1154 1 John 2:24

31. John held up before the people that counsel of old, "Of every tree of the garden thou mayest freely eat: but of the tree of the knowledge of good and evil, thou shalt not eat of it: for in the day that thou eatest thereof thou shalt surely die,"[1155] that is, die the death of the "eyes," "the eyes of your understanding."[1156] If the elders could know where they had fallen from, if they could study the history of apostasy against the LORD's voice to acknowledge from whence they are gathered, the counsel would be considered, "Have no fellowship with the unfruitful works of darkness,"[1157] and, "Be ye transformed by the renewing of your mind, that ye may prove what is that good, and acceptable, and perfect, will of God."[1158]

1155 Genesis 2:16,17
1156 Ephesians 1:18
1157 Ephesians 5:11
1158 Romans 12:2

8

Faith's Right End

1. Says the LORD, "Six days shall work be done, but on the seventh day there shall be to you an holy day, a Sabbath of rest to the LORD."[1159]

2. Again, the seventh day is to be held as what kind of day for the one who would observe it? It says, "The Sabbath is a holy day of rest."[1160] For, again, the LORD says, "Remember the Sabbath day, to keep it holy,"[1161] but one must question, if the Sabbath is "holy" and is to be reverenced as "holy," what must man first have in order to reverence that seventh day appointment? The Spirit answers, "Ye shall be holy men unto me."[1162] So then, how is that we are to be "holy"? What must we, as naturally damaged and unholy creations, do to be acknowledged of the Spirit as "holy"? Says the LORD our

---

[1159] Exodus 35:2
[1160] Exodus 35:2
[1161] Exodus 20:8
[1162] Exodus 22:32

Father, "Sanctify yourselves, and ye shall be holy; for I am holy."[1163] "Ye shall therefore be holy, for I am holy,"[1164] He says.

3. The Spirit counsels the believer to sanctify their conversation's heart, but what does the apostle say? At the sight of a corrupt spirit among the leadership of the early church, John writes, "Every man that hath this hope in him purifieth himself."[1165] The instruction is to purify the conscience of the conversation. The Spirit will not do this for us unless we confidently give His Word our active attention, consent, and cooperation. As the spirit of the conversation adopts the principle, "They which live should not henceforth live unto themselves, but unto him which died for them, and rose again,"[1166] that heart will receive the promise, "Then shalt thou delight thyself in the LORD,"[1167] and "in all holy conversation and godliness."[1168]

4. The Christian church, in the day of the apostle John, began to forward "those things which are not convenient; being filled with all unrighteousness, fornication, and all uncleanness, or covetousness,"[1169] "filthiness...foolish talking,"[1170] "envy, murder, debate, deceit, malignity."[1171] John saw the lack of respect towards the Spirit's pure instruction, and from being so near to the heart of heaven's throne, he knew that harmony failed among ministers because they refused to experience purification's right work and effect. Years before the activities John observed had found themselves openly manifested,

---

1163 Leviticus 11:44
1164 Leviticus 11:45
1165 1 John 3:3
1166 2 Corinthians 5:15
1167 Isaiah 58:14
1168 2 Peter 3:11
1169 Romans 1:28
1170 Ephesians 5:4
1171 Romans 1:28

Paul warned, "Of your own selves shall men arise, speaking perverse things, to draw away disciples after them."[1172] "Of your own selves," said Paul, but who was Paul talking to at this particular moment? Scripture tells us that Paul, "from Mile'tus he sent to Eph'esus, and called the elders of the church."[1173] Paul was speaking to the Christian leadership of Eph'esus, for a craft contrary to the doctrine of the Spirit's will and ministry would prosper from within their ranks, which is why the Spirit told John, concerning His warning for the churches, "Send it unto the seven churches which are in Asia,"[1174] and the first being sent unto Eph'esus.

5. Concerning Asia, we know how that the apostles "were forbidden of the Holy Ghost to preach the word in Asia,"[1175] for it says, "The Spirit suffered them not."[1176] What may have been the reason for the Spirit to resist the people of Asia? Well, "not alone at Eph'esus, but almost throughout all Asia,"[1177] "the great goddess Diana"[1178] was that which "all Asia and the world worshippeth."[1179] This is why John admonished the church, after observing church elders enjoying the craft of Asia, saying, "The whole world lieth in wickedness,"[1180] and why Paul advised them, "Have no fellowship with the unfruitful works of darkness,"[1181] and, "It is a shame even to speak of those things which are done of them in secret."[1182] Christian elders began meddling with the philosophy of them that had no knowledge

---

1172 Acts 20:30
1173 Acts 20:17
1174 Revelation 1:11
1175 Acts 16:6
1176 Acts 16:7
1177 Acts 19:26
1178 Acts 19:27
1179 Acts 19:27
1180 1 John 5:19
1181 Ephesians 5:11
1182 Ephesians 5:12

of the LORD's will, initiating commandments and mysteries with traditions and ceremonies by their inspiration, for "in the dark, every man in the chambers of his imagery"[1183] began "weeping for Tam'muz,"[1184] and teaching "to burn incense unto the queen of heaven, and to pour out drink offering unto her."[1185] Popular paganism was blending with a crude version of the apostles' doctrine, sweeping the Spirit's pure religion from the eyes and ears of ministers, leaving in its place a certain wine fermented with water and hemlock, for the people again began to worship "the brazen serpent that Moses had made."[1186] For this cause, Peter counseled the elders, "Be ye holy in all manner of conversation."[1187] "Not fashioning yourselves according to the former lusts in your ignorance; but as he which hath called you is holy, so be ye holy in all manner of conversation."[1188]

6. Paul confessed his fear for Christian elders, saying, "Lest by any means, as the serpent beguiled Eve, so your minds should be corrupted from the simplicity that is in Christ."[1189] The apostles knew that there was only one means whereby the Spirit's words may become subverted, therefore John wrote, "Whosoever transgresseth, and abideth not in the doctrine of Christ, hath not God."[1190] By adopting the principle, "Righteousness come by the law,"[1191] Paul knew that a corrupt spirit would enter in to the personal conversation of the elders to defile the church, and so wrote, "If ye bite and

---

1183 Ezekiel 8:12
1184 Ezekiel 8:14
1185 Jeremiah 44:17
1186 2 Kings 18:4
1187 1 Peter 1:15
1188 1 Peter 1:14,15
1189 2 Corinthians 11:3
1190 2 John 1:9
1191 Galatians 2:21

devour one another, take heed that ye be not consumed one of another,"[1192] for which cause John wrote, "This commandment have we from him, That he who loveth God love his brother also."[1193] And again, "If a man say, I love God, and hateth his brother, he is a liar."[1194]

7. When once heaven's pure doctrine became supplanted with a counterfeit, their apostasy was immediately evident. There is only one spirit attracted to the person by their acceptance of the LORD's voice, which is why Paul counseled, "Let brotherly love continue."[1195] Obedience to the Spirit's counsel for mental and moral redemption is ordained for the believer "to be conformed to the image of his Son."[1196] When the image of the LORD's Priest is known and confirmed within the reformer's conscience, "by this we know that we love the children of God,"[1197] because "every one that loveth him that begat loveth him also that is begotten of him."[1198] Herein is the only way that love could have left the church to have confusion with hatred enter in to it, for He that begat was rejected, leaving no man able to comprehend that vileness within their conversation, and so it was again fulfilled, "They hate him that rebuketh in the gate, and they abhor him that speaketh uprightly."[1199] Thus, "in those days, while Mor'decai sat in the king's gate,"[1200] when "the word that came to Jeremi'ah from the LORD"[1201] said, "Stand in the gate of the LORD's house,"[1202] "the Jews

---

1192 Galatians 5:15
1193 1 John 4:21
1194 1 John 4:20
1195 Hebrews 13:1
1196 Romans 8:29
1197 1 John 5:2
1198 1 John 5:1
1199 Amos 5:10
1200 Esther 2:21
1201 Jeremiah 7:1
1202 Jeremiah 7:2

stirred up the devout and honourable women, and the chief men of the city, and raised persecution against"[1203] "the apostles' doctrine and fellowship."[1204]

8. There is a reason why the LORD would have His assembly "holy," for He says, "Ye shall be holy unto me: for I the LORD am holy, and have severed you from other people, that ye should be mine."[1205] Should the believer confess His Christ's voice as a personal Savior, it is that they accept, and even long after, separation from the earth's manners through actively engaging self with His name. For, aren't we advised to "be dead with Christ from the rudiments of the world"?[1206] Of His assembly, the Spirit says, "The people shall dwell alone, and shall not be reckoned among the nations,"[1207] which is why John wrote to the churches that the love that is in the religious world, and the service of those flesh-based ordinances, are contrary to the LORD's name and wisdom, and is not of the doctrine of His Christ. It is for this reason that Peter counseled them, "Shew forth the praises of him who hath called you out of darkness into his marvelous light,"[1208] and why John also wrote, "The darkness is past, and the true light now shineth,"[1209] for by faith's learning and exercise we have "now have obtained mercy"[1210] for newness of heart and mind.

9. Look at and examine John's speech, for, he does not say that darkness is <u>passed</u>, but rather, that it is **past**, of former times and is now old and retired, being replaced by faith's higher learning, leaving the individual reformer as "now the

---

1203   Acts 13:50
1204   Acts 2:42
1205   Leviticus 20:26
1206   Colossians 2:20
1207   Numbers 23:9
1208   1 Peter 2:9
1209   1 John 2:8
1210   1 Peter 2:10

people of God,"[1211] "which in times past were not a people."[1212] That old religious manner for acceptance did sanctify "to the purifying of the flesh,"[1213] yet now by the Spirit's instruction, and through His Son's mediation, exists "a new and living way"[1214] that of old "could not make him that did the service perfect, as pertaining to the conscience."[1215] Because it is the Spirit's will to "purge your conscience form dead works to serve the living God,"[1216] a "holy" conversation, or a "godly" conversation, is in refraining the conversation from dead religious labors, which labors the LORD's Christ abolished by His passing flesh on the tree, "even the law of commandments contained in ordinances."[1217] The LORD's new covenant will is ordained to redeem or purchase the conversation's conscience from "the handwriting of ordinances"[1218] put together by priests and elders, which redemption is for the purpose of a conversation wholly devoted to the Word and not to the carnal policies of the religious world, which is why "pure religion and undefiled before God and the Father is"[1219] for one "to keep himself unspotted from the world."[1220] When we observe elders advancing what is abolished, we may understand that their conversation is contrary to the Spirit's will.

10. False leaders in the church compromised those principles advancing the true LORD's true Faith, for they inevitably crucified the body of the LORD's knowledge,[1221] "supposing

---

1211 1 Peter 2:10
1212 1 Peter 2:10
1213 Hebrews 9:13
1214 Hebrews 10:20
1215 Hebrews 9:9
1216 Hebrews 9:14
1217 Ephesians 2:15
1218 Colossians 2:14
1219 James 1:27
1220 James 1:27
1221 Hebrews 6:6

that gain is godliness."[1222] His Christ taught the precept, "If any man serve me, him will my Father honour,"[1223] yet by Christian ministers the Scripture is fulfilled, "Who hath believed our report?"[1224] It is written, "God is judge: he putteth down one, and setteth up another,"[1225] yet because the heads of the churches had become so consumed with theories and ordinances, with doctrines and suppositions, with supremacy and preeminence, John wrote, "Our fellowship is with the Father, and with his Son."[1226] The spirit in the church would not accommodate that Spirit of the LORD's High Priest; which "Spirit is truth"[1227] and which "Spirit is life";[1228] for the *name* of *the Spirit's Son* became a tool of psychological imprisonment for sensual wealth. Thus, the proverb was fulfilling before John's eyes, "The desire of the slothful killeth him; for his hands refuse to labour,"[1229] therefore he wrote to them, "He that saith, I know him, and keepeth not his commandments, is a liar, and the truth is not in him,"[1230] for he knew how it was written, "The robbery of the wicked shall destroy them; because they refuse to do judgment,"[1231] and, "Though hand join in hand, the wicked shall not be unpunished."[1232]

11. There is a unity and a labor that may be well, but in reality, it is of an injurious spirit. John saw how that all did "profess that they knew God; but in works they deny him";[1233]

1222 1 Timothy 6:5
1223 John 12:26
1224 Isaiah 53:1
1225 Psalms 75:7
1226 1 John 1:3
1227 1 John 5:6
1228 Romans 8:10
1229 Proverbs 21:25
1230 1 John 2:4
1231 Proverbs 21:7
1232 Proverbs 11:21
1233 Titus 1:16

denying His Spirit and His counsel to forward an employment contrary to His will. This is why John was moved to write to them, "This is his commandment, That we should believe on the name of his Son Jesus Christ, and love one another, as he gave us commandment."[1234]

12. The LORD needs no help to interpret His own self. For, "who hath directed the Spirit of the LORD, or being his counsellor hath taught him? With whom took he counsel, and who instructed him, and taught him in the path of judgment, and taught him knowledge, and shewed to him the way of understanding?"[1235] Every man without the LORD's Spirit needs an interpreter, which is why they need prescriptions expounding the pronunciation of *His* word by "philosophy and vain deceit, after the tradition of men, after the rudiments of the world."[1236] Therefore by failing to do heaven's course, they fulfill the saying, "They that are unlearned and unstable wrest, as they do also the other scriptures, unto their own destruction,"[1237] and, "Ever learning, and never able to come to the knowledge of the truth."[1238] Yet, says the Spirit, "Ye shall be holy men unto me,"[1239] and, "Sanctify yourselves, and ye shall be holy,"[1240] therefore Peter counseled them, "Sanctify the Lord God in your hearts."[1241]

13. As the times wore down the Christians, as they became "as the filth of the world"[1242] and "the offscouring of all things,"[1243] the "persecution against the church which was at

---

1234 1 John 1:23
1235 Isaiah 40:13,14
1236 Colossians 2:8
1237 2 Peter 3:16
1238 2 Timothy 3:7
1239 Exodus 22:31
1240 Leviticus 11:44
1241 1 Peter 3:15
1242 1 Corinthians 4:13
1243 1 Corinthians 4:13

Jerusalem";[1244] that is, "the churches of God which in Judae'a are in Christ Jesus";[1245] "in God the Father and in the Lord Jesus Christ";[1246] destroyed the hearts of her members to even provoke jealousy and envy against that which was honored among pagans. While the churches endured strange times against themselves, they were to remember, "Who is he that will harm you, if ye be followers of that which is good,"[1247] and we know how it is written of the Spirit's wisdom, "The law is good,"[1248] and that "there is none good but one, that is, God,"[1249] which is why it says, "The law is light,"[1250] and why John wrote, "God is light."[1251] "The Spirit of truth, which proceedeth from the Father,"[1252] is that understanding which men and women of faith are to take hold of for the accomplishment of righteousness. By fear, unconsecrated and unconverted ministers began to exalt the *doctrine of Christ* without the Spirit's light, which light is "the law of the Spirit of life."[1253] For, "fellowship of the Spirit"[1254] was to increase love and wisdom within the church "that their hearts might be comforted, being knit together in love, and unto all riches of the full assurance of understanding, to the acknowledgment of the mystery of God,"[1255] but if without that Spirit and knowledge of His will, wherein can a self-sacrificing union exist?

1244 Acts 8:1
1245 1 Thessalonians 2:14
1246 1 Thessalonians 1:1
1247 1 Peter 3:13
1248 1 Timothy 1:8
1249 Mark 10:18
1250 Proverbs 6:23
1251 1 John 1:5
1252 John 15:26
1253 Romans 8:2
1254 Philippians 2:1
1255 Colossians 2:2

14. This is why John wrote, "There is no fear in love,"[1256] for he knew that a new spirit had entered in to Christian assemblies. With the church forgetting the instruction, "Having your conversation honest among the Gentiles: that, whereas they speak evil of you, as of evildoers, they may be ashamed that falsely accuse your good conversation in Christ,"[1257] their blatant apostasy from heaven's right doctrine openly manifested itself to a pagan world, for the world saw the Christian as being no different in spirit and doctrine from them. For, who may believe the false criticisms against them and their doctrines but them that do not know the very doctrine they preach? Who may succumb to terror and fear of adversity but them that refuse the counsel, "None can keep alive his own soul"?[1258] Who may be offended at the Spirit's Faith but them that refuse to become first offended at self by His voice? Christian leadership was afraid of faith's exercise, wherefore the apostle wrote them, "Perfect love casteth out fear,"[1259] for he saw their prevailing spiritual illness and knew that there was fear, compromise, and disunity from the fact that the Holy Spirit's mind had been pushed out from their speech, and in so doing, none were receiving proper sanctification as ordained by the Father. Without receiving "sanctification of the Spirit,"[1260] none would know the science of the Spirit's will, and so by rejecting creation's course, none would come by justification's precepts, leaving no one to receive or care for the righteousness of faith's intercession, for they would rather be "made perfect by the flesh,"[1261] "justified by the law"[1262] of a legal religious tradition.

1256 1 John 4:18
1257 1 Peter 3:16
1258 Psalms 22:29
1259 1 John 4:18
1260 1 Peter 1:2
1261 Galatians 3:3
1262 Galatians 5:4

Faith's Right End • 137

15. To understand sanctification's course, it is necessary to connect the LORD's present purpose with His ancient will. Of old, "Moses took the anointing oil, and anointed the tabernacle and all that was therein, and sanctified them. And he sprinkled...to sanctify them. And he poured of the anointing oil upon Aaron's head, and anointed him, to sanctify him."[1263] Of all that Moses would sanctify, he "sanctified it, to make reconciliation."[1264]

16. There is a principle of sanctification that must be investigated and understood, for although the LORD, through the flesh of His Son, has made reconciliation a fact for every willing spirit, man can still fall short of that free privilege. Sanctification's course has been made freely available for every spirit to experience, but "all men have not faith"[1265] to know its blessing. Now, "we were reconciled to God by the death of his Son,"[1266] and this is true, but the Spirit's saying in Leviticus tells us that the matter of sanctification, and of reconciliation, is not complete until the anointing oil is poured upon the object to be reconciled. For "God was in Christ"[1267] and "hath reconciled us to himself"[1268] by His Son "in the body of his flesh through death,"[1269] to the end that we might have "the word of reconciliation."[1270] Every soul who soberly accepts, by faith, the illustration drawn by the Spirit's sacrifice, and the virtue of the merits of His Christ for spiritual recovery, are blessed of the LORD to know His Spirit's course. All of this is well, but unless the Spirit's anointing should be given consent to

---

1263 Leviticus 8:10-12
1264 Leviticus 8:15
1265 2 Thessalonians 3:2
1266 Romans 5:10
1267 2 Corinthians 5:19
1268 2 Corinthians 5:18
1269 Colossians 1:22
1270 2 Corinthians 5:19

swallow up the inward parts, there is no right reconciliation to His Spirit. This is why John wrote to the churches, "The anointing which ye have received of him abideth in you, and ye need not that any man teach you: but as the same anointing teacheth you of all things, and is truth, and is no lie, and even as it hath taught you, ye shall abide in him."[1271]

17. Notice John's words, for, this anointing of the living God's Spirit is what? It says that it is "truth." What else has John connected to that which is "truth"? He says, "The Spirit is truth."[1272] That which is to be the sign of reconciliation to the Spirit's ministry is the fact that His voice heals and instructs the conversation, and by His counseling, also seals within the believer's conscience His own mind and character as relayed by His High Priest. This is why Paul wrote, "The love of God is shed abroad in our hearts by the Holy Ghost,"[1273] for if the believer is in the Holy Ghost's understanding, they are receiving "the promise of the Holy Ghost,"[1274] which His Chief Priest "hath shed forth"[1275] on our inward parts, for it is the Father that "shed on us"[1276] this gift "abundantly through Jesus Christ our Saviour."[1277] As we "now have obtained mercy,"[1278] it is that "according to his mercy he saved us,"[1279] that is, "according to his abundant mercy";[1280] which is "abundance of grace and the gift of righteousness";[1281] that we may confess, "The Lord shall deliver me from every evil work, and will preserve me unto his

---

1271 1 John 2:27
1272 1 John 5:6
1273 Romans 5:5
1274 Acts 2:33
1275 Acts 2:33
1276 Titus 3:6
1277 Titus 3:6
1278 1 Peter 2:10
1279 Titus 3:5
1280 1 Peter 1:3
1281 Romans 5:17

heavenly kingdom,"[1282] and, "I will very gladly spend and be spent for you; though the more abundantly I love you, the less I be loved."[1283]

18. For, Scripture says of the heavenly ministration of the Spirit's Son, "To deliver their soul from death,"[1284] and, "He shall redeem their soul from deceit and violence."[1285] This work of redemption is to be completed in none other fashion but "by the washing of regeneration, and renewing of the Holy Ghost"[1286] "with the washing of water by the word,"[1287] for even "God anointed Jesus of Nazareth with the Holy Ghost."[1288] If the host of heaven's professors examine the counsel, "The disciple is not above his master,"[1289] it should be that none neglect the Spirit's anointing, of which when received, makes their reconciliation to His throne's religion complete for the purpose of sanctifying not only their inward members, but by the learning they are blessed to experience, all within their sphere may find their understanding refreshed to better honor God's voice, self, and one another, through them. This is why Paul counseled them, "Take heed unto thyself, and unto the doctrine; continue in them: for in doing this thou shalt both save thyself, and them that hear thee."[1290]

19. Moses sanctified in order to reconcile, and if "the redemption that is in Christ"[1291] is diligently experienced, then "being justified freely by his grace"[1292] "through faith in

---

1282 2 Timothy 4:18
1283 2 Corinthians 12:15
1284 Psalms 33:19
1285 Psalms 72:14
1286 Titus 3:5
1287 Ephesians 5:26
1288 Acts 10:38
1289 Matthew 10:24
1290 1 Timothy 4:16
1291 Romans 3:24
1292 Romans 3:24

his blood,"[1293] the believer will not only claim reconciliation, but will confess, "Much more, being reconciled, we shall be saved by his life."[1294] There is a primary condition to reconciliation that the personal religion must carry out, for it is not enough to say, "I have received atonement for my self-cultivated and inherited religious errors," but rather, now that you have become known of the LORD and have allowed self to feel after His cause, will you go to Him to learn of and do the purpose of His will? After you have believed whatever you have believed concerning His power and doctrine, will you receive that anointing understanding to let His Spirit recover your mind and soul temple? There is no reconciliation without sanctification, and if we are to become creations of the LORD's Word "through sanctification of the Spirit and belief of the truth,"[1295] it is then become an eternal fact that our inward parts, in order to own the atonement freely purchased for them, must pass through a course of learning, which is why it says, "Thou desirest truth in the inward parts: in the hidden part thou shalt make me to knowwisdom."[1296]

20. John knew that Christian elders rejected the Spirit of righteousness and sanctification while professing reconciliation. They that were of the church truly became "grievous wolves"[1297] "not sparing the flock,"[1298] for, because they left off examining the anointing within Christ's heavenly intercession, they forgot the counsel, "Feed the flock of God which is among you, taking the oversight thereof, not by constraint, but willingly; not for filthy lucre, but of a ready mind; neither

---

1293 Romans 3:25
1294 Romans 5:10
1295 2 Thessalonians 2:13
1296 Psalm 51:6
1297 Acts 20:29
1298 Acts 20:29

as being lords over God's heritage, but being ensamples of the flock."[1299] John saw the doctrine of Christ being trampled under their feet, and he knew that as heaven's simple truth was being disconnected from its LORD and Spirit, a false religion would enter in to the church to control the government of the heart for ruling the eyes, to the end that none would hear the Father's name and commandments. John understood that the church was developing laws and sentiments contrary to the LORD's throne, but similar to that of pagan ministers to gain public favor and acceptance, for it did not take long for them to cry out, "We also may be like all the nations."[1300]

21. There is and always will be one separating factor between the religious world and the LORD's host, and it His assembly's understanding that "God blessed the seventh day."[1301] This same John draws a distinction of days for us, writing, "The first day of the week cometh Mary,"[1302] and, "The first day of the week...came Jesus."[1303] John saw how unsanctified hearts would remember how Paul preached "upon the first day of the week,"[1304] and because of the ignorance in them built up from rejecting discernment's right medicine, would forget a day is as it is said, "The evening and the morning,"[1305] and so would overlook the fact that Paul preached "even till the break of day"[1306] and then "departed,"[1307] for the first apostles not only kept the seventh-day Sabbath, but also taught it. If there were none receiving the Spirit's purification because

---

1299 1 Peter 5:2
1300 1 Samuel 8:20
1301 Genesis 2:3
1302 John 20:1
1303 John 20:19
1304 Acts 20:7
1305 Genesis 1:31
1306 Acts 20:11
1307 Acts 20:11

they had rejected the Spirit of sanctification and the oil of reconciliation, it is that none were "holy," and if none were "holy," it is that the day blessed for celebrating sanctification's education would not be acknowledged, for one must be "holy" in conversation to care for rightly honoring that appointment, even as the LORD says of it, "My holy day."[1308] For, His precept reads, "Keep the Sabbath day to sanctify it,"[1309] but in order to sanctify the seventh day, one must be a subject of sanctification, and again, who is it that sanctifies? Paul writes, "Being sanctified by the Holy Ghost,"[1310] that is, "by the power of the Spirit of God."[1311]

22. John pleaded with the early church to remember, "Our fellowship is with the Father, and with his Son,"[1312] for he knew that the faithful should be "sanctified by God the Father, and preserved in Jesus Christ."[1313] It is well to personally learn of and do the Spirit's doctrine, but if the mind rejects purification by its LORD and Father, there is neither acceptance of His Christ's blood or of the will and ministry of His Spirit. This is why John writes, "He that acknowledgeth the Son hath the Father also,"[1314] for he was there when His Christ said, "All men should honour the Son, even as they honour the Father. He that honoureth not the Son honoureth not the Father which hath sent him."[1315] Would all professing Christ's name remember that He did not personally send His voice, nor did He appear to fulfill His own will, they would then "be filled with the knowledge of his will in all wisdom and spiritual

---

1308 Isaiah 58:13
1309 Deuteronomy 5:12
1310 Romans 15:16
1311 Romans 15:19
1312 1 John 1:3
1313 Jude 1:1
1314 1 John 2:23
1315 John 5:23

understanding."[1316] Upon receiving the wisdom of His mediation, the believer is to be, of the Father's Spirit, "translated into the kingdom of his dear Son."[1317] Without the LORD's Spirit, the heart will believe its throne is on earth to set up a reign in the flesh's mind and body. The believer is to be gathered under the wings of their High Priest by the knowledge of His grace within the heaven's Sanctuary, which knowledge He shares with us by His Father's Spirit, letting the reforming Christian know that the two; the LORD and His resurrected High Priest; are not separated, and that the Spirit of His intercession is that chain linking the soul to heaven's throne.

23. The LORD's wisdom is for the mind to understand and digest for the regulation of the members of the body. Should the church have centered itself on the fact of redemption's science, that only the Spirit of the Father may recover the spirit to love His precepts and His Son's character, they would not have needed to be "full of good works and almsdeeds."[1318] The priests of the churches were counseled to do "nothing by partiality,"[1319] but they judged the LORD unfaithful in His methods and purpose, and so rewrote His own Faith to suit their understanding, for they "changed";[1320] exchanged; "the truth of God into a lie."[1321]

24. John beheld unconverted ministers leading the churches, for their private actions gave witness that "these be they who separate themselves, sensual, having not the Spirit."[1322] Being sensual they were flesh-based and carnal in understanding, and the one that exists from the impulses and

---

1316 Colossians 1:9
1317 Colossians 1:13
1318 Acts 9:36
1319 1 Timothy 5:21
1320 Romans 1:25
1321 Romans 1:25
1322 Jude 1:19

inclinations of the flesh cannot hear the Spirit's commandments, for "the natural man receiveth not the things of the Spirit of God."[1323] Without receiving the necessary experience to teach, to preach, to comfort, and to uplift, John saw the churches venturing into a manner that embraced pagan rites and festivals, of which the church would establish Christian traditions for already existing pagan activities, secretly exalting the theological and philosophical gods of pagan institutions. It is for this reason that Paul was moved to write to them concerning those ministers that unlawfully handled heaven's Faith, "It is a shame even to speak of those things which are done of them in secret,"[1324] and, "Be not ye therefore partakers with them."[1325]

25. Paul let the churches know that as one is "strengthened with might by his Spirit in the inner man,"[1326] it then becomes proper to announce, "I delight in the law of God after the inward man."[1327] The inward heart of the conversation; the spirit of the mind; is that which is to be "saved," "redeemed," "delivered," "rescued," or "recovered" from religious practices that the death of the LORD's Man establishes as accursed to the Spirit's will and wisdom, to the end that within the conversation's conscience would rest every precept of the LORD for right godliness in manners of worship and service. The scriptures confess, concerning creation's present science, that it was "the great God that formed all things"[1328] by the name of His Son, for it was "God, who created all things by Jesus Christ."[1329] If the believer exercises faith in God; that

---

1323 1 Corinthians 2:14
1324 Ephesians 5:12
1325 Ephesians 5:7
1326 Ephesians 3:16
1327 Romans 7:22
1328 Proverbs 26:10
1329 Ephesians 3:9

is, in the Word of the Spirit; it is that they confess the LORD as God over the old and the new testaments, for there is no dispute that "God is the LORD."[1330] Now, "in the beginning was the Word, and the Word was with God, and the Word was God,"[1331] for at creation, both the LORD and His Word established the earth and the heavens. "God" was and still is the Word, and when hearing that "God was in Christ,"[1332] we are hearing that the Word dwelt within the spirit of God's Man, for, since "the Word of life"[1333] is "the Spirit of life,"[1334] and since "that which is born of the Spirit is spirit,"[1335] the Word can exist in none other body within man than that pertaining to the spirit of their mind, which is why we are counseled, "Be renewed in the spirit of your mind."[1336]

26. For this cause, if we are passing through the Spirit's course; which is the Word's higher learning; we understand why His Son says, "My words shall not pass away."[1337] Failure to accept the testimony of Scripture proves unbelief in Scripture and in the LORD and God of it. To be properly "holy," one must sanctify self according to the Spirit's charge; that is, with the experience contained within His Son's mediation; in order to cultivate a culture of learning to recover, within conversation's mind, a moral courage to overcome self and the religious world, and that course is "through sanctification of the Spirit and belief of the truth."[1338] Upon sincere reception of Christ's voice, the reformer is taken from an earthy

---

1330   Psalm 118:27
1331   John 1:1
1332   2 Corinthians 5:19
1333   1 John 1:1
1334   Revelation 11:11
1335   John 3:6
1336   Ephesians 4:23
1337   Mark 13:31
1338   2 Thessalonians 2:13

experience to dwell within the Spirit's presence within in His heavenly Place. The early church left off the course of righteousness, and in so doing, the members did not know the LORD or His Word as they should have, and for failing to learn humility and quietness of heart and mind by His voice, the LORD's ten precepts were dropped and forgotten, for only a people cleansed by His name can handle what is His. This is how the LORD's blessed Sabbath was replaced with a spurious *sabbath*, and how His voice found itself taken out of context. Because right fellowship remains only in learning of and doing the knowledge of His Son, by quitting faith's right training, ministers didn't have the ointment to discern the depth of redemption's plan and science.

27. "The natural man receiveth not the things of the Spirit of God: for they are foolishness unto him: neither can he know them, because they are spiritually discerned."[1339] "Their minds were blinded: for until this day remaineth the same veil untaken away in the reading of the Old Testament; which veil is done away in Christ."[1340] Elders corrupt in manners of worship and service were ordering their churches without the Spirit of the LORD's Faith, and without knowledge of a pure and living experience by faith on His voice, were destroying the flock of God for name, money, doctrines, and commandments. It is for this reason that Paul, observing the spirit motivating their devotion, wrote, "If any man have not the Spirit of Christ, he is none of his."[1341]

28. The Faith of Christ is after liberty of heart and conscience from former religious thought and manners, but the word was fulfilling, "Some shall depart from the faith, giving heed to seducing spirits, and doctrines of devils;

1339 1 Corinthians 2:14
1340 2 Corinthians 3:14
1341 Romans 7:9

speaking lies in hypocrisy; having their conscience seared with a hot iron."[1342] As the Christian religion began to blend with pagan and polytheistic Roman tradition, the sweet flavor that once gave the church an original taste was replaced with one most bitter. The church forgot how she was counseled, "Where the Spirit of the Lord is, there is liberty,"[1343] and because they took on laws of *justification* apart from heaven's true spiritual ordinances, the apostle wrote, "We have an advocate with the Father."[1344] When once the conversation finds itself needing no advocate or intercessor for understanding, but rather every mediator to keep up its appearance, it becomes free to declare itself king or queen over the throne of its heart. Such an individual is not the Spirit's convert or creation when found clinging to the religious error within them for a reason most personal, prescribing their own laws, and, ostentatiously with all stubbornness, keeping to their prescribed inherited or self-cultivated traditions. It was because of this spirit that every precept of heaven was done away with by Christian elders, eventually leading to even a changing of that commandment keeping the believer in the knowledge of the Spirit's creative and redemptive power, even His seventh day's Sabbath.

29. If the Spirit of the LORD's voice is not honored as the conversation's Creator, it is evident that His High Priest's ministry is not reverenced. If this Spirit is not honored as that One who spoke and it became, then a false *Christ* is honored, for his worshipper believes that they may liberate and justify self by self. Sanctification is but one of many steps that the LORD has prescribed for our present recuperation from the errors of the former religious age under Moses, which is why we have a High Priest consecrated "for the redemption of the

---

1342 1 Timothy 4:1
1343 2 Corinthians 3:17
1344 1 John 2:1

transgressions that were under the first testament."[1345] Personal and devotional sin will not magically evaporate from the mind, for the counsel is, "Break off thy sins by righteousness,"[1346] and we know how it is written, "All thy commandments are righteousness."[1347] This is why our LORD counsels, "My righteousness shall not be abolished,"[1348] which is why John wrote to the churches, "Every one that doeth righteousness is born of him."[1349]

30. So how is righteousness fulfilled? How are believers made "holy"? It is written, "Ye have purified your souls in obeying the truth through the Spirit."[1350] From willingly obeying the Spirit's voice, the believer will execute every law of the Spirit, and that execution will be done out of a love born of faith through a living experience. Above every thing, our personal harmony with heaven's voice is our LORD and Father's primary concern for us, that we will love His name by His Son's mediation, "and this is love, that we walk after his commandments."[1351] Where we see stoutness against the LORD's commandments, we may know that it is due to a failure to know His Spirit's will and righteousness, for if we are to "be dead with Christ from the rudiments of the world,"[1352] when found associated with the standards of the now abolished religious world from heaven's Faith, do we evince love for the LORD and Spirit of creation's present redemptive endeavor?

31. No one can tell a soul to do contrary to that which it has been taught by the living God, for because the church

---

1345 Hebrews 9:15
1346 Daniel 4:27
1347 Psalm 119:172
1348 Isaiah 51:6
1349 1 John 2:39
1350 1 Peter 1:22
1351 2 John 1:6
1352 Colossians 2:20

failed to know the LORD and Word of the first apostles, they found themselves so offended by His Christ that they found in Him no thing but evil, for "no man can say that Jesus is the Lord, but by the Holy Ghost."[1353] How then could ministers profess this Christ while knowing that they did not professes Him in reality? How can ministers claim the name and power of this Christ, yet remain self-centered and void of right feeling, receiving in their heart a confirmation of their wrong by practices of spiritual bondage? Scripture tells us that none display the character of God's High Priest without His LORD's Holy Ghost, and His character is one of self-sacrifice and self-denial for newness and regeneration not only within self, but also within the spirits of others. It is for this reason that John wrote, in order to provoke evidence of His Spirit within church elders, "This commandment have we from him, That he who loveth God love his brother also."[1354]

32. Creation and redemption revolve around the self-sacrificing benevolence within the heavenly ministry of the LORD's Son. Because ministers lacked that law of the Spirit's benevolence, it was only necessary that they should refuse the seventh-day's Sabbath of His love and science. For, the psalmist declares, "Thy name is near thy wondrous works,"[1355] and, "Thou, LORD, hast made me glad through thy work: I will triumph in the works of thy hands."[1356] How is it that the psalmist saw triumph for him in the Spirit's labor? How did the psalmist discern triumph through creation? When the Spirit's works are removed from our thoughts, when we "regard not the work of the LORD, neither consider the operation of his

---

1353 1 Corinthians 12:3
1354 1 John 4:21
1355 Psalms 75:1
1356 Psalms 92:4

hands,"[1357] the reason for upholding our faith by the authority of His voice is removed. His name is connected with His labor, and as the name of God's Spirit rests in His Sabbath, it is that in His Sabbath is constructed "the light of the knowledge of the glory of God in the face of Jesus Christ."[1358] In order to receive entrance into His seventh-day rest, the heart must consent to accept His doctrine for the purpose of writing His name and precepts within the spirit of the mind. No one without His anointing may declare complete reconciliation, for the will must consent to His will and manner of personal soul therapy. Because the early church consented to a sensual spirit, they would not hear the fact of salvation's matter, "wherefore God also gave them up to uncleanness through the lusts of their own hearts, to dishonour their own bodues between themselves."[1359]

33. Let the soul personally know godliness by faith in the virtue of the name of God's Man and the mind will accept every precept of His LORD and Father, despising every other believed route and policy for *right* worship and service. That we might learn how He says, "I am the LORD that sanctify them,"[1360] He gave us the Sabbath of His operation that we may know that the same creative power seen in the beginning is the same power that will create the conversation's heart afresh. The creations of the Spirit, by their course with faith on His Priest's words, will know, "The word of our God shall stand for ever,"[1361] and from knowing the LORD's will through a personal experience in the blessed liberty of His Son's name, life's principle will be, "Receive not the grace of

---

1357 Isaiah 5:12
1358 2 Corinthians 4:6
1359 Romans 1:24
1360 Ezekiel 20:12
1361 Isaiah 40:8

God in vain,"[1362] and, "Be ye transformed by the renewing of your mind."[1363]

34. "The promise of life which is in Christ Jesus"[1364] is "the grace that is in Christ Jesus,"[1365] and we should know that it is "the grace of God that bringeth salvation"[1366] for our conversation's conscience. There is only one power that can and will regenerate the members of our erroneous understanding, and that power rests in the knowledge of creation, which knowledge is sealed with His Sabbath to keep the mind cognizant of what completeness fills and surrounds heaven's throne. When once the mind accepts the Spirit's anointing, it will receive permission to know His doctrine, and in knowing His will, it will learn of and receive His rest, seeing as how, from surrendering to His will, we confess that self cannot cleanse self. We are to know that this LORD's Spirit sanctifies the character of our conversation's conscience by the instruction of His Son's heavenly priesthood, for the end of faith's learning is a "holy" conversation, and such a conversation is blessed with that "rest of the holy Sabbath unto the LORD,"[1367] which is why God, who is that same Word, blessed the seventh day of His earth in the beginning, and sanctified it for His thinking and feeling creation for ever.[1368] "A spirit that confesseth that Jesus Christ is come in the flesh"[1369] witnesses to the conversation of such a heart formed by faith's right intention.

1362 2 Corinthians 6:1
1363 Romans 12:2
1364 2 Timothy 1:1
1365 2 Timothy 2:1
1366 Titus 2:11
1367 Exodus 16:23
1368 Genesis 2:3
1369 1 John 4:2

9

Like Mother, Like Daughter

1. Anciently the Spirit counseled, "Of every tree of the garden thou mayest freely eat: but of the tree of the knowledge of good and evil, thou shalt not eat of it: for in the day that thou eatest thereof thou shalt surely die."[1370]

2. The tree that held the Spirit's curse was "the tree of knowledge of good and evil,"[1371] or, it is rather better understood that this tree contained a substance for "knowing good and evil."[1372] Such a tree would catch the eye of Eden's newly formed pair, for its separation from all of the other trees would magnify its *dignity* to their conscience. The LORD said, "In the day you eat of it, you will die a death," and, concerning the word "day," as we see how it is said, "In the day that the LORD God made the earth and the heavens,"[1373] it is that the word "day"

1370 Genesis 2:17
1371 Genesis 2:17
1372 Genesis 3:5
1373 Genesis 2:4

means season or time, for creation was not accomplished in a literal day, but rather in a period of time, a season of days. Scripture tells us that the lights of heaven's firmament are to "be for seasons, and for days, and years,"[1374] and it was that in the season, or in the day, or in the year that the tree should be eaten, "death" would find the willingly negligent, and their inward stumbling at the Spirit's commandment would be known.

3. Whenever the LORD's charge concerning that accursed tree should find itself masticated and then digested, at that season, or at that period of time, the individual would die the death ordained of the LORD's voice. As the command came, "Thou shalt not eat of it,"[1375] the woman's attention was hurled towards the side of curiosity. Her actions lay the foundation for the precept that God's Christ taught concerning the wandering of the eyes, for He says, "Whosoever looketh on a woman to lust after her hath committed adultery with her already in his heart."[1376] This is why the LORD would have man comprehend the commandment, "Thou shalt not commit adultery,"[1377] for Eve did not have to physically eat of the tree to taste it, but in her mind she cultivated an intemperate spirit that swayed her heart and perverted her imagination. In Eve, the proverb is fulfilled, "As a man thinketh in his heart, so is he."[1378]

4. It is evident that transgression does not begin outside of man, but rather within the heart of their thoughts and imaginations. Because Eve constantly held the tree in her mind, she fed her self on thoughts and possibilities of what consuming such an understanding should do for her. If she was not thinking on the tree, Eve could be found looking at it with ambitious

---

1374 Genesis 1:14
1375 Genesis 2:17
1376 Matthew 5:28
1377 Exodus 20:14
1378 Proverbs 23:7

eyes, for she thought, "Ye shall not eat of it, neither touch it, lest ye die."[1379] The stubbornness of her heart pronounced a person within the members of her flesh that she had no idea existed within her person, for she longed to lawfully honor her LORD's commandment, but for some reason she could not. She desired to bring her self to a thorough investigation of creation by "rightly dividing the word of truth,"[1380] but, "The good that I would I do not: but the evil which I would not, that I do,"[1381] she repeatedly said to herself. By sensually looking on the tree, her fantasies of its *brilliance* amounted to her consumption of it, foreshadowing the inevitable error she should physically accomplish.

5. Appetite was the ruin of man. It did not take long for Eve to burden her mental and moral faculties by consuming her own imaginations, for as soon as she had heard from Adam that there was a tree of a supposedly different quality among them, the mind behind her character, and the hope of her devotion, became known. She wanted to possess a conversation dawning both good and evil, doing contrary to what one of old time spoke concerning faithfulness to what is "good," saying, "I cannot go beyond the commandment of the LORD, to do either good or bad of my own mind."[1382] That knowledge of good and evil moves the heart to persuade the mind to go above or below the LORD's commandment, and to accept exchanging knowledge of His Spirit's true revelation for a presumptuous lie. This state of mind owns the belief that what the Spirit decrees is not a legitimate judgment, and seeing as though I, because of my persuasion, may now acknowledge that counsel according to my own perception, I can take that

---

1379 Genesis 3:3
1380 2 Timothy 2:15
1381 Romans 7:19
1382 Numbers 24:13

counsel and do as I please with it, even taking it out of context, or out the way of its usefulness, as I so choose, altering it to fit my circumstance; this is a lewd mind. For, of old, the Spirit said, "If it be a beast, whereof men bring an offering unto the LORD...he shall not alter it, nor change it, a good for a bad, or a bad for a good."[1383] To do good and bad is to alter what the LORD has said and done so that good and bad meet in the center as one, and this work is a work of "death" against the heart and the conscience, as it says, "God hath given them the spirit of slumber, eyes that they should not see, and ears that they should not hear."[1384]

6. Again, it was during a search for a wife for Abraham's son that it was said, "If ye will deal kindly and truly with my master, tell me: and if not, tell me; that I may turn to the right hand, or to the left. Then Laban and Bethu'el answered and said, The thing proceedeth from the LORD: we cannot speak unto thee bad or good. Behold, Rebekah is before thee, take her, and go."[1385]

7. No thing could be spoken contrary to the LORD's voice because it had been accepted as coming from Him, yet if that commandment had not been accepted by faith, then it would not have been that they told the servant yes or no, but would have cultivated an in-between language for their own benefit or gain. To do "right" is to tell or to do yes or to tell or do no concerning the LORD's voice, but to do "wrong" against another is to withhold the pure right and the pure wrong for a blend of the two, creating a philosophy most comfortable for the members of the heart to accept, yet detrimental for the health of the heart and mind, for "the heart is deceitful above

---

1383 Leviticus 27:9,10
1384 Romans 11:8
1385 Genesis 24:49,50

all things, and desperately wicked."[1386] This is why the apostle writes, "Did I use lightness? or the things that I purpose, do I purpose according to the flesh, that there should be yea yea, and nay nay? But as God is true, our word toward you was not yea and nay."[1387] Paul knew that the instruction of good and evil was after a service warning no one of the left and turning no one to the right, but was a course keeping them in the middle of religious error and far from a right experience with the LORD's Son and Spirit, which is why he handled every church like "as a nurse cherisheth her children."[1388]

8. For this cause, "God is true,"[1389] said Paul, "for all the promises of God in him are yea,"[1390] which is why John wrote, "The darkness is past, and the true light now shineth."[1391]

9. There was no need for the early church to cultivate an intemperate and unsanctified spirit of self-preservation, yet in the church, John saw the entrance of such a spirit. Before his death, Peter had placed the church in remembrance to their relation with the Spirit's knowledge, saying, "Whereby are given unto us exceeding great and precious promises: that by these ye might be partakers of the divine nature, having escaped the corruption that is in the world through lust."[1392] It would be that, "through the knowledge of him that hath called us to glory and virtue,"[1393] the inwards of the conscience would receive an edifying learning and the spirit of the mind would regain order for the body's good, and this work occurring through the promises of life given of the Spirit, should ministers check their

---

1386   Jeremiah 17:9
1387   2 Corinthians 1:17,18
1388   1 Thessalonians 2:7
1389   2 Thessalonians 1:18
1390   2 Corinthians 1:20
1391   1 John 2:8
1392   2 Peter 1:4
1393   2 Peter 1:3

appetite at the door of His heavenly Temple. John saw how priests didn't care to apply to the Father's promises by faith's exercise. Instead of studying after "the unity of the faith, and of the knowledge of the Son of God,"[1394] the fruits accursed of the Word became tantalizing due to a lack of exercising faith on that Word. The early church transgressed in their manners of worship and service after the fashion of their mother Eve, for they blended heaven's pure counsel with a crude and disapproved form of devotion, accepting their translated alteration of heaven's will as a means to shun both temporal and spiritual persecution, and to avoid the work necessary for acceptance with the true LORD and His Spirit, even as it is written of them, "As many as desire to make a fair shew in the flesh, they constrain you to be circumcised; only lest they should suffer persecution for the cross of Christ."[1395]

10. The Spirit once said, "Let your communication be, Yea, yea; Nay, nay: for whatsoever is more than these cometh of evil."[1396] This Spirit was there in the garden to see the end of such perversity, making note of how "the woman saw that the tree was good for food, and that it was pleasant to the eyes, and a tree to be desired to make one wise."[1397]

11. Originally, the Spirit had made "every tree that is pleasant to the sight, and good for food,"[1398] but her imaginations added more to the accursed tree than what was ordained, and the construction of her thoughts knew only an evil or empty work. This is why the apostle sought to warn church leaders by saying, "There be some that trouble you, and would pervert

---

1394 Ephesians 4:13
1395 Galatians 6:12
1396 Mathew 5:37
1397 Genesis 3:6
1398 Genesis 2:9

the gospel of Christ."[1399] To pervert heaven's tidings is to transgress or violate the doctrine of heaven's High Priest, and such perversion is after the saying, "Now are made perfect by the flesh,"[1400] when in reality it is "the grace of God that bringeth salvation,"[1401] and this salvation is to make one "perfect, as pertaining to the conscience."[1402] Even Paul was disrespected for the fact of the Spirit's Faith, saying, "We be slanderously reported, and as some affirm that we say, Let us do evil, that good may come,"[1403] for the unconverted ear oddly heard Paul say, "Continue in sin, that grace may abound."[1404] The apostle confirmed that his teaching was in the LORD's new will and promise, saying, "In him was yea,"[1405] for the churches desired outward shows of devotion as a proof of *piety*, and as former religious manners of worship and service mingled with *heaven's Faith*, again a middle wall of partition was created between the living God and them that would know His name.

12. Eve wanted freedom of speech within her conversation not to honor the LORD's voice, but to live out "the imagination of the thoughts of the heart,"[1406] and when she heard the serpent's doctrine, "His words are weighty and powerful,"[1407] she thought. The corrupt or irreverent heart will always find a reason to skip out of a learning experience with the LORD's sayings, and this is what Eve wanted to do. As she saw the tree desirous to make one wise in spiritual understanding, she imagined herself and her husband above the creation and wiser

---

1399 Galatians 1:7
1400 Galatians 3:3
1401 Titus 2:11
1402 Hebrews 9:9
1403 Romans 3:8
1404 Romans 6:1
1405 2 Corinthians 1:19
1406 1 Chronicles 29:18
1407 2 Corinthians 10:10

than the Creator, and being the first to eat the fruit above the man, women and men may now equally idolized her as Adam. She at first timidly imagined eating from the accursed tree, and then carelessly for days without end, saying to her man, and as "she lay sore upon him,"[1408] "I will fetch wine, and we will fill ourselves with strong drink; and to morrow shall be as this day, and much more abundant."[1409]

13. Eve desired to be a "god" in show and in understanding, for we see that on one occasion "Ra'chel had stolen the images that were her father's,"[1410] and when her father knew that they were missing he said, "Hast thou stolen my gods?"[1411] There is only one reason to erect an image, and that is for worship, therefore Scripture concludes, "They that make a graven image are all of them vanity; and their delectable things shall not profit; and they are their own witnesses."[1412] A "god" is a chief religious judge or minister among the people, as it says, "Thou shalt not revile the gods, nor curse the ruler of thy people,"[1413] and, "Who made thee a ruler and a judge?"[1414] Eve desired to be the sole witness of her conversation, and to be one greatly revered for the appearance of that witness.

14. In clear language, Scripture tells us that one who would conceal an image, or subscribe to its use, is one desiring to be his or her own conversation's witness. Because John saw the error arising from *justification* by works, along with *justification* by faith "through philosophy and vain deceit, after the tradition of men,"[1415] he wrote to the churches, "It is the Spirit the beareth

---

1408 Judges 14:17
1409 Isaiah 56:12
1410 Genesis 31:19
1411 Genesis 31:30
1412 Isaiah 44:9
1413 Exodus 22:28
1414 Acts 7:35
1415 Colossians 2:8

witness,"[1416] and, "Old things are passed away,"[1417] and, "Let no man deceive you: he that doeth righteousness is righteous."[1418] By repairing old religious manners condemned by the offered flesh of God's Man; for, "that which decayeth and waxeth old is ready to vanish away";[1419] Christian leadership evinced their opinion of the present "time of reformation,"[1420] which time teaches us that "by the deeds of the law there shall be no flesh justified in his sight,"[1421] but that justification rather appears as one honors the counsel, "Worship God in the spirit."[1422] The flesh of God's Man upon that tree represents the fact that every legal religious commandment of every *Moses* for every age is abolished, defining the re-establishment of such religious manners as "sin" and religious error to the Spirit's new covenant will. Therefore observing Christian elders falling in their understanding by their violation of the LORD's present commandment for sanctification, the apostle counseled them, "Whosoever abideth in him sinneth not: whosoever sinneth hath not seen him, neither known him."[1423]

15. Heaven's good will was received by Gentile pagan converts to Judaism who opened their heart to feel after a right service free from the burdensome persuasion they had come to know under the law of Moses, for they understood that such religious manners "could not make him that did the service perfect, as pertaining to the conscience."[1424] For, before heaven's Faith arrived and was ratified, such pagan converts to

---

1416 1 John 5:6
1417 2 Corinthians 5:17
1418 1 John 3:7
1419 Hebrews 8:13
1420 Hebrews 9:10
1421 Romans 3:20
1422 Philippians 3:3
1423 1 John 3:6
1424 Hebrews 9:9

the Jews' religion "were without Christ, being aliens from the commonwealth of Israel, and strangers from the covenants of promise, having no hope, and without God in the world."[1425] To these people the message came and was accepted, "In Christ Jesus ye who sometimes were far off are made night by the blood of Christ,"[1426] and because they had received this confirmation of reconciliation, Paul told them, "Having abolished in his flesh the enmity, even the law of commandments contained in ordinances,"[1427] "through him we both have access by one Spirit unto the Father."[1428] The apostles longed to confess of every believer, "Ye turned to God from idols to serve the living and true God,"[1429] for commandments, and rites, and sacrifices to that which is against heaven's Faith, governed these converts to Judaism, and his own people. Such a service declared the one who did them to be a witness to their own religion and practice, to their own *wisdom* and *piety*, wherefore John, observing Christian elders continuing in what is accursed by the offering and high priestly mediation of the LORD's Christ, counseled them, "We know that he abideth in us, by the Spirit which he hath given us."[1430]

16. If the churches maintained that simplicity of worship and learning as given by the LORD's Spirit, they would not have left the only acceptable medicine for a pure character and conscience. In the garden, Eve, because she inwardly adhered to accursed religious practices, was fast exhibiting the marks of religious self-exaltation, which is why the Spirit today counsels His assembly, "Thou shalt have no other gods before me."[1431]

1425 Ephesians 2:12
1426 Ephesians 2:13
1427 Ephesians 2:15
1428 Ephesians 2:18
1429 1 Thessalonians 1:9
1430 1 John 3:24
1431 Exodus 20:3

Eve desired not only to be above Adam and the Spirit's instruction, but she cared to be worshipped for generations to come. To be as that form of "god" that the serpent references, it is to possess attributes of self-governance and independence from heaven's will and wisdom, as if the heart now becomes immune to ordering and sincerely doing every word of God's Spirit due to the fact that it believes the invention of its own devising. To the "god," their religious standard is of greater benefit for self-economy than what the Spirit is able to provide. For, it is written, "He called them gods, unto whom the word of God came,"[1432] allowing us to understand that Eve's heart desired to uphold the Word by her own sensual religious understanding, which understanding became old the moment the LORD said, "Do not eat."

17. This is "death" and its course — believing that self's rationale is the *Supreme Being* of the personal religion — for when Eve began eating of the tree within her person, the "death" pronounced against the tree began to confiscate her judgment. An eye lusting after a charge contrary to the LORD's, or a stubbornness manifested towards refusing to investigate His decree, is proof that the heart wants to govern self's conversation apart from His throne's wisdom and counsel. It was because he saw this seed in the church that John pleaded, "Little children, keep yourselves from idols,"[1433] for he saw that the ambition of the early church had become no different from the mother of sin's name and character.

18. As Eve believed the fruit of this cursed tree would help provide independence from the supposed box that the LORD's charge held her in, she readily accepted the saying, "Your eyes shall be opened,"[1434] or rather, as she may have

---

1432 John 10:35
1433 1 John 5:21
1434 Genesis 3:5

heard and interpreted it, "The eyes of your understanding being enlightened."[1435] Eve saw an escape through this tree. Whereas we are to "have escaped the pollutions of the world through the knowledge of the Lord and Saviour Jesus Christ,"[1436] this woman saw her liberation from the Spirit's course by the *knowledge* of an accursed doctrine. If she could let the substance of this tree mingle with her self then she would have all understanding, leaving her knowledgeably free from the LORD's Spirit that it may be as it is said, when others see the outward adornment of her conversation, "He opened the rock, and the waters gushed out."[1437] At this thought, Eve imagined herself with a flood of *light* and *knowledge*. Before the woman had physically tasted the blood of this cursed tree, she herself was already "dead," and this "death" is explained to us by how the LORD went about forming her, for it says, "The LORD God caused a deep sleep to fall upon Adam, and he slept."[1438] Henceforward, the person hopeful to reform from her train of thought would have to pray, in order to find self loosened from the flesh's irrational chain, "Lighten mine eyes, lest I sleep the sleep of death."[1439]

19. Eve heard how she came to be. She heard from Adam about the work of their God's hands before they both owned a breath of consciousness, and of the power of His voice concerning right consciousness. But from her actions and inward philosophy, there is enough proof to ascertain that this woman silenced her higher faculties for an appetite contrary to her being and purpose. As soon as her eyes and heart had

---

1435 Ephesians 1:18
1436 2 Peter 2:20
1437 Psalms 105:41
1438 Genesis 2:21
1439 Psalms 13:3

consensual intercourse with that course denounced by God's voice, she was "dead" within those parts of her person that she sacrificed for greed through inordinate affection. But heaven's faithful pray, "I cannot go beyond the commandment of the LORD, to do either good or bad of mine own mind";[1440] the same cannot be said for *heaven's* negligent. For, when the LORD's creation, when a professed servant of *His* name, said to Eve, "Ye shall not surly die,"[1441] because she was spiritually dead, she discerned no error of that knowledge of good and evil within the creature's sentiment. Her heart did not like to retain knowledge of His operation, and for her failure, she was unable to recognize a voice that was blatantly contrary to His. The more she thought on the tree, the more she began to see *wisdom* and *life* in that which had no wisdom or life. For her stubbornness she honored fear, and for laziness she coveted an *instrument* of *wisdom*, for she believed, "Stolen waters are sweet, and bread eaten in secret is pleasant."[1442]

20. This is why the apostle counsels, "It is a shame even to speak of those things which are done of them in secret. But all things that are reproved are made manifest by the light: for whatsoever doth make manifest is light."[1443]

21. By allowing both the tree and the serpent to remain in Eden, the living God displays the highness of His mind. That which He curses will reveal the character of the one professing love for *Him*, while at the same time shining light on the error of the ones caught by that cursed creature, for "we do know that we know him, if we keep his commandments."[1444] Such a work of the Word is done among us "that they which are

---

1440 Numbers 24:13
1441 Genesis 3:4
1442 Proverbs 9:17
1443 Ephesians 5:12,13
1444 1 John 2:3

approved may be made manifest,"[1445] which is why John wrote of Christian elders, "They went out, that they might be made manifest that they were not all of us."[1446] As the churches began to carry themselves in the name of *Christ* while reverencing not only that nailed to the tree, but also the pagan secrets and mysteries of ministers around them, a spirit of error captivated their judgment and hid virtue by unnecessary fear. Such actions to abide by the tradition of flesh above the Spirit's voice express wrongful independence from His will, for which cause John wrote, "If we say that we have no sin, we deceive ourselves."[1447] If we will to lawfully admit that our conversation is without "sin," then we admit service to the LORD as no transgressor of His Spirit's name, but the dialect of the early church; as a faith re-establishing "sin" presently abolished by the passing and regenerating flesh of the LORD's Man; is of the belief that "righteousness come by the law,"[1448] confessing open sin and apostasy within that religion professing service to *His name* and *Son's confidence*.

22. The purpose of Christ's offering was to vindicate the name of His Father in the sight of the religious world, and through an experimental faith on His mission and ministration's doctrine, bring every believer into harmony with His precepts of right devotional sobriety while exhibiting the character of the One in whom they trust, as it says, "They that know thy name will put their trust in thee."[1449] Refusing to allow the heart to consent to sanctification's science, and by faith on the end promised of that course, is to reject the fact that it was necessary for the Son of God to pass away for an ungrateful

---

1445   1 Corinthians 11:19
1446   1 John 2:19
1447   1 John 1:8
1448   Galatians 2:21
1449   Psalm 9:10

spirit within ignorant flesh, which flesh and ungratefulness we all naturally own. To reject His manner of righteousness by faith's exercise, and to adhere to the policy of *righteousness* by the religious law of some *Moses*, is to reject the course of heaven-appointed salvation for the inward parts and to apply *salvation* to the flesh; even as it was done of old; leaving man as governor over his own religious hopes for his own prescribed desire. Man confesses himself innocent within himself when refusing to apply the Spirit's saying to his own heart for right spiritual understanding, and such a soul is "in the gall of bitterness, and in the bond of iniquity"[1450] not knowing their error, for "a deceived heart hath turned him aside, that he cannot deliver his soul, nor say, Is there not a lie in my right hand?"[1451]

23. As Eve inwardly encouraged excessive indulgence, her senses became numb and her higher faculties slept, for in her it was fulfilled, "He hath shut their eyes, that they cannot see; and their hearts, that they cannot understand."[1452] It was because of this perverse spirit and inward illness that Paul wrote, "For this cause many are weak and sickly among you, and many sleep."[1453] Eve, even before she had touched the tree, was in this state of "death," for had she exercised self-restraint to independently approach the LORD's throne, she would have become aware of the fact that the knowledge she lusted after was already within her. Eve had the mental power to resist her self, she had an undefiled form that had great power to activate a defense against every irrational thought and imagination, but at last that strange part of humanity won the war. Her immediate "death" was visible to no eye but God's, for He knew that

---

1450 Acts 8:23
1451 Isaiah 44:20
1452 Isaiah 44:18
1453 1 Corinthians 11:30

soon she would physically do that which ceaselessly flourished within her heart.

24. The record of their fall is for us alive today to examine. The LORD has given His counsel for revival and reform by His own voice, yet He has not removed every *creation* that He has allowed, and which He has given a voice in its time. It is His own voice that says, "I will lay stumblingblocks before this people, and the fathers and the sons together shall fall upon them."[1454] Every one who professes the name of His Son should know that it is His Spirit who knows His faithful, which is why we are counseled, "Study to shew thyself approved unto God, a workman that needeth not to be ashamed, rightly dividing the word of truth."[1455]

25. There are things inspired and ordained of *the Spirit* that are given life by ministers who will not open their understanding to His voice for fear of learning that what they reverence, and that what they invent, is not His inspiration. This is why it is well for us, if we are moved, and if we have any thing in our heart moving us to learn of His Faith, to personally pick up His words. He has, by the passing flesh of His Christ on that tree, removed that fashioned by flesh from His throne's higher learning, revealing that there is no longer a service in these things for what He hopes to do within our heart and mind, for it is His intention to "purge your conscience from dead works to serve the living God."[1456] Eve's example proves that such a heart will honor that uninspired creation above the blessed Word and Spirit of the Creator, leaving the conscience paralyzed and asleep to the spiritual understanding contained within His throne's will. The believer should know how to properly order His voice for their conversation's good and

---

1454 Jeremiah 6:21
1455 2 Timothy 2:15
1456 Hebrews 9:14

wellbeing, for if the effort to diligently investigate the Spirit's commandment is forsaken, Eve is proof that the heart will receive a delusional observance, and without embracing thorough humility and repentance for personal and devotional error, will find no escape from that wrong.

26. Thus, at the rise of the adoption of legal religious superstitions and traditions, and at the sign of openly accepting a mind that rests in the religious world, the apostles counseled, "I write unto you, little children, because your sins are forgiven you for his names sake."[1457] "All of you be subject one to another, and be clothed with humility: for God resisteth the proud, and giveth grace to the humble. Humble yourselves therefore under the mighty hand of God, that he may exalt you in due time."[1458] "I write unto you, fathers, because ye have known him that is from the beginning. I write unto you, young men, because ye have overcome the wicked one. I write unto you, little children, because ye have known the Father."[1459]

1457 1 John 2:12
1458 1 Peter 5:5,6
1459 1 John 2:13

10

The Theology Of The Compromised Church

1. It is written of old, "Deb'orah said unto Ba'rak, Up; for this is the day in which the LORD hath delivered Sis'era into thine hand: is not the LORD gone out before thee? So Ba'rak went down from mount Ta'bor, and ten thousand men after him. And the LORD discomfited Sis'era, and all his chariots, and all his host, with the edge of the sword before Ba'rak; so that Sis'era lighted down off his chariot, and fled away on his feet."[1460]

2. This lesson from the ancient record is for us who care to approach heaven's will by faith on the name of heaven's High Priest. Ba'rak confidently believed the word given him that said, "The LORD has delivered Sis'era into thine hand,"[1461] for

---

1460 Judges 4:14,15
1461 Judges 4:14

170 • A Fallen Record: The Christian Transgression

"God subdued on that day"[1462] to the praise of His name, and for us the LORD has promised, "Even to your old age I am he; and even to hoar hairs will I carry you: I have made, and I will bear; even I will carry, and will deliver you."[1463]

3. The words of the then mother of Israel are today yet applicable: "Is not the LORD gone out before thee?"[1464] It is written, "We might have a strong consolation, who have fled for refuge to lay hold upon the hope set before us: which hope we have as an anchor of the soul, both sure and stedfast, and which entereth into that within the veil; whither the forerunner is for us entered, even Jesus, made an high priest for ever."[1465] The LORD's Christ is Governor and High Priest over the LORD's heavenly Sanctuary; there is none other consecrated priests or priesthoods of the LORD on earth. The churches of Rome had put forth a theoretical theological outlook that taught *the kingdom of God* was on earth and to be led by elected elders, and that their church was the earthly representation of that *kingdom*. Yet it is that, concerning the Spirit's Christ, "if he were on earth, he should not be a priest,"[1466] seeing as how of old every priest did "serve unto the example and shadow of heavenly things."[1467] That establishment "made with hands, which are the figures of the true,"[1468] was to stand as that representative substance of the LORD's Faith for the times to come, for this Christ confessed, "My kingdom is not of this world."[1469]

4. To claim any structure on earth for that of *God* and of His *Christ* is to confess no pure diet and conversation with the

---

1462 Judges 4:23
1463 Isaiah 46:4
1464 Judges 4:14
1465 Hebrews 6:18-20
1466 Hebrews 8:4
1467 Hebrews 8:5
1468 Hebrews 9:24
1469 John 18:36

LORD's Word, and to announce an impure heart with strange ambitions, for, isn't it written, "We have an altar, whereof they have no right to eat which serve the tabernacle"?[1470] The church had early on grown tired of remaining faithful to the principles of the doctrine of Christ. Because of their growing unpopularity, because of persecution against them in various forms, Christian elders took it upon themselves to agree on one point, "If the LORD be with us, why then is all this befallen us? and where be all his miracles which our fathers told us of, saying, Did not the LORD bring us up from Egypt? but now the LORD hath forsaken us."[1471] This is why Peter warned, "There shall come in the last days scoffers, walking after their own lusts, and saying, Where is the promise of his coming? for since the fathers fell asleep, all things continue as they were from the beginning of the creation."[1472] John saw the foul spirit of unbelief and unsanctified ambition taking root in the churches, therefore, recognizing the age that he was in; for what was prophesied of certain elders and priests was fulfilling as it was spoken; he said, "It is the last time,"[1473] for the times were ordained to fulfill the saying, "A woman that sitteth in the midst of the e'phah. And he said, This is wickedness."[1474]

5. The spirit working within Christian elders was determined to build this woman articulated by Zechari'ah; which "woman" is a church estranged from the doctrine of the Spirit's Christ; "an house in the land of Shi'nar: and it shall be established, and set there upon her own base."[1475] Now, in the land of Shi'nar sat the empire of Babylon, and when Nebuchadnez'zar

---

1470 Hebrews 13:10
1471 Judges 6:13
1472 2 Peter 3:3,4
1473 1 John 2:18
1474 Zechariah 5:7,8
1475 Zechariah 5:11

had conquered ancient Israel, he took their valuables and their treasures "into the land of Shi'nar to the house of his god."[1476] Babylon, other than its beautifully ordered State, is spiritually known for its god and system of pagan worship, and the god of Babylon is as it is written, "Will ye plead for Ba'al? will ye save him? he that will plead for him, let him be put to death whilst it is yet morning: if he be a god, let him plead for himself."[1477] Babylonian worship is dedicated to Ba'al; if it is in the "morning" that Ba'al should be able to fight and deliver his own enemy to death, why is there an emphasis on the morning? The "morning" denotes the "sun," even as it is written, "As the light of the morning, when the sun riseth,"[1478] and, "In the morning, as soon as the sun is up."[1479] Whatsoever is therefore founded in Shi'nar, it is well to know that it is in service to the god of the sun.

6. Pagan nations have always devoted their religion to the sun. This is why in the morning this god should have come to his own defense, for the sun shining in its brightness is an open indicator of his presence, and this god should have had full consciousness to have taken knowledge of an act against him when it was day. For this cause, it is well to know how it says, "The sun, and the moon, and the stars, even all the host of heaven...the LORD thy God hath divided unto all nations under the whole heaven."[1480] This was the lot of the religious world, even that they "saith to the wood, Awake; to the dumb stone, Arise, it shall teach!"[1481] As the church began saying, because of apparent public disapproval, "Wherefore dost thou

---

1476 Daniel 1:2
1477 Judges 6:31
1478 2 Samuel 23:4
1479 Judges 9:33
1480 Deuteronomy 4:19
1481 Habakkuk 2:19

forget us for ever, and forsake us so long time?"[1482] growing tired of enduring for heaven's promise, she began to foster a spirit that said, "I am, and none else beside me; I shall not sit as a widow."[1483] Thus, it would inevitably happen that, to gain public approval and political favor, she would embrace all that was necessary of the Roman world to fund her universal triumph. The saying, as it was said of old, was again fulfilled in Christian ministers: "Saying to a stock, Thou art my father; and to a stone, Thou hast brought me forth: for they have turned their back unto me."[1484] Seeing the development of this spirit, before the church would make her impure endeavors officially public, years before she would seal her separation from heaven's LORD and High Priest, John wrote to church elders, "Keep yourselves from idols."[1485]

7. If their back is turned from the LORD's heavenly Sanctuary, what are they now doing, and where is there face now found? It is written, "At the door of the temple of the LORD, between the porch and the altar, were about five and twenty men, with their backs toward the temple of the LORD, and their faces toward the east; and they worshipped the sun toward the east."[1486] As the church would move from the first apostles' pure spirit and doctrine, the LORD's Spirit would report of her, "I know thy works, and where thou dwellest, even where Satan's seat is: and thou holdest fast my name, and hast not denied my faith."[1487] As the vision showed twenty-five priests at the door of the LORD's Temple, but with their backs to the Building of His name while reverencing the god of the sun,

---

1482 Lamentations 5:20
1483 Isaiah 47:8
1484 Jeremiah 2:26,27
1485 1 John 5:21
1486 Ezekiel 8:16
1487 Revelation 2:13

so too the Christian church would keep by the *Temple's fame*, but only in name, for these elders initiated a most disastrous compromise between Roman paganism and their apostate religion, which religion deviated from "the apostles' doctrine and fellowship."[1488]

8. Because the church had lost the Spirit's power and understanding due to the spurious heart working within her, she had to get *power* from another source, namely, her government. The Spirit's Faith "is the power of God unto salvation,"[1489] and by "the fullness of the blessing of the gospel of Christ,"[1490] "ye are complete in him"[1491] who is "a great high priest, that is passed into the heavens."[1492] It is "the grace of God that bringeth salvation,"[1493] that delivers liberty and understanding to the heart and conscience for obtaining an undefiled personal religion within the name of the Father and His Son. Herein is the reason why Paul wrote to the churches under Roman religious doctrine, "There is therefore now no condemnation to them which are in Christ Jesus, who walk not after the flesh, but after the Spirit,"[1494] for it is "the Spirit of grace"[1495] that embalms the inward parts with "the grace of life"[1496] to soberly love the LORD's name, self, and others; not that possessing "power and authority."[1497]

9. Where no condemnation exists, there is absolution, acquittal, pardon, and release for recuperation. Such

---

1488 Revelation 2:13
1489 Romans 1:18
1490 Romans 15:29
1491 Colossians 2:10
1492 Hebrews 4:14
1493 Titus 2:11
1494 Romans 8:1
1495 Hebrews 10:29
1496 1 Peter 3:7
1497 Luke 20:20

a benefit is conferred upon the person's inwards after they have sincerely believed on and examined heaven's decree for spiritual recovery, trusting in that saying to have self placed in to the hand of the LORD's Spirit for revival and reform. Why should Paul write to elders on such matters as pardon and forgiveness for religious negligence? Why did he have to remind them, "Ye are complete in him, which is the head of all principality and power"?[1498] He saw the fruit that Christian teachers were bearing from the branches of their conversation's character, and, for their spiritual error, was compelled to place them in remembrance on just what Christ's sacrifice represented, counseling, "By the deeds of the law there shall no flesh be justified in his sight."[1499]

10. God's Man has abolished from His LORD's Faith; by His passing flesh; all legal religious ethics of ministers, perpetually "blotting out the handwriting of ordinances."[1500] Because it is written, "He that is hanged is accursed of God,"[1501] the LORD's Man on that tree is a figurative illustration of the fact that every handwritten ordinance of every *Moses*; "not only in this world, but also in that which is to come";[1502] is accursed and condemned by the living God's Faith. Paul, observing Christian elders subscribing to what has become cursed by the LORD's Word, needed to counsel them on right religious manners, for these elders took a condemned practice to be for their *righteousness*, evincing that they did not rightly understand the body of the Spirit's knowledge, and for their misunderstanding, were misrepresenting the Spirit's will, so much so that Paul was moved to say to them, "The name of God is blasphemed among

---

1498 Colossians 2:10
1499 Romans 3:20
1500 Colossians 2:14
1501 Deuteronomy 21:23
1502 Ephesians 1:21

the Gentiles through you, as it is written."[1503] Gross devotional error against the LORD's new covenant will was creeping into the churches of professed Jewish and Gentile Jewish converts of the apostles' speech. A fleshly ambition compelled Christian elders to pick up the order established of old, blatantly rejecting the counsel, "The priesthood being changed, there is made of necessity a change also of the law."[1504]

11. With God's Man brought into His Father's heavenly Temple and anointed as His Faith's High Priest, what fleshly tradition or commandment of elders can today suffice for the reception and execution of heaven's will? There is no longer any form of earthy religion ordained after the order of Aaron, which services "stood only in meats and drinks, and divers washings, and carnal ordinances";[1505] in "gifts and sacrifices, that could not make him that did the service perfect, as pertaining to the conscience."[1506] The apostles saw the elders of the churches placing pagan rites, feasts, and ceremonies, for Christian ordinances that are not meant; according to heaven's right Faith; to be ritualized or inordinately coveted. The apostles saw a spirit forming that would embrace a denial of the Spirit's Faith, re-directing man from understanding that this Christ's mediation is their only intercessor and hope for heaven-appointed and heaven-ordained righteousness.

12. Sensing the stoutness settling into Christian factions, Paul understood that it was necessary to place ministers in remembrance that "there is one God, and one mediator between God and men, the man Christ Jesus; who gave himself a ransom for all, to be testified in due time."[1507] It is this Christ

---

1503 Romans 2:24
1504 Hebrews 7:12
1505 Hebrews 9:10
1506 Hebrews 9:9
1507 1 Timothy 2:5,6

who has gone before us in to the LORD's true Temple to assume the role as High Priest that we may chase every religious error out of our heart. As of old, how the Spirit wrought a victory for Israel based upon absolute faith, so today, for His assembly, the Spirit will yet work a victory by our diligent and experimental faith on the hope of redemption from personal and devotional sin against heaven's Word. Thus, John would have the churches know, "We have an advocate with the Father, Jesus Christ the righteous,"[1508] and, "Your sins are forgiven you for his name's sake."[1509]

13. For, the new faith among Christian leadership was, "You are justified by the law,"[1510] but, in reality, "the law made nothing perfect"[1511] "and the law is not of faith,"[1512] and because "whatsoever is not of faith is sin,"[1513] to uphold what is not of faith; which is the legal religious bill; is to evince the conversation as unjust and sinful before the Word. Since "without faith it is impossible to please him,"[1514] the longer Christian doctrines remained without faith's right exercise and stayed on legal religious canons, the longer the Spirit's displeasure rested on them, for what blessing can appear by what is condemned and accursed? To claim *righteousness* by what is abolished; as it says, "Blotting out the handwriting of ordinances";[1515] and as satisfying the Spirit's precepts, is to call Him and His Son a liar, in that He need not have gone through all that He did to recover even one spirit from religious error. And this is why John wrote, "He that believeth not God hath made him a

---

1508   1 John 2:1
1509   1 John 2:12
1510   Galatians 5:4
1511   Hebrews 7:19
1512   Galatians 3:12
1513   Romans 14:23
1514   Hebrews 11:6
1515   Colossians 2:14

liar; because he believeth not the record that God gave of his Son,"[1516] and, "If we say that we have not sinned, we make him a liar, and his word is not in us."[1517]

14. It was the growing disbelief against the Spirit's doctrine that allowed John to discern the reason for the lacking of godly unity. The elders were serving another god that demanded another spirit for his religion, and the apostles knew that such a course would only lead into relations with that abolished craft of the religious world. The *new* theology concocted by Christian elders hid the fact of Christ's right name, along with the course of that name's learning, as being man's only surety to quit "the corruption that is in the world through lust."[1518] The new religious laws and traditions of the church were full of sensual labors and appointments to place the carnal heart at ease, but, again, no thing done without faith in the Spirit's voice may return any benefit to the doer, and since these were the edicts of men, "The LORD hath rejected thy confidences, and thou shalt not prosper in them,"[1519] said the Spirit. Deeds done in the body, and by the imagination of priests, were to account for *justification* before *God*, when in reality all that is necessary is to hear and do the counsel, "Seek ye out of the book of the LORD, and read,"[1520] and, "Be ye doers of the word."[1521] The counsel is, "He is gone into the Spirit's Building to appear in the Word's presence for us,"[1522] and as the heart becomes touched at the Father's kindness, and as His voice rains down medicine onto the conscience; as it says, "My doctrine shall

---

1516   1 John 5:10
1517   1 John 1:10
1518   2 Peter 1:4
1519   Jeremiah 2:37
1520   Isaiah 34:16
1521   James 1:22
1522   Hebrews 9:24

drop as the rain";[1523] it is that faith on the Spirit's praise will satiate the soul and forward the experience.

15. As the church turned away from doing the Spirit's righteousness for the power of His grace, it is that they began "to eat things sacrificed unto idols, and to commit fornication."[1524] Her elders sought "fellowship with the unfruitful works of darkness,"[1525] communing with "those things which are done of them in secret,"[1526] and in turn retained their god and his yoke in exchange for political prowess to assert their perceived earthly dominion. And the Spirit, who says of her priests, "Thou hast there them that hold the doctrine of Ba'laam, who taught Ba'lac to cast a stumblingblock, "[1527] gives us a clear revelation of the movements within the Christian church at this time. As the Revelation is a vision of no literal illustration, but is a spiritual delineation finding accomplishment in a real way, it is our responsibility to examine history to understand just what the Spirit is saying. Ba'laam and Ba'lac have been dead a very long time by the time we reach the year of the Revelation; which year is around 100 A.D.; allowing us to look for a false prophet; the Christian church; coming into contact with a pagan king; Constantine; to establish a legal compromise between paganism and the already apostate Christian religion.

16. Understanding where ministers should find themselves if they did not at once learn heaven's new will, Paul counseled all elders, "The law maketh men high priests which have infirmity";[1528] this counsel is both personal and for the church. Any law that the heart may develop to maintain its religion is a

---

1523 Deuteronomy 32:2
1524 Revelation 2:14
1525 Ephesians 5:11
1526 Ephesians 5:12
1527 Revelation 2:14
1528 Hebrews 7:28

policy formed out of fear and error. Laws that are so internally advocated, due to an evident laziness to investigate Scripture and to examine the path of the feet, will decree the heart as high priest over the entire mind and body. This heart of error will place itself; the mind of the flesh that is naturally full of spiritual infirmity; as governor over the members of the body and conscience. That which is born in us will rule if there is no mind to stimulate a thought to hear the counsel, "This is the victory that overcometh the world, even our faith."[1529] To defeat the natural spirit that works within the members of the heart, the eye of our faith must remain "looking unto Jesus the author and finisher of our faith."[1530] This means more than mindlessly idolizing a traditional *man*, and this is why our Priest counsels, "If a man love me, he will keep my words,"[1531] and, "Ye are clean through the word which I have spoken."[1532] Such counsel allows us to understand that the LORD's Chief Apostle would have every one owning confidence in His name with an intelligent faith, which cannot take place within any one unless they are willing to examine the Spirit's Bible, "rightly dividing the word of truth."[1533] Heaven's right baptism is not by literal water, nor is it by the impression of flesh, but we are counseled, "Of his own will begat he us with the word of truth."[1534] Because no word or counsel is innately physical, and because "that which is born of the Spirit is spirit,"[1535] right sanctification is through "the washing of water by the word,"[1536] which is why the Spirit's creation prays, "I will meditate in thy precepts, and

---

1529 1 John 5:4
1530 Hebrews 12:2
1531 John 14:23
1532 John 15:3
1533 2 Timothy 2:15
1534 James 1:18
1535 John 3:6
1536 Ephesians 5:26

have respect unto thy ways."[1537] This is why we are told, "Set your affection on things above, not on things on the earth."[1538]

17. "Our conversation is in heaven"[1539] "where Christ sitteth on the right hand of God,"[1540] for "we have such an high priest, who is set on the right hand of the throne of the Majesty in the heavens; a minister of the sanctuary, and of the true tabernacle, which the Lord pitched, and not man."[1541] "The eyes of your understanding"[1542] should be turned to this heavenly Place; every heart should long for the knowledge of this Sanctuary's acceptable Faith; even as it is written, "I will worship toward thy holy temple, and praise thy name for thy lovingkindness and for thy truth."[1543] For, "after that the kindness and love of God our Saviour toward man appeared"[1544] among men, it is the LORD our Father "who will have all men to be saved, and to come unto the knowledge of the truth."[1545]

18. "The word of the truth of the gospel"[1546] states: "By grace are ye saved through faith; and that not of yourselves."[1547] Therefore "according to the truth of the gospel,"[1548] "we might be justified by the faith of Christ, and not by the works of the law"[1549] of priests and elders. There is no doctrine of flesh, and there is no superstition or stubborn presumption, that can produce the Spirit's grace to cleanse the inward parts. The

---

1537 Psalm 119:15
1538 Colossians 3:2
1539 Philippians 3:20
1540 Colossians 3:1
1541 Hebrews 8:1,2
1542 Ephesians 1:18
1543 Psalms 138:2
1544 Titus 3:4
1545 1 Timothy 2:4
1546 Colossians 1:5
1547 Ephesians 2:8
1548 Galatians 2:14
1549 Galatians 2:16

intended purpose of the Spirit's redemption is for the LORD to personally perform a lasting creation within the spirit of man's mind, which is why we are "to be strengthened with might by his Spirit in the inner man."[1550] Indeed "the new man, which after God is created in righteousness and true holiness,"[1551] will not have a superficial experience in His Son's name, but will be with His Priest where He is, giving the Captain of their salvation full reign over their soul temple.

19. There is therefore no condemnation within heaven's will; there is no required religious sentence or judgment for the one bearing right faith and confidence in the Spirit's doctrine; for "by the righteousness of one the free gift came upon all men unto justification of life."[1552] For this cause the apostle writes, concerning them that care to personally learn of heaven's will, to do it, "Not by works of righteousness which we have done,"[1553] and, "By grace are ye saved through faith; and that not of yourselves: it is the gift of God."[1554] The gift of justification[1555] is released into the soul for correction "of sin, and of righteousness, and of judgment"[1556] by the Spirit of our High Priest's ministry. "They which receive abundance of grace and of the gift of righteousness"[1557] are blessed of the Spirit "with all spiritual blessings in heavenly places in Christ"[1558] to hear, "Look upon Zion, the city of our solemnities: thine eyes shall see Jerusalem a quiet habitation, a tabernacle that shall not be taken down; not one of the stakes thereof shall

---

1550 Ephesians 3:16
1551 Ephesians 4:24
1552 Romans 5:18
1553 Titus 3:5
1554 Ephesians 2:8
1555 Justification is another term for sanctification
1556 John 16:8
1557 Romans 5:17
1558 Ephesians 1:3

ever be removed, neither shall any of the cords thereof be broken."[1559] This is why Paul writes, "Ye are come unto mount Si'on, and unto the city of the living God, the heavenly Jerusalem...to the general assembly and church of the firstborn, which are written in heaven...and to Jesus the mediator of the new covenant,"[1560] wherein rests "the spirits of just men made perfect."[1561]

20. What individuals dwell within the Spirit's City with His Christ as that Head over His New Covenant Church? It is written, "Just men made perfect."[1562] And what of them receives health? Again, it says, "The spirits of just men."[1563] The justified, or the sanctified, exist by "the knowledge of the Son of God"[1564] and accept the fact that their reconciliation to His Spirit is the means whereby they are brought "into the kingdom of his dear Son"[1565] to be "perfect, as pertaining to the conscience."[1566] For, the reign of this Christ is as it is said, "The LORD hath sworn, and will not repent, Thou art a priest for ever after the order of Melchiz'edek."[1567]

21. Looking at that Melchiz'edek, we see that he was "king of Sa'lem...and he was the priest of the most high God,"[1568] and with this office also, to Abraham he "brought forth bread and wine,"[1569] which is why our Priest says, "The bread that I will give is my flesh,"[1570] and, "He that eateth me, even he shall live

---

1559 Isaiah 33:20
1560 Hebrews 12:22-24
1561 Hebrews 12:23
1562 Hebrews 12:23
1563 Hebrews 12:23
1564 Ephesians 4:13
1565 Colossians 1:13
1566 Hebrews 9:9
1567 Psalms 110:4
1568 Genesis 14:18
1569 Genesis 14:18
1570 John 6:51

by me."[1571] To whom was substance given but to Abraham, and he representing them that should, "through the righteousness of faith,"[1572] subscribe to One "after the similitude of Melchis'edec."[1573] To the one of faith is conferred the benefit of the Spirit's heavenly ministry, for the name and wisdom of His High Priest's intercession is now become to the believer, "Wonderful, Counsellor, The mighty God, The everlasting Father, The Prince of Peace,"[1574] even their "wisdom, and righteousness, and sanctification, and redemption."[1575]

22. Notice that Melchiz'edek personally gave to Abraham bread and wine, and that such was not already in Abraham's possession at that time. To them that are actively exercising faith on the Spirit's will and saying; the Spirit's bread and the wine; which are the complete principles of the doctrine of Christ and the experience of that learning; will be given them by His mediation through their long-suffering with "patience and comfort of the scriptures."[1576] For, "the just shall live by faith";[1577] that is, the blessed and the sanctified; for "ye have need of patience, that, after ye have done the will of God, ye might receive the promise."[1578] This is why John wrote, "He that doeth the will of God abideth for ever,"[1579] because He who should be the Head of the Spirit's House "abideth a priest continually"[1580] after that figure of old, leaving no shortage of support for the believer, seeing as how it is "the Son, who is

---

1571 John 6:57
1572 Romans 4:13
1573 Hebrews 7:15
1574 Isaiah 9:6
1575 1 Corinthians 1:30
1576 Romans 15:4
1577 Hebrews 10:38
1578 Hebrews 10:36
1579 1 John 2:17
1580 Hebrews 7:3

consecrated for evermore."[1581] He is that King[1582] of that "city which hath foundations, whose builder and maker is God,"[1583] and is the Minister "of the true tabernacle, which the Lord pitched and not man."[1584] True acceptable faith is ordained of His LORD and Father to keep His reformer in this Sanctuary, that by faith's course, the spirit of the mind created after the law of His mediation would shine through them as a good and benevolent service reveals the character of their personal religion.

23. Under the jurisdiction of His intercession, the spirit of the believer will be made perfect, for faith in His name is that process leading to a self-sacrificing ministry. Though no religious law or commandment may produce redemption's blessing, it is "that faith without works is dead,"[1585] for a right and spiritually benevolent labor is proof of the Faith in the sight of the Word. Now, the works of the Spirit are not the works of men, for it is counseled, "Shew out a good conversation his works with meekness of wisdom."[1586] Wisdom is not physical or tangible. Wisdom is not contained within an image or a custom, a day or a dress, an article of food, the outward frame of the stature or the handcrafted policy. The counsel is, "Let the word of Christ dwell in you richly in all wisdom,"[1587] for wisdom manifests itself "without dissimulation,"[1588] being "kindly affectioned one to another with brotherly love."[1589] Should one display wisdom "in love,

---

1581 Hebrews 7:28
1582 A King of the LORD is another term for High Priest
1583 Hebrews 11:10
1584 Hebrews 8:2
1585 James 2:20
1586 James 3:13
1587 Colossians 3:16
1588 Romans 12:9
1589 Romans 12:10

and in the spirit of meekness,"[1590] it is that we are "to bear the infirmities of the weak, and not to please ourselves,"[1591] fulfilling the counsel, "Bear ye one another's burdens, and so fulfill the law of Christ."[1592] Being sanctified by faith on the LORD's voice, the mind becomes His Son's apprentice to observe His ways and labors that it may then work as He works and live as He lives.

24. The works of the Spirit are witnessed by the mind of the Spirit, even as that done by man is a witness of self, which is why John writes to the churches, "It is the Spirit that beareth witness."[1593] That done without faith is done without the Spirit's cause moving the heart, and if without the Spirit's will, it is done without right affection, seeing as how "the love of God is shed abroad in our hearts by the Holy Ghost."[1594] Our responsibility is not simply to lethargically and idolatrously believe in *Christ* and that is all, for His Man owns a living office to be understood, and the reformer has a responsibility to know their conversation's relation to that office. Because the church violated the doctrine of this Christ, souls were removed from observing the Spirit's Temple in heaven, wherein the only Mirror for a correct worship and service exists. Thus, for removing their understanding from heaven's Sanctuary, their new theology taught, "Righteousness come by the law."[1595] The labor of any legal religious law and ordinance is without faith and right love for the inward person, becoming, because of fear, a numbing ritual and superstition to hide self from self and the heart from its Creator. There-

---

1590 1 Corinthians 4:21
1591 Romans 15:1
1592 Galatians 6:2
1593 1 John 5:6
1594 Romans 5:5
1595 Galatians 2:21

fore seeing "the throne of iniquity have fellowship"[1596] with *the Word*, Paul wrote, "If righteousness come by the law, then Christ is dead in vain,"[1597] for, isn't it that this Christ of the living God was "made of a woman, made under the law, to redeem them that were under the law"?[1598]

[1596] Psalms 94:20
[1597] Galatians 2:21
[1598] Galatians 4:4,5

11

Reconciliation's Administration

1. Says our High Priest, "I have given you an example, that ye should do as I have done";[1599] "give me thine heart, and let thine eyes observe my ways."[1600] For we understand that this Man "lifted up his eyes to heaven,"[1601] and for the reformer it is counseled, "Seek those things which are above, where Christ sitteth on the right hand of God."[1602]

2. There is a reason why the eyes of our faith and understanding[1603] should be found in the Spirit's heavenly Court. It is the LORD who, "according to the eternal purpose which he purposed in Christ"[1604] "when he raised him from

---

1599 John 13:15
1600 Proverbs 23:26
1601 John 17:1
1602 Colossians 3:1
1603 Ephesians 1:18
1604 Ephesians 3:11

the dead, and set him at his own right hand in the heavenly places,"[1605] called "us unto the adoption of children"[1606] "with the word of truth, that we should be a kind of first fruits of his creatures."[1607] The purpose of His Christ's sacrifice did not end with Him on the tree, for what occurred at His crucifixion only ratified that purpose the LORD pronounced in Eden, saying, "I will put enmity between thy seed and her seed."[1608] Thus, by that accomplished through the passing flesh of this Christ, the Word's eternal purpose for man should find itself established by His Son's name through an experimental faith on the Spirit science, seeing as how "of his own will begat he us with the word of truth."[1609] By actively believing on and examining His name, the process of sanctification within the organs of the inward person will commence, and where this learning takes place, it is known that "there is no more offering for sin."[1610]

3. Now, "the law having a shadow of good things to come";[1611] which law did "serve unto the example and shadow of heavenly things";[1612] "in the dispensation of the fullness of times,"[1613] it was that the Spirit's Christ should become "an high priest of good things to come."[1614] The "good things" of old, as determined by Moses, were a figure for this Christ's vocation in the LORD's heavenly Sanctuary, for He told Moses, "Make me a sanctuary"[1615] "according to all that I shew thee, after the

---

1605 Ephesians 1:20
1606 Ephesians 1:5
1607 James 1:18
1608 Genesis 3:15
1609 James 1:18
1610 Hebrews 10:18
1611 Hebrews 10:1
1612 Hebrews 8:5
1613 Ephesians 1:10
1614 Hebrews 9:11
1615 Exodus 25:8

pattern."[1616] That tabernacle on earth was formed after the fashion of the heavenly Temple, and to understand the season in which we today live, it is necessary to examine the movements of old. Therefore, concerning sanctification, it is written, "Moses took the anointing oil and anointed the tabernacle and all that was therein, and sanctified them. And he sprinkled... to sanctify them."[1617] "He poured of the anointing oil upon Aaron's head, and anointed him, to sanctify him."[1618] Of all that Moses did to sanctify the tabernacle, its instruments, and the ones ordained for its service, Moses "sanctified it, to make reconciliation upon it."[1619]

4. Belief on the LORD's Man is not enough. His Christ "hath given himself for us an offering and a sacrifice to God"[1620] that we may be "reconciled to God"[1621] for an intelligent purpose. Concerning the LORD's right operation, "now hath he reconciled in the body of his flesh through death"[1622] every one who will trust on and investigate that fact by an experimental faith, and He did this for our reconciliation to His Spirit for creation's course, making "peace through the blood of his cross, by him to reconcile all things unto himself."[1623] Christ offered the flesh of His name that all things should be given a right chance to commune with His Father's name, which is why Paul writes, "I bow my knees unto the Father of our Lord Jesus Christ, of whom the whole family in heaven and earth is named."[1624] Who is the reformer named after? All

---

1616 Exodus 25:9
1617 Leviticus 8:10,11
1618 Leviticus 8:12
1619 Leviticus 8:15
1620 Ephesians 5:2
1621 2 Corinthians 5:20
1622 Colossians 1:21,22
1623 Colossians 1:20
1624 Ephesians 3:14,15

are become, through sanctification, creations consecrated to His LORD and Father, which is why "unto him"; the Father; "be glory in the church by Christ"[1625] through the knowledge of His Son, which is why this Christ prays to His LORD, "Keep through thine own name those whom thou hast given me."[1626] "Him"; this Christ; "hath God exalted with his right hand to be a Prince and a Saviour, for to give repentance to Israel, and forgiveness of sins."[1627] Did not the literal nation of Israel cease to be in favor with God after Christ? How is it that "Israel" yet remains as the LORD's inheritance, and for a specific plan of redemption? "The Israel of God"[1628] is joined to their LORD through the Faith of His High Priest, "who is even at the right hand of God, who also maketh intercession for us."[1629]

5. Such a people are no literal earthy denomination, but are, by their faith's higher learning, members of "the general assembly and church of the firstborn, which are written in heaven."[1630] This is why the believer must know that there exists "an high priest over the house of God."[1631] More important than the image of the tree; or of the cross; is the Priest removed from its wood, even that law and counsel maintained "through the blood of the everlasting covenant."[1632] The believer of the Spirit's will grows "unto a perfect man, unto the measure of the stature of the fullness of Christ,"[1633] and Scripture tells us that right growth and development cannot commence until the

---

1625 Ephesians 3:21
1626 John 17:11
1627 Acts 5:31
1628 Galatians 6:16
1629 Romans 8:34
1630 Hebrews 12:23
1631 Hebrews 10:21
1632 Hebrews 13:20
1633 Ephesians 4:13

process of sanctification begins, which sanctification occurs only within the heavenly Sanctuary at this present time.

6. Moses sanctified to reconcile, therefore one can be reconciled to the Spirit, yet only in name and not in fact. Until faith receives and exercises self within the Spirit's anointing, allowing that wisdom to flow over and within the conscience, reconciliation does not exist, for Moses "sanctified it, to make reconciliation."[1634] It is true that by God's Man we are now "reconciled to God by the death of his Son,"[1635] but this Man's offering is a general sacrifice for whoever should feel after His LORD's will and promise. As a general sacrifice, because the flesh of man was offered, His spilt blood binds humanity to His heaven's throne for heaven's course of learning; this sacrifice did not fulfill the end of this course and the promise of that throne within any one. As a general offering, the Spirit's will is open for all to know, leaving the reception of that will's promise, and the experience of that learning, up to the person to individually forward by an experimental faith. Earth's mission is finished; flesh's constitution is bound by blood to heaven's new will for an amendment; yet He was brought up to the Spirit's Building for a reason. The Father's will; because He is LORD of heaven and earth; must find itself finished within man's inward parts as their conversation is joined to His Son's heavenly ministry; this is why it says, "By his knowledge shall my righteous servant justify many."[1636]

7. There is no such thing as justification; which is sanctification; by a lame and undemanding belief on the man *Jesus*; this is illogical due to the fact that "God is a Spirit,"[1637] for

---

1634 Leviticus 8:15
1635 Romans 5:10
1636 Isaiah 53:11
1637 John 4:24

"that which is born of the Spirit is spirit."[1638] Paul found Christian churches establishing their creed by a lazy approach to heaven's throne, finding it necessary to write, "Wherefore henceforth know we no man after the flesh: yea, though we have known Christ after the flesh, yet now henceforth know we him no more."[1639] Christian elders; because these were Jews and pagan converts to Judaism owning a religious heritage formerly subject to "meats and drinks, and divers washings, and carnal ordinances";[1640] sought to honor *God's Faith* according to the manners under the former will, which was a covenant pronouncing blessing "by works of righteousness which we have done."[1641] The sacrificed flesh of God's Man abolished such manners of worship and service, opening up the worshipper of His LORD and Father to an entirely spiritual practice, for which cause we are counseled, "Worship God in the spirit,"[1642] and, "Have no confidence in the flesh,"[1643] that is, quit "your vain conversation received by tradition"[1644] and "live according to God in thespirit."[1645]

8. Right baptism is today by the voice of the LORD's Spirit working within the spirit of the mind, which is why we are counseled, "That which is born of the Spirit is spirit,"[1646] and, "Be renewed in the spirit of your mind."[1647] It is therefore a carnal practice to keep after the legal ordinances of flesh, for such adherence witnesses to the fact that we do not own confidence

---

1638 John 3:6
1639 2 Corinthians 5:16
1640 Hebrews 9:14
1641 Titus 3:5
1642 Philippians 3:3
1643 Philippians 3:3
1644 1 Peter 1:18
1645 1 Peter 4:6
1646 John 3:6
1647 Ephesians 4:23

or a right understanding in the act of God's Man. Justification; which is sanctification; because blessing is wholly confined to the spirit of the mind, must find itself accomplished by a better manner, for it is the Spirit's will to "purge your conscience from dead works to serve the living God."[1648] What physical routine, or what tradition of flesh, can then suffice for what the Spirit intends? Sanctification commences by mentally examining and physically acting out His voice, allowing us to understand that the mind must wrestle with the Spirit's voice in order to obtain the conception promised by heaven's mediation, which is why "through knowledge shall the just be delivered,"[1649] for the Spirit's voice is "spiritually discerned."[1650] "Deliverance" is herein understood to be from lame religious practices halting the effect of faith's right learning, which practices God's Man has for ever nailed to the tree. Therefore, if we fail to acquire knowledge of His name, must we believe that we should own deliverance from religious error to know liberty of conscience to properly honor heaven's course?

9. This is why it says, "As many as received him, to them gave he power to become the sons of God, even to them that believe on his name."[1651] The name of God's Son is the knowledge of His intercession, wherefore belief is herein understood to be; because no name is physical; a mental course, even as God's Man once said to the Jews, "If ye believe not his writings, how shall ye believe my words?"[1652] We may place confidence on writings only as we examine them, and because the Jews failed to meditate on the former will, they could not discern the new will and promise that His Christ pronounced. So too we, by failing to

---

1648 Hebrews 9:14
1649 Proverbs 11:9
1650 1 Corinthians 2:14
1651 John 1:12
1652 John 5:47

familiarize self with His voice, will find our conversation without His ministry of healing, which is why His Faith counsels, "Ye are clean through the word which I have spoken,"[1653] and, "Be ye transformed by the renewing of your mind."[1654]

10. Upon accepting His sacrifice as that means for our reconciliation to the heavenly Sanctuary, and His doctrine as our conversation's Savior, the reformer is reconciled to His Father's Spirit for "the days of their purification,"[1655] which is why the apostle would have the churches remember, "The anointing which ye have received of him abideth in you."[1656] Now, when should this anointing have been received, and what is it? It is written, "After that ye believed, ye were sealed with that holy Spirit of promise, which is the earnest of our inheritance,"[1657] for our Priest says, "I send the promise of my Father upon you."[1658] Wherefore today, "being by the right hand of God exalted, and having received of the Father the promise of the Holy Ghost, he hath shed forth this"[1659] benevolent promise "that we might live through him,"[1660] to the end our conversation should find itself diligently upheld by His name. This is why it is written, "Ye might believe that Jesus is the Christ, the Son of God; and that believing ye might have life through his name,"[1661] for "the Spirit is life,"[1662] and this "life" being "the light of men,"[1663] for "the light shineth in darkness."[1664]

1653 John 15:3
1654 Romans 12:2
1655 Esther 2:12
1656 1 John 2:27
1657 Ephesians 1:13
1658 Luke 24:49
1659 Acts 2:33
1660 1 John 4:9
1661 John 20:31
1662 Romans 8:10
1663 John 1:4
1664 John 1:5

11. Herein is the reason why the apostle wrote, after observing the idolatrous and covetous spirit within the Christian camp, "If we say that we have fellowship with him, and walk in darkness, we lie, and do not the truth."[1665] "Fellowship is with the Father, and with his Son,"[1666] meaning our "fellowship of the Spirit"[1667] is by "the communion of the Holy Ghost."[1668] "The unfruitful works of darkness"[1669] do not exist in the Father's Faith because "God is light,"[1670] and being light, His voice is an illuminator of religious negligence because "all things that are reproved are made manifest by the light: for whatsoever doth make manifest is light."[1671] There is light in the Spirit's sayings because His voice reproves and corrects personal and devotional error, and there is only one Spirit of the LORD given the office of Educator, and that being the Comforter, for "when he is come, he will reprove."[1672] Therefore by the fellowship of the Spirit, one should possess the mind of the Spirit, "for the Spirit searcheth all things, yea, the deep things of God."[1673] For this cause, it is well to know that "the things of the Spirit of God"[1674] "are spiritually discerned,"[1675] and by daily communing with the Spirit's Word, the thoughts and intentions of the heart will be made manifest, for, now "old things are passed way; behold, all things are become new."[1676] This is why our confidence is not only on the doctrine of His

---

1665 1 John 1:6
1666 1 John 1:3
1667 Philippians 2:1
1668 2 Corinthians 13:14
1669 Ephesians 5:11
1670 1 John 1:5
1671 Ephesians 5:13
1672 John 16:8
1673 1 Corinthians 2:10
1674 1 Corinthians 2:14
1675 1 Corinthians 2:14
1676 2 Corinthians 5:17

Christ's name, but our fellowship is also with the name of His Father's throne, for the reformer is to be "sanctified by God the Father."[1677]

12. The Spirit's pure counsel rejects every notion to adopt legal religious tenets and ordinances for devotional rituals and superstitions to the *praise* of *the Word*. There is only One that may cleanse the soul, and this sanctification "with the washing of water by the word,"[1678] wherefore the reformer is made clean "being sanctified by the Holy Ghost."[1679] For, "by the power of the Spirit of God,"[1680] "the righteousness of the law"[1681] will conquer our inward parts, which "righteousness" is "the kindness and love of God our Saviour toward man."[1682] That old will is nailed to the tree, for the LORD, understanding that the former manner did no good thing for the conversation's mind, sought a better will for man by a better priesthood owning better promises. Herein is the reason why it was needful that the LORD bring up His Son from that tree, for by leaving behind an accursed religious manner, we not only "have a great high priest, that is passed into the heavens,"[1683] but we also "have not an high priest which cannot be touched with the feeling of our infirmities; but was in all points tempted like as we are, yet without sin."[1684] If we did not have Him, we would be confined to that on the tree, yet we have "a merciful and faithful high priest in things pertaining to God,"[1685] allowing us

---

1677 Jude 1:1
1678 Ephesians 5:26
1679 Romans 15:16
1680 Romans 15:19
1681 Romans 8:4
1682 Titus 3:4
1683 Hebrews 4:14
1684 Hebrews 4:15
1685 Hebrews 2:17

to lawfully pass through creation's science by the Spirit of His mediation's wisdom and power.

13. Unless the soul would "be filled with the Spirit,"[1686] unless the believer is "filled with all the fullness of God"[1687] by that name of whom it is written, "In him dwelleth all the fullness of the Godhead,"[1688] reconciliation to the Spirit is not complete, for it is the Father's Spirit that sanctifies, even as it says, "Through sanctification of the Spirit."[1689] "God anointed Jesus of Nazareth with the Holy Ghost,"[1690] and because this Man loved righteousness and hated every wrong decree against righteousness' course, it is said, "God, even thy God, hath anointed thee with the oil of gladness above thy fellows."[1691] The believer is to observe the mind of the Spirit and of His Christ, because what was done for Him will be done for them through His name's learning. Unless "the oil of joy"[1692] is received into the spirit of the mind to work conversion in to the conversation's conscience; which oil is "abundance of grace and of the gift of righteousness";[1693] there is no right inward reconciliation. Reconciliation is forwarded when the reconciled object is sanctified, and if what is to be sanctified fails to acknowledge sanctification's course, then there is indeed no gathering to the Spirit's Word, but *reconciliation* existing only in name until that object should surrender to its anointing.

14. There is a Place for sanctification, and there is a substance and an Agent for cleanliness, and it is only "by the

---

1686 Ephesians 5:18
1687 Ephesians 3:19
1688 Colossians 2:9
1689 1 Peter 1:2
1690 Acts 10:38
1691 Hebrews 1:9
1692 Isaiah 61:3
1693 Romans 5:17

washing of regeneration, and renewing of the Holy Ghost"[1694] within that Building "which the Lord pitched, and not man."[1695] Various Christian tribes openly transgressed the LORD's Faith and remained "not in the doctrine of Christ"[1696] when declaring, "Righteousness come by the law,"[1697] and, "Ye now made perfect by the flesh."[1698] "The Circumcision in the flesh made by hands"[1699] taught, "You are justified by the law,"[1700] yet, "according to the truth of the gospel,"[1701] these ministers preached a rule contrary to that of man's Intercessor, which rule is of "another gospel"[1702] magnifying "another Jesus."[1703] For, by the Spirit and High Priest of the heavenly Temple, "we might be justified by the faith of Christ"[1704] "with the circumcision made without hands"[1705] within that "greater and more perfect tabernacle, not made with hands."[1706] Any thing else other than what the LORD's Spirit has established is evidently a forced lie, and Paul, upon hearing this lie taught by Christian elders, said, "This persuasion cometh not of him that calleth you."[1707]

15. It is important to know that on earth rests no place or minister for salvation's science, "for unto which of the angels said he at any time, Thou art my Son, this day have I begotten thee? And again, I will be to him a Father, and he shall be

---

1694 Titus 3:5
1695 Hebrews 8:2
1696 1 John 1:9
1697 Galatians 2:21
1698 Galatians 3:3
1699 Ephesians 2:11
1700 Galatians 5:4
1701 Galatians 2:14
1702 2 Corinthians 11:4
1703 2 Corinthians 11:4
1704 Galatians 2:16
1705 Colossians 2:11
1706 Hebrews 9:11
1707 Galatians 5:8

to me a Son?[1708] An "angel" is a term denoting a minister or teacher, for it says, "To which of the angels said he at any time, Sit on my right hand, until I make thine enemies thy footstool? Are they not all ministering spirits, sent forth to minister for them who shall be heirs of salvation?"[1709] Paul was moved to write such a message because he observed angels, or priests and ministers, performing a role that is already filled. This Christ of the living God is gone "into heaven itself, now to appear in the presence of God for us,"[1710] "that in all things he might have the preeminence,"[1711] but the Christian spirit was revealed to the apostles, so much so that John even writes of one elder, "Who loveth to have the preeminence among them, receiveth us not."[1712]

16. The word was being fulfilled within the Christian church, "In the latter times some shall depart from the faith."[1713] The ground of the Faith is baptism by faith's exercise "according to the promise of life which is in Christ."[1714] Now, that promise of life in Christ's voice is "the grace that is in Christ,"[1715] and this grace in His doctrine is "the salvation which is in Christ,"[1716] for it is "the grace of God that bringeth salvation."[1717] "The gift of the grace of God"[1718] is shed forth on us by "the Spirit of grace,"[1719] for within the Spirit's voice is "the grace of life"[1720]

1708 Hebrews 1:5
1709 Hebrews 1:13,14
1710 Hebrews 9:24
1711 Colossians 1:18
1712 3 John 1:9
1713 1 Timothy 4:1
1714 2 Timothy 1:1
1715 2 Timothy 2:1
1716 2 Timothy 2:10
1717 Titus 2:11
1718 Ephesians 3:7
1719 Hebrews 10:29
1720 1 Peter 3:7

"unto justification of life"[1721] that the believer may say, "I delight in the law of God after the inward man,"[1722] for it is purposed of the Father that, "through faith in his blood,"[1723] we should be "strengthened with might by his Spirit in the inner man."[1724] The inner man, the mind of the conversation, is the Word's object and sanctification's subject. The righteousness of the Spirit is to be fulfilled within our inward parts as there is an acceptance of the Spirit's will and the anointing joined to it, to the end the heart may examine self for learning how "to be confirmed to the image of his Son."[1725]

17. A conversation arranged around a legal religious routine to honor the LORD's name and ten laws is abolished, "for finding fault with them, he saith, Behold, the days come, saith the Lord, when I will make a new covenant."[1726] We will reverence these laws of heaven's Church and State by "obeying the truth through the Spirit,"[1727] for, concerning the Spirit's "law of truth,"[1728] the LORD anciently prophesied, "A law shall proceed from me, and I will make my judgment to rest for a light of the people."[1729] This law and judgment is the Spirit's will and commandment, and because "we have received a commandment from the Father,"[1730] His Chief Apostle came preaching, "For judgment I am come into this world."[1731] His mission was to establish that judgment to lead the doer of it into the heavenly Sanctuary to love and respect the LORD

1721 Romans 5:18
1722 Romans 7:22
1723 Romans 3:25
1724 Ephesians 3:16
1725 Romans 8:29
1726 Hebrews 8:8
1727 1 Peter 1:22
1728 Malachi 2:6
1729 Isaiah 51:4
1730 2 John 1:4
1731 John 9:39

of His intercession, "and this is love, that we walk after his commandments."[1732]

18. No man or woman can bring self to reverence the LORD's commandments according to the required standard established by the Author of those laws. To devise carnal and sensual means to do that which only His Spirit can do is to turn the religion over to "wisdom in will worship"[1733] "after the commandments and doctrines of men."[1734] This is the "sin" and "transgression" that we may today commit against the Spirit's doctrine and science, that by means of flesh-based inventions; which religious concoctions are nailed to the tree; man may decree a *righteousness* fulfilling the perceived demand of *righteousness*, when in fact Christ "gave himself for our sins"[1735] "to declare his righteousness for the remission of sins."[1736] What "righteousness" is given for our spiritual negligence? The course of His name's learning is given for the recovery of our understanding from religious error, which learning is "even the righteousness of God which is by faith of Jesus Christ unto all and upon all them that believe."[1737] This is why, if we today are subscribing to the religious laws, traditions, and doctrines of priests and ministers, it is well to know that "Christ is the end of the law for righteousness to every one that believeth."[1738]

19. When one fails to actively believe on the name and knowledge of His Son, then that one will desire their own legal ordinance for their own imagined *righteousness*, and this is why the LORD's first will failed among the Israelites. The priests under the old will took the ordinance to be their righteousness

---

1732 2 John 1:6
1733 Colossians 2:23
1734 Colossians 2:22
1735 Galatians 1:4
1736 Romans 3:25
1737 Romans 3:22
1738 Romans 10:4

for the LORD's manner of righteousness, and so bogged down the ultimate intention of that covenant by various traditions and handwritings of ordinances. This is crucial to understand, for, when observing priests advancing legal religious traditions, and enjoining such laws to *the LORD's Christ*, we may understand that, because the sacrifice of His Christ abolished such manners from His Father's Faith, these ministers "are the enemies of the cross of Christ: whose end is destruction, whose God is their belly, and whose glory is in their shame, who mind earthly things."[1739] This is why "God hath not given us the spirit of fear; but of power, and of love, and of a sound mind."[1740] Wherefore John, suspecting that many elders feared to place themselves under the rule of the Spirit's learning, wrote, "There is no fear in love,"[1741] and, "These things have I written unto you concerning them that seduce you."[1742]

20. Because of fear; of inward fear for the unknown result of faith, of a fear of the then pagan ministers and philosophers, and of a fear of the Roman government; the early church was falling away from heaven's throne religion. And aside from their failing heart, debates and divisions were flourishing among their various camps, for the elders of the churches wanted to be that head bishop above their members and colleagues, making it necessary for them to hear, "No man taketh this honour unto himself, but he that is called of God, as was Aaron. So also Christ glorified not himself to be made an high priest; but he that said unto him, Thou art my Son, to day have I begotten thee. As he saith also in another place, Thou art a priest for ever after the order of Melchis'edec."[1743] Church

---

1739 Philippians 3:18
1740 2 Timothy 1:7
1741 1 John 4:18
1742 1 John 2:26
1743 Hebrews 5:4-6

elders needed to hear, "Be mindful of the words which were spoken before by the holy prophets, and of the commandment of us the apostles,"[1744] for Paul tried to warn them of the spirit advancing within them by referencing the mind of past ministers mishandling the LORD's name, saying of ancient ministers, "Backbiters, haters of God, despiteful, proud, boasters, inventors of evil things, disobedient to parents, without understanding, covenantbreakers, without natural affection, implacable, unmerciful: who knowing the judgment of God, that they which commit such things are worthy of death, not only do the same, but have pleasure in them that do them."[1745]

21. Herein it was necessary to remind them, "Ye were as sheep going astray; but are now returned unto the Shepherd and Bishop of your souls."[1746] If these were once astray, it is that they were once contrary to heaven's right manners, making it needful for them to hear, "Ye who sometimes were far off are made night by the blood of Christ." [1747]All who should come after the Spirit's first apostles; which is all of us; are truly pagans and Gentiles by birth and heritage, yet it is that by exercising faith on the virtue of the name and merits of "the last Adam";[1748] the LORD's High Priest; through His heavenly ministry "we have boldness and access with confidence by the faith of him"[1749] unto the LORD His Father for "the spirit of wisdom and revelation in the knowledge of him."[1750] If indeed there is access to the Father, then that means there is a Temple and an administration by which He is to be reached, for like as "the first covenant had also ordinances of divine service, and

---

1744 2 Peter 3:2
1745 Romans 1:30-32
1746 1 Peter 1:25
1747 Ephesians 2:13
1748 1 Corinthians 15:45
1749 Ephesians 3:12
1750 Ephesians 1:17

a worldly sanctuary,"[1751] so under the new covenant we have a Minister of the heavenly Sanctuary, which is why the LORD's Spirit "hath raised us up together, and made us sit together in heavenly places in Christ."[1752]

22. This Christ "gave himself for our sins, that he might deliver us,"[1753] but deliver us where? If "we have a great high priest, that is passed into the heavens,"[1754] is it not then become an eternal fact that we too are to find our conversation passed into this same Place? If "Christ our passover is sacrificed for us,"[1755] we evince that His name is no means for passing over by our strict reliance to what is nailed to that tree on earth, for He "abolished in his flesh the enmity, even the law of commandments contained in ordinances."[1756] For this cause we bless the LORD and Father of this Christ, "who hath delivered us from the power of darkness, and hath translated us into the kingdom of his dear Son."[1757]

23. His Christ confesses, "My kingdom is not of this world,"[1758] for within the LORD's heavenly Building rests "the kingdom of Christ and of God"[1759] with the Spirit's Minister as "the mediator of the new covenant."[1760] The reformer is entered in to this Building through faith on this Priest's name, and by the power and wisdom of His LORD's Spirit, to become a citizen and member of "the city of the living God, the heavenly Jerusalem,"[1761] and of "the general assembly and church of the

---

[1751] Hebrews 9:1
[1752] Ephesians 2:6
[1753] Galatians 1:4
[1754] Hebrews 4:14
[1755] 1 Corinthians 5:7
[1756] Ephesians 2:15
[1757] Colossians 1:13
[1758] John 18:36
[1759] Ephesians 5:5
[1760] Hebrews 12:24
[1761] Hebrews 12:22

firstborn,"[1762] where they have "such an high priest, who is set on the right hand of the throne of the Majesty in the heavens; a minister of the sanctuary, and of the true tabernacle, which the Lord pitched, and not man."[1763] Within this Sanctuary is "such an high priest who became us,"[1764] "who is consecrated for evermore,"[1765] who "is able also to save them to the uttermost that come unto God by him, seeing he ever liveth to make intercession for them."[1766]

24. Upon a sober and sincere reception of the Spirit's doctrine, the believer is taken into this Place that their reconciliation to the Godhead may be made perfect, and "perfect, as pertaining to the conscience."[1767] As of old there were "ordinances of divine service, and a worldly sanctuary,"[1768] "in which were offered both gifts and sacrifices,"[1769] so there is also a true City and Church above the earth, "whose builder and maker is God,"[1770] and wherein, for the doer of the Spirit's judgment, are ordained "ordinances of justice"[1771] "to offer up spiritual sacrifices, acceptable to God by Jesus Christ."[1772]

1762 Hebrews 12:23
1763 Hebrews 8:1,2
1764 Hebrews 7:26
1765 Hebrews 7:28
1766 Hebrews 7:25
1767 Hebrews 9:9
1768 Hebrews 9:1
1769 Hebrews 9:9
1770 Hebrews 11:10
1771 Isaiah 58:2
1772 1 Peter 2:5

12

Justification's Acknowledged Character

1. Says our High Priest, "The Father himself loveth you,"[1773] but how and why? He continues, "Because ye have loved me, and have believed that I came out from God."[1774] How is it that one may experience His Father's kindness? He says, "Have believed that I came out from God."[1775] Why is it that we are cared for by His Father? He says, "Because ye have loved me."[1776] For this cause we are counseled, "He that loveth me shall be loved of my Father,"[1777] and, "If a man love me, he will keep my words.[1778]

1773 John 16:27
1774 John 14:21
1775 John 14:21
1776 John 14:21
1777 John 14:21
1778 John 14:23

2. In order to be "loved" of the Spirit, right love must be given to the Spirit. "Because thou desiredst me,"[1779] says our Priest, "My Father 'had pity on thee.'"[1780] Is this a lie? "That he might be just, and the justifier of him which believeth in Jesus,"[1781] it was the LORD His Father who ordained "his righteousness";[1782] the righteousness of His Son's name; "for the remission of sins."[1783]

3. How is this "love" pronounced to us? It is exposed by the gift of His Son's praise, in that from believing on and actively investigating the name of His Son, the pleasure of His mediation will be given by active faith on the hope of that intercession, which hope is "even the righteousness of God which is by faith of Jesus Christ unto all and upon all them that believe."[1784] A longing to silence self-righteousness and self-sufficiency to pick up the consolation offered by His name will secure the blessing and attention of the Father to our inward parts. "Because you love my name," says this Christ; that is, because you have cherished the knowledge and understanding of my ministry; "the wisdom and power of my Father will recover your heart. You accepting my priesthood's good intention will erase from your mind 'imaginations, and every high thing that exalteth itself against the knowledge of God,'[1785] and 'because I live, ye shall live also.'"[1786] Our Priest counsels us to believe on "Him," and this is not advice to lethargically or sensually accept the fleshly person of a man as our confidence. The "I" and the "me" that are mentioned speak of no direct

---

1779 Matthew 18:32
1780 Mathew 18:32
1781 Romans 3:26
1782 Romans 3:25
1783 Romans 3:25
1784 Romans 3:22
1785 2 Corinthians 10:5
1786 John 14:19

reference to flesh, but to His doctrine, even as He says, "He that rejecteth me, and receiveth not my words,"[1787] and, "If a man love me, he will keep my words,"[1788] and, "If ye abide in me, and my words abide in you."[1789] To love "Him" is to learn of and do the sayings of His Father's Spirit, which, if we diligently and soberly do, because words are firstly mental, will result in the eyes of our understanding being enlightened.[1790] This is why He says, "He that loveth me not keepeth not my sayings."[1791]

4. It is for this reason that He says, "Be ye therefore perfect, even as your Father which is in heaven is perfect,"[1792] but one must ask, "How can I be as perfect as the Majesty of His mediation?" We are to be "perfect, as pertaining to the conscience,"[1793] and in order to obtain such a conversation, His Spirit's voice must "purge your conscience from dead works to serve the living God."[1794] This purging is "the kindness and love of God our Saviour towards man,"[1795] allowing us to understand that the Father's manner of love is demonstrated to our inward person and is fallen upon our understanding. So long as we personally examine and do the name of His Son's knowledge, the Spirit of the Father will educate our heart that we "might be filled with the knowledge of his will in all wisdom and spiritual understanding";[1796] this is the kingdom and righteousness of His Spirit. To "love one another"[1797] is to "comfort

---

1787 John 12:48
1788 John 14:23
1789 John 15:7
1790 Ephesians 1:18
1791 John 14:24
1792 Matthew 5:48
1793 Hebrews 9:9
1794 Hebrews 9:14
1795 Titus 3:4
1796 Colossians 1:9
1797 1 Thessalonians 4:9

yourselves together, and edify one another,"[1798] and the "love" of the Spirit is in edifying the spirit of the mind for dressing and perfecting our personal religion to the LORD His Father.

5. For this cause our Father says, concerning a right conversation, "Perfect through my comeliness, which I had put upon thee."[1799] What is this comeliness, or loving-kindness, that only He beautifies our mind and character with? He says, "I clothed thee also with broidered work,"[1800] and, "I girded thee about with fine linen,"[1801] "for the fine linen is the righteousness of saints,"[1802] "And their righteousness is of me, saith the LORD."[1803] The only way that religiously erroneous men and women may be considered "perfect" in the sight of the LORD is by His own name and righteousness within their conscience and covering the body of their ignorance, and He pronounces this covering by saying, "My righteousness is near; my salvation is gone forth,"[1804] which "righteousness" He states by saying, "A law shall proceed from me."[1805] Thus, by dressing the organs of the heart and mind with "the law of the Spirit of life,"[1806] His Spirit will edify the inwards "to present you holy and unblameable and unreproveable in his sight."[1807]

6. Now, it is a depressing thought to consider the complexity of the human heart in relation to its natural rebellion against the LORD's voice, to then think on the highness of obtaining His manner of righteousness. The LORD's new will states

---

1798 1 Thessalonians 5:11
1799 Ezekiel 16:14
1800 Ezekiel 16:10
1801 Ezekiel 16:10
1802 Revelation 19:8
1803 Isaiah 54:17
1804 Isaiah 51:5
1805 Isaiah 51:4
1806 Romans 8:2
1807 Colossians 1:22

the creation of a new heart and mind absolutely keeping and dressing the conversation by every word that has ever fallen out of His mouth, for He promises, "I will put my spirit within you, and cause you to walk in my statutes, and ye shall keep my judgments, and do them."[1808] This is "the mystery of his will, according to his good pleasure which he hath purposed in himself,"[1809] and it is after the birth of a "new man, which after God is created."[1810] Now, in the beginning, "the Word was with God, and the Word was God,"[1811] and today, the Word is still God. To be created after "God" is to be conceived after the LORD's Word, and seeing as how "God is a Spirit,"[1812] this birth can only commence within the spirit of the mind, which is why "that which is born of the Spirit is spirit."[1813]

7. Would the LORD utter any thing to have that thing never come to pass? Or would the living God set a law and a judgment that cannot be followed, or that He cannot create us for? The LORD's Christ confessed the God of His conversation by saying, "I know him, and keep His saying,"[1814] for this Man blessed His conversation with the saying of His Father's Spirit, so much so that He confesses, "I know that his commandment is life everlasting."[1815] His Christ kept His Word, and the end of that course was knowledge of the Word's LORD and Father, which is why our Priest says, "I have kept my Father's commandments, and abide in his love."[1816] It is our Father's will to correct our manners of worship and service to His name,

---

1808 Ezekiel 36:27
1809 Ephesians 1:9
1810 Ephesians 4:24
1811 John 1:1
1812 John 4:24
1813 John 3:6
1814 John 8:55
1815 John 12:50
1816 John 15:10

and it may seem as though we are too pitiful or ignorant to soberly reverence Him, or to learn His mind, but this is why He first labored through Abraham, for when this man "had patiently endured, he obtained the promise."[1817] Likewise we are promised a new heart and mind through His Son's mediation, and it is our responsibility to personally acquaint our mind with His voice, which is why we are counseled, "Be renewed in the spirit of your mind."[1818]

8. Herein is the reason why it was necessary that the flesh of God's Man find itself passed away on the tree, "for he that is hanged is accursed of God."[1819] As His flesh is upon that tree and passed away, this body represents the fact that legal religious bills handwritten by priests and elders have given up their ghost from out of the Spirit's higher learning. On that tree, this Man represents the fact that legal religious laws and commandments are accursed by the Word and His LORD, for, today, the Spirit of this LORD will engrave His name upon our heart and mind by an instrument "written not with ink, but with the Spirit of the living God."[1820] Because this manner of creation is not physical or natural, it must find itself accomplished within the spirit of the mind through "the washing of water by the word."[1821]

9. For "if there had been a law given which could have given life, verily righteousness should have been by the law,"[1822] but "Christ hath redeemed us from the curse of the law (of the handwritten code of priests and elders), being made a curse for us: for it is written, Cursed is every one that hangeth on

---

1817 Hebrews 6:15
1818 Ephesians 4:23
1819 Deuteronomy 21:23
1820 2 Corinthians 3:3
1821 Ephesians 5:26
1822 Galatians 3:21

a tree."[1823] All that was anciently prescribed under types and figures, all that was recorded and written for instruction to follow, all of the "precepts, statutes, and laws, by the hand of Moses";[1824] whether that ancient man or any modern *one* from any age; awards none who does them *righteousness*, or else our LORD's Spirit is a liar, for it says, "Through this man";[1825] through the Faith of His Son's name; "is preached unto you the forgiveness of sins: and by him all that believe are justified from all things, from which ye could not be justified by the law of Moses,"[1826] which is why the first apostles collectively taught, "There is none other name under heaven given among men, whereby we must be saved."[1827] Again, a name is not physical, for, concerning "name," the Spirit says, "Thou holdest fast my name, and hast not denied my faith,"[1828] and, "Hast kept my word, and hast not denied my name."[1829] The "name" of the Word's Priest is the Faith of His mediation, and as the mind examines and proves the knowledge of His name, the understanding will find itself edified to love the LORD and Father of His ministry, "and this is love, that we walk after his commandments."[1830]

10. The entire point of the old will was to educate the people on how and why to keep the LORD's ten commandments, but the people perverted that manner, taking the written tradition of Moses to be the end of the LORD's intention for them. Such a flesh-based form of religion is nailed to the tree, opening up the person to learn of the opportunity to have the Spirit of this

---

1823 Galatians 3:13
1824 Nehemiah 9:14
1825 Acts 13:38
1826 Acts 13:38,39
1827 Acts 4:12
1828 Revelation 2:13
1829 Revelation 3:8
1830 2 John 1:6

LORD personally seal their heart to His throne, which sealing no tradition or commandment of self or of elders can accomplish, which is why Paul taught, concerning the name of God's Son diligent living within the mind, "All that believe are justified from all things, from which ye could not be justified by the law of Moses."[1831] The apostles observed Christian elders continuing that spirit of Moses' religion, and understanding that such a routine is now accursed by the *One* they profess to honor, the apostles said to them, "If ye be dead with Christ from the rudiments of the world, why, as though living in the world, are ye subject to ordinances...after the commandments and doctrines of men?"[1832]

11. The Spirit's law teaches liberty from the legal religious bill for personally advancing in creation's science, which science is the Spirit's righteousness, which righteousness will move the mind to say, "Why is my liberty judged of another man's conscience?"[1833] to then pick up the confession, "The law of the Spirit of life in Christ Jesus hath made me free from the law of sin and death."[1834] Heaven's new covenant promise demands the exercising of faith on the Spirit's law and commandment, but because the former manners of worship and service are undemanding, it is evident that "the law is not of faith."[1835] It takes no intelligent faith to do a religious charge, for, if I may capture *righteousness* from simply doing a commandment, then, whether I care for the commandment or not, I will do that commandment for *righteousness*, and am therefore *righteous* by the commandment. If I do the law of the elders, then I am *just*, for my faith is in the commandment, but

---

1831 Acts 13:39
1832 Colossians 2:20-22
1833 1 Corinthians 10:29
1834 Romans 8:2
1835 Galatians 3:12

if I fail to do the charge, then I have fallen away from what is *just*, for I deviate from the ordinance. But it is well to know that "whatsoever is not of faith is sin,"[1836] therefore if "the law is not of faith,"[1837] and if I devoutly revere the legal religious charge, then I plainly commit "sin" against the Spirit's new will and transgress the doctrine of His Son's name, seeing as how "no man is justified by the law in the sight of God."[1838] For this cause we are rather counseled, concerning heaven's Faith, "By his knowledge shall my righteous servant justify many."[1839]

12. Why then should these things of old have justified them that followed them? "Wherefore then serveth the law? It was added because of transgressions, till the seed should come to whom the promise was made."[1840] Moses' brand of religion was to last until the LORD's Christ should anoint His new manner by His passing on the tree, wherefore if we are subscribing to what is nailed to that tree; which is Moses' accursed brand of religion; then we plainly transgress the Spirit's will, for, "if I build again the things which I destroyed, I make myself a transgressor."[1841] This Paul writes because the passing flesh of God's Man abolishes the fashion of legal religious traditions from heaven's will, but the regeneration of God's Man witnesses to the fact "that we should serve in newness of spirit, and not in the oldness of the letter."[1842]

13. By that old routine, there was a figure of liberty from sin, in that those laws "sanctifieth to the purifying of the flesh,"[1843] leaving the inward man yet condemned without aid

---

[1836] Romans 14:23
[1837] Galatians 3:12
[1838] Galatians 3:11
[1839] Isaiah 53:11
[1840] Galatians 3:19
[1841] Galatians 2:18
[1842] Romans 7:6
[1843] Hebrews 9:13

to overcome its religious error. So we see that, in reality, there was no full work of spiritual redemption for the ones that participated in these ordinances, "because that the worshippers once purged should have had no more conscience for sins."[1844] Works of *justification* served their purpose "until the time of reformation,"[1845] for these rites and ordinances were ordained to serve as "our schoolmaster to bring us unto Christ";[1846] unto the knowledge of that Faith within the heavenly Sanctuary; "that we might be justified by faith"[1847] on the knowledge of that Faith within the heavenly Sanctuary. That "which stood only in meats and drinks, and divers washings, and carnal ordinances,"[1848] "in which were offered both gifts and sacrifices, that could not make him that did the service perfect, as pertaining to the conscience,"[1849] enclosed "the faith which should afterwards be revealed."[1850] That Faith is the Spirit's doctrine confessing the righteousness of His ministry as the only purifying judgment of redemption. Herein it is well to notice how such works under Moses' direction can only *purify* the conversation of the flesh, yet that will of the Spirit is ordained to "purge your conscience from dead works,"[1851] even from those same works used to *bless* the flesh.

14. For this cause, one professing Christ's name needs right knowledge of His name in order to benefit from both His Father and the ministry of His Spirit. This is why it is well to understand that image begets image and shadow begets original. Like as of old there were "ordinances of divine service,

---

1844 Hebrews 10:2
1845 Hebrews 9:10
1846 Galatians 3:24
1847 Galatians 3:24
1848 Hebrews 9:10
1849 Hebrews 9:9
1850 Galatians 3:23
1851 Hebrews 9:14

and a worldly sanctuary,"[1852] so too now "Christ is not entered into the holy places made with hands, which are the figures of the true; but into heaven itself, now to appear in the presence of God for us."[1853] The language of the apostle reveals that Christ Himself is today "a minister of the sanctuary, and of the true tabernacle, which the Lord pitched, and not man."[1854] The only way to be received into the congregation of this High Priest is to have the Spirit's righteousness over and within the conversation's conscience, which is why the Spirit "hath consecrated for us"[1855] "a new and living way"[1856] "through the veil, that is to say, his flesh,"[1857] or rather, "through the offering of the body of Jesus"[1858] "he hath perfected for ever them that are sanctified."[1859] By examining the Spirit's Faith, one is blessed to receive His righteousness, for "whom he justified, them he also glorified"[1860] with His same mind and ministry.

15. There is full hope and assurance for the one tired of their lame heart and paralyzed eyes. Yes the conscience needs the righteousness of the Father if the conversation would be perfect according to His standard, and for the possibility of this perfect desire rising up within any one, the Father sent His Son "to declare his righteousness, for the remission of sins,"[1861] that we might do the judgment that He preaches in order to obtain His Spirit's benevolent will. There is no thing that can be done to purchase this goodness unless the inwards are

---

1852 Hebrews 9:1
1853 Hebrews 9:24
1854 Hebrews 8:2
1855 Hebrews 10:20
1856 Hebrews 10:20
1857 Hebrews 10:20
1858 Hebrews 10:10
1859 Hebrews 10:14
1860 Romans 8:30
1861 Romans 3:25

baptized "through faith in his blood."[1862] If indeed we love this Christ, if the virtue of His name and merits should be taken into the soul's temple and treasured, it is that knowledge of His name will be given to alleviate our conversation's conscience from religious error. Therefore as you stand before the Word as new creatures of His Spirit, He will bring up your thoughts to match the image of His Son, and "shall also quicken your mortal bodies by his Spirit."[1863]

16. "Through sanctification of the Spirit"[1864] the mind will regain right conciseness to operate our faith's body. With the Spirit's Faith nourishing the conversation's heart, the personal religion does not stall or retard, for His name is given "to keep you from falling, and to present you faultless,"[1865] that the spirit of the mind may become that new ark holding His ten laws, and that the temple of the character may be established upon the ordinances of heaven-approved justice and charity.

17. The perfecting righteousness of the Father is given and is available by an experimental faith through the doctrine of His Son and Spirit. His Christ saying, "Be perfect," is just as if He says, "Take My righteousness, and take the commandment of my voice, for purging your faith's conscience," for one is "perfect, as pertaining to the conscience."[1866] In order for us to have that perfection pertaining to the inward man, it is that the Spirit's saying must become "high priest in things pertaining to God"[1867] for our conversation, for only then can we who are erroneous to heaven's right way confess, "I delight in the law of God after the inward man."[1868] Indeed "his Spirit in the inward

---

1862 Romans 3:25
1863 Romans 8:11
1864 1 Peter 1:2
1865 Jude 1:24
1866 Hebrews 9:9
1867 Hebrews 2:17
1868 Romans 7:22

man"[1869] is to awaken the eyes to life and regeneration by reformation, for "the Spirit is life because of righteousness,"[1870] and the Spirit is ordained to seal within the mind those precepts of "the word of righteousness,"[1871] certifying how it says, "All thy commandments are righteousness."[1872]

18. To be "loved" of the Father is to receive "the love of God, and the communion of the Holy Ghost,"[1873] to keep and dress the mind with His commandments, "for this is the love of God, that we keep his commandments."[1874] By doing creation's law and judgment, the reformer is blessed to receive the power and wisdom of that law's Spirit for grace to overcome sin against heaven's manners, for if there should be only forgiveness from error without creative power to rescue the conscience from spiritual error, and without a course for the mind to quit former patterns of thinking and feeling, then the act of God's Man is done in vain. But since we have a complete law of salvation through that blood of the new covenant, "Be ye transformed by the renewing of your mind,"[1875] we are counseled.

19. As the believer holds dear to heaven's Faith, it is that they will find their conversation adopted into the Spirit's assembly to commune with Him for newness of heart and mind. Written in the log of membership within the LORD's heavenly Church are those who subscribe and appropriate the name of His Son to their conversation as their Savior and Counselor. God's Man "is set on the right hand of the throne of the Majesty in the heavens,"[1876] shedding light on the fact that His reformer

---

1869 Ephesians 3:16
1870 Romans 8:10
1871 Hebrews 5:13
1872 Psalms 119:172
1873 2 Corinthians 13:14
1874 1 John 5:3
1875 Romans 12:2
1876 Hebrews 8:1

is joined to His Father just as much as He is joined to them. If this is not so, then our Priest lies when saying, "I ascend unto my Father and your Father; and to my God, and your God."[1877] All things concerning the LORD and Father of this Christ are as much of a concern to the one believing on His name as they are to His heavenly ministry. So as "God anointed Jesus of Nazareth with the Holy Ghost,"[1878] He says to all who should trust on His Spirit, "Ye shall receive power, after that the Holy Ghost is come upon you."[1879] For, "being by the right hand of God exalted, and having received of the Father the promise of the Holy Ghost, he hath shed forth this"[1880] blessing that our conversation might be "sanctified by the Holy Ghost,"[1881] purified "by the power of the Spirit of God."[1882]

20. The believer is "conformed to the image of His Son"[1883] "through sanctification of the Spirit and belief of the truth."[1884] In reality, the one professing loyalty to His Son's heavenly doctrine is "sanctified by God the Father,"[1885] which is why "we have received a commandment from the Father."[1886] Because "that which is born of the Spirit is spirit,"[1887] sanctification is wholly for the spirit of the mind, which sanctification is the Spirit's righteousness. Without obtaining the Spirit's righteousness by an experimental faith "through the redemption that is in Christ,"[1888] there will be no reception of "the promise

---

1877 John 20:17
1878 Acts 10:38
1879 Acts 1:8
1880 Acts 2:33
1881 Romans 15:16
1882 Romans 15:19
1883 Romans 8:29
1884 2 Thessalonians 2:13
1885 Jude 1:1
1886 2 John 1:4
1887 John 3:6
1888 Romans 3:24

of the Spirit through faith."[1889] The believer needs to personally know, and to also sincerely believe the fact of redemption's inward work, if they should excel in fellowship with the Father's Spirit, for the counsel of truth teaches "that we might be justified by the faith of Jesus Christ,"[1890] and by no thing else. Such counsel allows us to understand that if sanctification arises by the Faith of God's Man, that it is of great importance to comprehend just what the Faith of the LORD's Christ is, which is why the apostle counseled the elders, "Be ye not unwise, but understanding what the will of the Lord is."[1891]

21."The promise by faith of Jesus Christ might be given to them that believe"[1892] to "receive abundance of grace and of the gift of righteousness,"[1893] for without rightly applying self to righteousness' offering, the conversation will offer for *righteousness*. It is that after the heart has set itself to occupy faith's ground, that being faithful holders of a benevolent commandment in confidence of the end of that saying, the LORD's Spirit will be given to work into the soul temple what that done by hand and flesh can never do. The fullness of the power and wisdom of the Spirit is given for mental and moral recovery, which fullness contains the creative material of grace to erase the knowledge of sin from the conscience. Again, this is our LORD and Father's manner of "love," even the "mystery of his will, according to his good pleasure which he hath purposed in himself."[1894] As "the Spirit of truth, which proceedeth from the Father,"[1895] is "life" because of righteousness' course and

---

1889 Galatians 3:14
1890 Galatians 2:16
1891 Ephesians 5:17
1892 Galatians 3:22
1893 Romans 5:17
1894 Ephesians 1:9
1895 John 15:26

effect,[1896] it is that within the Spirit is "the grace of life"[1897] that we may acknowledge and forward what, according to the Father, is "good."

22. His Christ suffered in the flesh and died the death of the tree to confirm to us what is just, to the end man would find harmony with His Father's throne from honoring the precepts of His doctrine. The Spirit's witness once testified, "He whom God hath sent speaketh the words of God,"[1898] and of old Moses said of the event at Si'nai, "I stood between the LORD and you at that time, to shew you the word of the LORD."[1899] The commandment of the Son is the saying of this same LORD's Spirit, for the Spirit's good will is "according to his good pleasure which he hath purposed in himself."[1900] Therefore it is not *Moses* that rules the Spirit's dominion, but it is "Jesus the mediator of the new covenant,"[1901] who will build up the one "that cometh unto God by him,"[1902] that is, that seeks to honor heaven's Word by the faith and confidence of His name. This is the Spirit's manner of love, "and this is love, that we walk after his commandments."[1903]

23. Again, who is the believer gathered to by their High Priest? It says, "That come unto God by him,"[1904] for He indeed suffered "that he might bright us to God."[1905] Now, to whom was the ordained priesthood of the Levites consecrated? The LORD said, "The Levites are mine."[1906] Again, the Spirit said,

---

1896 Romans 8:10
1897 1 Peter 3:7
1898 John 3:24
1899 Deuteronomy 5:5
1900 Ephesians 1:9
1901 Hebrews 12:24
1902 Hebrews 7:25
1903 2 John 1:6
1904 Hebrews 7:25
1905 1 Peter 3:18
1906 Numbers 3:12

"I have taken your brethren the Levites from among the children of Israel: to you they are given as a gift for the LORD, to do the service of the tabernacle of the congregation";[1907] "in the tabernacle of the congregation, and to make an atonement for the children of Israel."[1908] Why was this priesthood given to Israel? It was known that "perfection were by the Levit'ical priesthood,"[1909] for by them, those things concerning the LORD's voice were to be carried out to educate on the LORD's ten precepts, which precepts every ordinance, statue, and judgment, returned to. Now, that of old served its purpose "having a shadow of good things to come,"[1910] but today His Christ is become "an high priest of good things to come."[1911] Just as that of old served as a vehicle to educate on the nature of "sin" in relation to the violation of the LORD's precepts, so now that true Priesthood within the heavenly Temple, and headed by the LORD's true High Priest, serves to bring His congregation to the same respect, and no longer by the works of the flesh, as of old, but by an experimental faith on His name.

24. It should be understood how it also says that the Levites were given to make atonement before the LORD, for no other type of priest or ministry satisfied atonement to the LORD. This is why Scripture tells us that it is through His High Priest that "we have now received the atonement,"[1912] that is, "We were reconciled to God by the death of his Son"[1913] "that we might live through him."[1914] Scripture's language conceals

---

[1907] Numbers 18:6
[1908] Numbers 8:19
[1909] Hebrews 7:11
[1910] Hebrews 10:1
[1911] Hebrews 9:11
[1912] Romans 5:11
[1913] Romans 5:10
[1914] 1 John 4:9

the fact of reconciliation, yet the believer does not hear this and quit learning of how to maintain reconciliation, believing that *Christ* has somehow fully handled their inward condition, or that His offering has somehow opened up a lazy route to *recovery*. We all must hear, and will hear upon our honest reception of His voice, "Leaving the principles of the doctrine of Christ, let us go on unto perfection."[1915]

25. After the counsel of spiritual ransom is believed on, know that "ye were sealed with that holy Spirit of promise"[1916] to pick up the demeanor, "I have suffered loss of all things"[1917] "that I may know him, and the power of his resurrection."[1918] The believer is conceived "by the word of God, which liveth and abideth for ever,"[1919] that they may know, "He that doeth the will of God abideth for ever."[1920] By that righteousness of "the law of Christ,"[1921] the believer has boldness to approach the Word from admitting their conversation to a living faith in that law's expected benevolence. No thing, concerning the LORD's hope for us, has changed, except that now the shadow of redemption has met the figure from which it is drawn. As there were ordinances and precepts to bring the doer of that tradition to a higher knowledge of the LORD's character to love His name, so today, by the doctrine of His Christ, the one actively examining the name of His intercession will come into personal contact with His LORD's Spirit to have His laws engraved within their conversation's conscience. Is this not what is promised to us? Isn't it written, "I will give them one

---

1915 Hebrews 6:1
1916 Ephesians 1:13
1917 Philippians 3:8
1918 Philippians 3:10
1919 1 Peter 1:23
1920 1 John 2:17
1921 Galatians 6:2

heart, and one way, that they may fear me for ever,"[1922] and, "I will put my law in their inward parts, and write it in their hearts; and will be their God, and they shall be my people"?[1923]

26. That of old was an established waymark that led to reverencing His throne's Ten Commandments, and the Faith of His Son is yet established to do the same thing by "a better and an enduring substance"[1924] poured forth from the Spirit under "a more excellent ministry,"[1925] for this Christ "is the mediator of a better covenant, which was established upon better promises."[1926] "Verily the first covenant had also ordinances of divine service, and a worldly sanctuary,"[1927] yet by the death of the LORD's Christ, "he taketh away the first, that he may establish the second."[1928] Through the new covenant is "given unto us exceeding great and precious promises"[1929] for our "holy conversation and godliness,"[1930] and from exercising faith on the knowledge acquired by proving His name, we may rightly serve the living LORD God in the spirit of our mind, as opposed to traditions and ordinances perceived to be a means for proof of *loyalty* and *devotion*. This is why our Priest counsels, "The true worshippers shall worship the Father in spirit and in truth: for the Father seeketh such to worship him."[1931]

27. The apostle John saw the church turning to "the works of their hands"[1932] for *justification*, and because he knew that only One was foreshadowed to be that Preeminent Minister

---

1922 Jeremiah 32:39
1923 Jeremiah 31:33
1924 Hebrews 10:34
1925 Hebrews 8:6
1926 Hebrews 8:6
1927 Hebrews 9:1
1928 Hebrews 10:9
1929 2 Peter 1:4
1930 2 Peter 3:11
1931 John 4:23
1932 Revelation 9:20

and High Priest of man for the Word's righteousness; which baptism is a "circumcision made without hands";[1933] he told them, "We have an advocate with the Father."[1934]

28. There is only One called after Aaron's office, "and no man taketh this honour unto himself, but he that is called of God, as was Aaron."[1935] There is only One "after the similitude of Melchis'edec,"[1936] for "Christ glorified not himself to be made an high priest; but he that said unto him, Thou art my Son, to day have I begotten thee."[1937] John saw that the church, because of adhering to religious error condemned by the passing, regenerating, and priestly anointing of the LORD's Christ, lusted after a place and a position not given to her, for in her heart brewed the spirit of that disappointment "who opposeth an exalteth himself above all that is called God, or that is worshipped; so that he sitteth in the temple of God, shewing himself that he is God."[1938]

29. Without the Spirit, the church existed by a spirit that was strange to the Spirit's religion. A new doctrine was forming within the church, and with commandments and traditions of a faith that would teach *salvation* only through her dogma, and with regard to the bishops, that their charge was *divine*. Because he discerned the making of a most dreadful beast, the apostle counseled, "He who loveth God love his brother also,"[1939] for the Spirit's love is seen by how He passed away from *righteousness* to establish a right course for all to know, and John knew this manner of edifying consolation convicted the heart to understand that "we ought also to lay down our

---

1933 Colossians 2:11
1934 1 John 2:1
1935 Hebrews 5:4
1936 Hebrews 7:15
1937 Hebrews 5:5
1938 2 Thessalonians 2:4
1939 1 John 4:21

lives for the brethren."[1940] God's Man on the tree, resurrected, and then brought up in to the Spirit's Sanctuary, represents a passing away from one religious conversation and the regeneration of a more benevolent manner wholly devoted to the Word for personal edification. For, observing elders not only staying in manners now accursed by the offering of this Word, but also creating a religious tradition by that condemnation, the apostle was moved to write, in order for them to see their wrong course, "In that he died, he died unto sin once: but in that he liveth, he liveth unto God."[1941]

30. The Spirit's labor for man did not end at the cross, or at Him purged from that tree to be found in a grave. The credit for reconciliation by faith on salvation's fact is free for all who will diligently investigate the name of that Priest within the heavenly Sanctuary, for after that reconciliation is accepted, and after the individual makes a personal covenant with the Word of that reconciliation, then the work of righteousness begins with He who "ever liveth to make intercession for them."[1942] We have full and unadulterated access, by our involvement with law of His mediation, to all of the riches for spiritual wisdom and knowledge concerning the will of His LORD and Father for our mental and moral wellbeing. From simple and diligent faith on the Spirit's sacrifice, the LORD's Priest will impute His virtue onto the believer that they may be given into the hands of His Spirit to be raised in figure as He is, and with the same mind of character that is in Him. This is why it is written, "Like as Christ was raised up from the dead by the glory of the Father, even we also should walk in newness of life. For if we have been

---

1940 1 John 3:16
1941 Romans 6:10
1942 Hebrews 7:25

planted together in the likeness of his death, we shall be also in the likeness of his resurrection."[1943]

31. What distinguishes the sincere doer of heaven's will from the liar is that their existence is not devoured by a mind forcing a legal religious policy to establish *righteousness*. Their energies will not be spent on doing this or that for *justification*, or for creating this or that for *piety*, which error is proof that they are without the teaching and sealing Spirit of the LORD's new covenant promise, for it is evident that they do reject personally investigating the Faith of His Son's name. Our thoughts and feelings are "to be conformed to the image of his Son,"[1944] and this is why the Captain of our salvation says, "By this shall all men know that ye are my disciples, if ye have love one to another."[1945] The clearest proof of the Spirit's "love" working within our spirit is witnessed by the counsel, "Thou shalt in any wise rebuke thy neighbour, and not suffer sin upon him."[1946] If today, even as it was of old, every legal religious "law is not is not of faith,"[1947] and if "whatsoever is not of faith is sin,"[1948] then I, by not only adhering to what is "sin," but also encouraging others to do the same, do not reveal my stewardship to be under wings of the Spirit's Son. Wherefore the apostle, observing Christian ministers doing contrary to the kindness preached by God's Priest, wrote to them, "Let us not therefore judge one another any more,"[1949] that is, "Let us no longer hold dominion over the conscience of any one any longer."

32. True godly benevolence is a revelation that both the LORD's Faith and Ten Commandments are in harmony with

---

1943 Romans 6:4,5
1944 Romans 8:29
1945 John 13:35
1946 Leviticus 19:17
1947 Galatians 3:12
1948 Romans 14:23
1949 Romans 14:13

the personal religion. Such communion with one another can only be had if redemption's learning quenches the spirit of self-righteousness. As the church held dear to its political ambitions to support its spurious theory of being the *kingdom of God* on earth, she forsook the counsel, "Let us consider one another to provoke unto love and to good works,"[1950] and, "Let no corrupt communication proceed out of your mouth, but that which is good to the use of edifying."[1951]

33. As did the Christian church; and as she and her daughters continue to do; so too the heart may organize itself as an impregnable empire if the knowledge and virtue of the Spirit's Son isn't applied to. Because that which expresses the living God's name was put aside for that which emphasized self-justification, the church did contrary to heaven's good tidings and left off unity and faithful compassion. To the church, *righteousness* came from laws of circumcision, from feasts, from days and ordinances, from *sabbaths*, which spirit, because of its intercourse with enmity, eventually demanded obedience to doctrines backed by civil Roman authority. As time passed away from the apostle John, the church would serve as the conscience of its members, for by joining to the State of Rome, she became a crowd of strangers to heaven's goodness. To say that *piety* found expression from such things was to call the Spirit and High Priest of creation a liar, and because the church existed in religious manners that halted sanctification by an active and experimental faith, there was plague among her elders and church members, for the Spirit promised her; for her continued spiritual negligence; "I will cast her into a bed, and them that commit adultery with her into great tribulation, except they repent of their deeds. And I will kill her children

---

1950 Hebrews 10:24
1951 Ephesians 4:29

with death."[1952] For this cause, to this day, "God hath given them the spirit of slumber,"[1953] for their fathers "repented not of the works of their hands."[1954]

34. Yet remember the position of Aaron, how that during a gross plague he "stood between the dead and the living; and the plague was stayed."[1955] The congregation of the heavenly assembly of "Aaron"; that is, of Christ the LORD's Chief Minister and Son; is without plague, for "in the way of righteousness is life; and in the pathway thereof is no death."[1956] What is it that this Christ says concerning "death"? Doesn't He counsel, "If a man keep my saying, he shall never taste of death"?[1957] Our primary responsibility is to seek first the Spirit's righteousness, and because He says, "I leave the world, and go to the Father,"[1958] must we fail to understand that it is our assignment to "seek those things which are above, where Christ sitteth on the right hand of God"?[1959] The only Faith without religious error is found within the heavenly Sanctuary, which is why it says, "Thy way, O God, is in the Sanctuary."[1960] For, by adhering to that nailed to the tree, Christian elders prevented themselves and their congregations from taking the body of the Spirit's knowledge to be that means for their passing over from a conversation now negligent before the Word, to one ultimately drawing the Spirit's benevolence. Such elders suffered sin against the LORD's name on themselves

---

1952 Revelation 2:22
1953 Romans 11:8
1954 Revelation 9:20
1955 Numbers 16:48
1956 Proverbs 12:28
1957 John 8:52
1958 John 16:28
1959 Colossians 3:1
1960 Psalm 77:13

and others, allowing us to understand their rebellion against heaven's doctrine.

35. The name of the Father justifies the ministry of His High Priest, and the professed of His Son's Faith will be known by their communion with that mind resting within the doctrine of His mediation. Therefore let the one touched by the Spirit's sacrifice know and remember, "Ye are washed, but ye are sanctified, but ye are justified in the name of the Lord Jesus, and by the Spirit of our God."[1961] This "God sent his only begotten Son into the world"[1962] "to declare his righteousness for the remission of sins,"[1963] "and hereby we know that he abideth in us, by the Spirit which he hath given us."[1964] "If any man sin, we have an advocate with the Father"[1965] "who is gone into heaven, and is on the right hand of God; angels and authorities and powers being made subject unto him."[1966]

[1961] 1 Corinthians 6:11
[1962] 1 John 4:9
[1963] Romans 3:25
[1964] 1 John 3:24
[1965] 1 John 2:1
[1966] 1 Peter 3:22

13

Transgression's Fever

1. Paul once wrote, "It hath been declared unto me of you, my brethren...that there are contentions among you,"[1967] and although writing to the Corinthian elders, he was speaking to every minister of the Corinthian spirit. For their mind of conversation was so bad that he wrote, "There is fornication among you, and such fornication as is not so much as named among the Gentiles."[1968]

2. The apostles saw, among church elders, the saying again finding fulfillment, "Hath a nation changed their gods, which are yet no gods? but my people have changed their glory for that which doth not profit,"[1969] therefore Paul counseled, "Cast off the works of darkness...rioting and drunkenness... chambering and wantonness...strife and envying,"[1970] and,

---

[1967] 1 Corinthians 1:11
[1968] 1 Corinthians 5:1
[1969] Jeremiah 2:11
[1970] Romans 13:12-14

"Fornication, and all uncleanness, or covetousness, let it not be once named among you."[1971] In the place of such strange and unprofitable works, he counseled, "Put on the armour of light,"[1972] that is, "Put ye on the Lord Jesus Christ."[1973] John also observed the same contrary spirit within Christian elders, and wrote, "This then is the message which we have heard of him, and declare unto you, that God is light,"[1974] for the armor of light that Paul would have believers put on is "even the righteousness of God."

3. Because there was a failure among Christian leaders to properly and personally appropriate the law of Christ's voice to their personal religion, the churches existed in spiritual confusion. If indeed the elders had submitted to wearing the acceptable garment of heaven's doctrine over the spirit of their mind, they would have known that such virtue educates against "provision for the flesh, to fulfill the lusts thereof."[1975] Instead of maintaining the mind of the members of the conversation through unprofitable religious policies, "fulfilling the desires of the flesh and of the mind,"[1976] Paul counseled them, "Fulfill the law of Christ,"[1977] which law John plainly pronounced for their observation, saying, "This is the message that ye heard from the beginning, that we should love one another."[1978]

4. The Corinthian spirit compelled Paul to write, "Ye are full, now ye are rich";[1979] "ye are strong; ye are honourable,

---

1971 Ephesians 5:3
1972 Romans 13:12
1973 Romans 13:14
1974 1 John 1:5
1975 Romans 13:14
1976 Ephesians 2:3
1977 Galatians 6:2
1978 1 John 3:11
1979 1 Corinthians 4:8

but we are despised";[1980] therefore he challenged the churches, "We then that are strong ought to bear the infirmities of the weak,"[1981] for the law and doctrine of Christ teaches, "Bear ye one another's burdens."[1982] Yet the church could not hear the end of the counsel because she could not follow the example that taught, "Israel which followed after the law of righteousness, hath not attained to the law of righteousness. Wherefore? Because they sought it not by faith."[1983]

5. Again Paul tried to awaken their understanding to their doctrinal error, saying, in reference to them under the former will that stumbled at the LORD's commandment for them, "They being ignorant of God's righteousness, and going about to establish their own righteousness, have not submitted themselves to the righteousness of God."[1984]

6. Paul uses this illustration because he saw the church falling after the same example of unbelief as his own natural kin. Throughout their generations, Israel had "a zeal for God, but not according to knowledge,"[1985] for the Spirit testified of them, "Full well ye reject the commandment of God, that ye may keep your own tradition."[1986] The Spirit's apostles were seeing, among Christian elders, a movement to form hierarchies and ranks of positions, along with doctrines and traditions that removed the mind from pure labors to procure repentance for spiritual recovery, in exchange for that which gratified the ambitions of an unconverted heart. The word was fulfilling, "Remember ye the words which were spoken before of the apostles of our Lord Jesus Christ; how that they told you there should be mockers in

---

1980 1 Corinthians 4:10
1981 Romans 15:1
1982 Galatians 6:2
1983 Romans 9:31,32
1984 Romans 10:3
1985 Romans 10:2
1986 Mark 7:9

the last time, who should walk after their own ungodly lusts."[1987] The church was moving from "the righteousness which is of faith"[1988] to "works of righteousness,"[1989] "the works of their own hands,"[1990] for *faith's righteousness*. The result of such an exchange of fellowship; that is, exchanging "fellowship of the Spirit"[1991] to commune with "lasciviousness, lusts, excess of wine, revelings, banquetings, and abominable idolatries";[1992] so exposed their conversation that the apostle wrote, "If a man say, I love God, and hateth his brother, he is a liar,"[1993] and, "If any man have not the Spirit of Christ, he is none of his."[1994]

7. Persecution against the church by Jews and pagans under the Roman age had made her tired. When it came to heaven's assembly, all "perceived that they were unlearned and ignorant,"[1995] and Christian elders were feeling the backlash brought upon them because of the Spirit's Faith. For Paul wrote of the times, saying of his band, "We are made as the filth of the world, and are the offscouring of all things unto this day,"[1996] which is why John tried to console the church by saying, "Marvel not, my brethren, if the world hate you."[1997] Paul noticed how weariness rested among the ranks of the church, and so he counseled, "Bless them which persecute you: bless, and curse not."[1998] The apostles knew that all things happening; both in the church and without; were of the LORD's will for

---

1987 Jude 1:17,18
1988 Romans 9:30
1989 Titus 3:5
1990 Acts 7:41
1991 Philippians 2:1
1992 1 Peter 4:3
1993 1 John 4:20
1994 Romans 8:9
1995 Acts 4:13
1996 1 Corinthians 4:13
1997 1 John 3:13
1998 Romans 12:14

this denomination, for they would have Christian elders know, "Whom the Lord loveth he chasteneth,"[1999] "therefore the world knoweth us not, because it knew him not."[2000]

8. Knowing the despair that His believers should face, and also the frailty of the human heart, God's Man, looking into the future, counseled, "If the world hate you, ye know that it hated me before it hated you."[2001] To His soldiers, salvation's Captain still delivers the same counsel of old: "They have not rejected thee, but they have rejected me, that I should not reign over them."[2002] An unconsecrated heart will find injury against it in any form of persecution. A spirit without a personal religion blessed by the name of the Spirit's Son will, from a wearied state of mind, desire vengeance against what it perceives to be hostility against it, which is why Paul counseled them, "Avenge not yourselves, but rather give place unto wrath: for it is written, Vengeance is mine; I will repay, saith the Lord."[2003] Because ministers had allowed the mind of Christ's mediation to fail from within them, and with also that communion of the Father's Spirit, every attack brought against the church was taken personally and stored within a place where wisdom and understanding should have dwelt by faith.

9. The elders remembered scenes such as those "which came to pass in the days of Claudius Caesar";[2004] that same Claudius who was the uncle of Caligula; and how false Jews banded together against the word of one rightly representing the Spirit's speech "and beat him before the judgment seat"[2005] of one named Gal'lio, the deputy of Acha'ia. The record

---

1999 Hebrews 12:6
2000 1 John 3:1
2001 John 15:18
2002 1 Samuel 8:7
2003 Romans 12:19
2004 Acts 11:28
2005 Acts 18:17

states, "Gal'lio cared for none of those things."[2006] This was the condition of the times if you were a Christian in that very early age of the church. They who rightly honored both the Father and His Son were, of the Romans, and of "certain of the sect of the Pharisees which believed,"[2007] terribly despised. It was this cup allotted to the Christian tribe that compelled Peter to write, "If any man suffer as a Christian, let him not be ashamed,"[2008] and likewise Paul counseled, "Be not thou therefore ashamed of the testimony of our Lord...but be thou partaker of the afflictions of the gospel according to the power of God."[2009]

10. The church fainted because of persecution, and because she rejected communion with the Spirit's Word for continual conversational sustenance, her impure heart desired her own form of support coupled together with her own form of reverence. Though she would hear no thing concerning surrendering her heart for the purification of the members of her body, she gladly took hold of the words, "Let every soul be subject unto the higher powers. For there is no power but of God: the powers that be are ordained of God. Whosoever therefore resisteth the power, resisteth the ordinance of God: and they that resist shall receive to themselves damnation."[2010]

11. Tired of suffering for the sake of some LORD and Christ that she didn't know, tired of feigning a spirit desiring to become familiar with a Spirit that she didn't care for, the church longed after a political arm to stretch over the conscience of the world to finally hear her voice. Whoever should resist the counsel of the one perceived to be upheld by *God* for order; as

---

2006 Acts 18:17
2007 Acts 15:5
2008 1 Peter 4:16
2009 2 Timothy 1:8
2010 Romans 13:1,2

it says, "Let every soul be subject unto the higher powers";[2011] if she could have a place among those legislative powers, then she would exist next to *that* "minister of God, a revenger to execute wrath upon him that doeth evil."[2012] Those that then reject her doctrines should not be taken for "Christians," but rather heretics, "traitors, heady, highminded, lovers of pleasures more than lovers of God."[2013]

12. The church had rejected the counsel, "Bless, and curse not,"[2014] for because of impure ambitions, the elders suffered a curse on themselves and all joined to them, even as it says, "Leanness into their soul."[2015] It was this leanness that caused her elders to involve themselves with pagan philosophies to invent a species of creatures for their own consumption, of which would serve as meats "carried about with divers and strange doctrines."[2016] Soon enough the prophecy would be fulfilled, "There went out another horse...and power was given to him that sat thereon to take peace from the earth, and that they should kill one another."[2017] This is why it says, concerning Rome's "son of perdition,"[2018] "His power shall be mighty, but not by his own power,"[2019] and, "Through his policy also he shall cause craft to prosper in his hand,"[2020] and, "He shall also stand up against the Prince of princes."[2021]

13. This *power* was civil or legislative, and as the church forsook Him that had all right power to exalt her according to

---

2011 Romans 13:1
2012 Romans 13:4
2013 2 Timothy 3:4
2014 Romans 12:14
2015 Psalms 106:15
2016 Hebrews 13:9
2017 Revelation 6:4
2018 2 Thessalonians 2:3
2019 Daniel 8:24
2020 Daniel 8:25
2021 Daniel 8:25

His own design, being impatient and intemperate in relation to the Spirit's will and counsel, she took the necessary steps to join to that which would give her *power* according to her own perception of what power was. Again the body of the LORD's name and knowledge was sold to death by Judas to "both Herod and Pon'tius Pilate, with the Gentiles, and the people of Israel."[2022] Therefore, observing the events leading up to this compromise, the apostle was moved to advise her elders, "For meat destroy not the work of God."[2023]

14. Such actions to claim a political seat confessed that her elders believed their own untrained theories and uninspired expositions of *Scripture*, that the *kingdom of God* had come to earth through them, and that they were the stewards of it. For this mistake in judgment, Paul wrote, "The kingdom of God is not meat and drink; but righteousness, and peace, and joy in the Holy Ghost."[2024]

15. The kingdom or denomination of priests and ministers is but one of anxious self-righteous agitation with joy in a flesh-based stimulus, but to the one who subscribes to the virtue of Christ's name and is joined to that Temple within the Spirit's heavenly City, Paul writes, "We are the circumcision, which worship God in the spirit, and rejoice in Christ Jesus, and have no confidence in the flesh."[2025] The ministers of the churches confessed confidence in the flesh's constitution by joining hands with the ultimate *power* of flesh for their glory and admiration, for by State assistance, they would further remove from men that good will concerning heaven's kindness towards them, doing contrary to the LORD's High Priest, who

---

2022 Acts 4:27
2023 Romans 14:20
2024 Romans 14:17
2025 Philippians 3:3

"came and preached peace,"[2026] that is, who "set at liberty them that are bruised."[2027] "Abundance of grace"[2028] is "abundance of peace,"[2029] and grace; which is "the gift of righteousness";[2030] is received by a faith exercising confidence on the doctrine of His Son's mediation. Because the church removed herself from observing that Faith accomplished only through faith, admitting, "Righteousness come by the law,"[2031] she removed herself from receiving the Spirit's grace to newly create an *understanding* on heavenly things, seeing as how "he scorneth the scorners: but he giveth grace unto the lowly."[2032] For this cause the apostle counseled her elders, "All of you be subject one to another, and be clothed with humility: for God resisteth the proud, and giveth grace to the humble."[2033]

16. Slowly the science of salvation was being replaced with "fables, and commandments of men, that turn from the truth."[2034] The word of the truth is the word of creation's Faith, and this counsel announces justification[2035] and liberty to the spirit of the mind only by experimenting with faith on the name of the Father and His Son, and by no thing else. Because the church had put off from her self a right "love in the Spirit,"[2036] she turned to honor that persuasion "in the flesh made by hands,"[2037] and to "worship devils, and idols of gold, and silver, and brass, and stone, and of wood: which neither can see, nor

---

[2026] Ephesians 2:17
[2027] Luke 4:18
[2028] Romans 5:17
[2029] Psalms 72:7
[2030] Romans 5:17
[2031] Galatians 2:21
[2032] Proverbs 3:34
[2033] 1 Peter 5:5
[2034] Titus 1:14
[2035] Which is another word for sanctification
[2036] Colossians 1:8
[2037] Ephesians 2:11

hear, nor walk."[2038] For this cause it was fulfilled in them that held to their universal creed, "They that make them are like unto them: so is every one that trusteth in them."[2039] The elders grew tired of the saying, "These men, being Jews, do exceedingly trouble our city, and teach customs, which are not lawful for us to receive, neither to observe, being Romans,"[2040] therefore they began to fulfill the prophecy of themselves, which vision spoke of "them that hold the doctrine of Ba'laam, who taught Ba'lac to cast a stumblingblock before the children of Israel, to eat things sacrificed unto idols, and to commit fornication."[2041]

17. The Romans were of a pagan heritage, subscribing to the god of the sun and all other gods they come across as they conquered the lands of other pagan people. As Christians of Rome preached blessing from one LORD and Spirit above all gods, they were looked upon as traitors to their heritage, as a people most perverse and confused, for the Romans held their State to be divine, and to reject the legal idolatrous polytheistic religion of the State of Rome would be just as much of an injustice as to reject the laws of the Sate itself. The State was the highest authority, and the Emperor, being known as that chief symbol of both Rome's law and religion, added on to the divinity of the governmental laws and religious ordinances. To subscribe to a doctrine preaching One above that connected to the Roman Emperor and Empire was therefore treason. The church knew all this, yet because she didn't care to endure in the peculiar light that she was privileged to receive, she gave up heaven's good Faith and subscribed to that spirit of religious error, consenting to its bargain that promised, "If thou

---

2038 Revelation 9:20
2039 Psalms 135:18
2040 Acts 16:21
2041 Revelation 2:14

therefore wilt worship me, all shall be thine."[2042] She took falsehood's plea, which event fulfilled the saying, "I know thy works, and where thou dwellest, even where Satan's seat is,"[2043] for she now assumed the distinction, "The people of the prince,"[2044] that is, that sect of "the prince of the power of the air, the spirit that now worketh in the children of disobedience."[2045]

18. He to whom the events of the church were revealed did not sit back in silence or idleness, but he would counsel the elders, "Whosoever shall confess that Jesus is the Son of God, God dwelleth in him, and he in God,"[2046] and, "The Father sent the Son to be the Saviour of the world."[2047]

19. The confession of the church testified to the fact that the Spirit's Word was not in the heart of her conversation, and that she had no right communion with the Father to have placed in her mind the character of His Son and Spirit. The church was existing where "Satan" was, and the confession of his religion is, "I will ascend into heaven, I will exalt my throne above the stars of God: I will sit also upon the mount of the congregation."[2048] A throne and a congregation, these are a church and a civil government, and as it is yet in the heart of Satan to rule over the LORD's earth by these means, in the Roman churches this philosophy found servants willing to say, "I am a God, I sit in the seat of God."[2049] Herein that spirit of error had a wife to build a house for their son, even a church

---

2042 Luke 4:7
2043 Revelation 2:13
2044 Daniel 9:26
2045 Ephesians 2:2
2046 1 John 4:15
2047 1 John 4:14
2048 Isaiah 14:13
2049 Ezekiel 28:2

preaching "the image which fell down from Jupiter"[2050] under the legal religious rule of "that man of sin, the son of perdition; who opposeth and exalteth himself above all that is called God, or that is worshipped."[2051]

20. As Satan said, "My throne will be above heaven's stars,"[2052] so the Spirit lets us know, "The seven stars are the angels of the seven churches."[2053] Now, "angels" are ministers and apostles of the Spirit's Faith. The church began to blot out the true revelations of the Spirit from His chosen apostles to erect feigned teachings "from fornication, and from things strangled, and from blood."[2054] John saw this work and counseled, "He that dwelleth in love dwelleth in God, and God in him,"[2055] for the Spirit's doctrine of benevolence is not without the Spirit's blessing to the inward parts, wherefore he wrote, "Our fellowship is with the Father, and with his Son."[2056] There is an order of the living God for His faithful, and to every believer are stages of continual advancement ordained for them "to offer up spiritual sacrifices"[2057] by "the knowledge of his will in all wisdom and spiritual understanding."[2058] The work of disregarding exercising faith on the voice of the LORD's High Priest was destroying all that the Spirit had established for man. For, the church confessed, "I justify myself,"[2059] and to gain public favor, she transformed His instruction into "another

---

[2050] Acts 19:35
[2051] 2 Thessalonians 2:3,4
[2052] Isaiah 14:13
[2053] Revelation 1:20
[2054] Acts 15:20
[2055] 1 John 4:16
[2056] 1 John 1:3
[2057] 1 Peter 2:5
[2058] Colossians 1:9
[2059] Job 9:20

gospel,"[2060] becoming them that "changed the truth of God into a lie."[2061]

21. Paul knew, because of her failure to learn of and do heaven's will, the storm awaiting the church, and so wrote, "I say, through the grace given unto me, to every man that is among you, not to think of himself more highly than he ought to think; but to think soberly, according as God hath dealt to every man the measure of faith."[2062] And Peter, sensing the same wrath, counseled, "Wherefore gird up the loins of your mind, be sober, and hope to the end for the grace that is to be brought unto you at the revelation of Jesus Christ; as obedient children, not fashioning yourselves according to the former lusts in your ignorance."[2063]

22. A sober mind is one existing in and by a knowledgeable confidence. The only way that the heart may have a chance to magnify self against the Word of Christ's mediation is if it casts off faith's learning and applies to another principle of subjection, which principle is formed out of a policy by fear and fables to obtain self-validation. This is why Paul counseled her elders, "Neither give place to the devil,"[2064] for by disappointment and anxiety, the heart will suppress every promise of the Godhead to encourage weighty thoughts driven by irrational emotions. Because of persecution for the character and doctrine of His Christ, Christian elders had lost any love for His name. They carried their understanding partially considering His Son's face, casting off the original confidence and righteousness preached to them by the first apostles, and with the gifts and promises of that Faith, for another *confidence* of no value and

---

2060 Galatians 1:6
2061 Romans 1:25
2062 Romans 12:3
2063 1 Peter 1:13,14
2064 Ephesians 4:27

accursed of the LORD by His Word, even as it says, "The flesh profiteth nothing,"[2065] and, "They that are in the flesh cannot please God."[2066] This is why the apostle would have her men remember, "The angels which kept not their estate, but left their habitation, he hath reserved in everlasting chains under darkness."[2067]

23. This example was to provoke thought for the current "home" of the believer, and how that of old typified that which would later come to be. The estate of the faithful is found in that Place where the LORD's Christ, "when he had purged our sins, sat down on the right hand of the Majesty on high,"[2068] leaving the believer, through faith on His name and office, to "have attained to righteousness, even the righteousness which is of faith."[2069] When once the counsel of justification by an experimental faith on the Spirit's saying was silenced, then should come darkness over the church to fulfill the prophecy, "They should kill one another."[2070]

24. Scripture says, "Love one another,"[2071] but in reality this saying means, "Comfort yourselves together, and edify one another."[2072] Therefore, seeing the developing error in Christian manners of worship and service, Paul counseled them, "Follow after the things which make for peace, and things wherewith one may edify another,"[2073] but prophecy was being fulfilled. The work of peace, or rather, "the work of faith with power,"[2074]

2065 John 6:63
2066 Romans 8:8
2067 Jude 1:6
2068 Hebrews 1:3
2069 Romans 9:30
2070 Revelation 6:4
2071 1 Thessalonians 3:9
2072 1 Thessalonians 4:11
2073 Romans 14:18
2074 2 Thessalonians 1:11

was being removed from the church due to her rejecting the praise of the Spirit's name, fulfilling the saying, "The time will come when they will not endure sound doctrine,"[2075] and, "They shall turn away their ears from the truth, and shall be turned unto fables."[2076] Herein is the end of self-righteousness, even that spirit and tradition nailed to the tree forwarded by the conversation. Failure to do the Spirit's will and saying therefore opens us up to have it said of us, "I gave them up unto their own hearts' lust: and they walked in their own counsels."[2077]

25. Heaven's LORD and Father will notice persistent rejection of the conditions to accept His benevolent promise. Therefore "leaving the principles of the doctrine of Christ, let us go on unto perfection,"[2078] and as perfection is blessed to the conversation's conscience by faith's exercise, the reformer is to serve the Father out of their spirit by faith on the end of His Son's name. Such a religion calls for a reform in learning if heaven-appointed revival would be seen within the conversation, for "God imputeth righteousness without works."[2079] "Therefore it is of faith, that it might be by grace,"[2080] "and if by grace, then it is no more of works: otherwise grace is no more grace."[2081]

[2075] 2 Timothy 4:3
[2076] 2 Timothy 4:4
[2077] Psalms 81:12
[2078] Hebrews 6:1
[2079] Romans 4:6
[2080] Romans 4:16
[2081] Romans 11:6